Black migrants: white natives

Black migrants: white natives

A study of race relations in
Nottingham

DANIEL LAWRENCE
Lecturer in Sociology, Nottingham University

CAMBRIDGE
UNIVERSITY PRESS

Published by the Syndics of the Cambridge University Press
Bentley House, 200 Euston Road, London NW1 2DB
American Branch: 32 East 57th Street, New York, N.Y. 10022

Library of Congress Catalogue Card
Number: 73–89005

ISBNs:
0 521 20353 8 hard covers
0 521 09847 5 paperback

First published 1974

Text set in 10/12 pt. Photon Times Roman, printed by photolithography,
and bound in Great Britain at The Pitman Press, Bath

To my Mother
and in memory of
my Father

Contents

List of tables

List of maps

Acknowledgements

It was during a conversation with Professor Julius Gould that I first began to think about a study of race relations in Nottingham. I am grateful to him for his suggestion and for his subsequent advice and encouragement. I am also indebted to several other colleagues and friends. I have benefited greatly from my conversations with Michael King and from his comments on drafts of the manuscript. Jonathan Silvey's willingness to give advice on data collection and analysis made my task very much easier. Julia Evetts, Michael McDougall and Dorothy M. Wood made very helpful comments on drafts of some of the chapters.

The survey on which much of the book is based was made possible by a grant of £750 from the Social Science Research Council. Of those who helped me with the interviews my thanks are especially due to Margaret Reckord, U. S. Dougal and J. S. Dosanjh. I am also grateful to the Commonwealth Citizens Consultative Committee for allowing me access to its Minutes and to all those people in Nottingham who agreed to be interviewed or who provided me with information in other ways. Since I cannot name all of them I have decided not to single out specific individuals for mention. I can only hope that they feel that the outcome is worth the efforts which they made.

I am also grateful to Florence (and Alan) Watkin who battled with my ailing typewriter to prepare the final typescript; to Mrs Eileen Davis for her work on an earlier draft; and to Mrs Peggy Saunders and Mrs Maureen Ward who turned my code sheets into neat tabulations. Finally, I must thank my wife Helen for so very much: without her the book would not have been written.

NOTE ON TABLES

If respondents gave more than one answer to a question (as in reply to that on which Table 1 is based) totals in % columns may exceed 100.

1
Introduction

This is not the first investigation which has been concerned with race relations in Nottingham. There have already been studies of the employment experiences of coloured workers,[1] of housing,[2] and of the Commonwealth Citizens Consultative Committee,[3] and Nottingham was one of six places selected by the Survey of Race Relations for a study of English attitudes towards coloured people.[4] What distinguishes it is that it is not limited to a single aspect of race relations and makes use of a different perspective from that of any previous investigation. There is an obvious need for a study of this kind. In 1958 there were racial disturbances in the St Anns Well Road area and Nottingham was dubbed the 'race-war city'.[5] Yet, since the early 1960s, it has acquired a reputation for tolerance and racial harmony. It is not easy to know how to interpret this change in reputation. Much depends on the significance which is attached to the 1958 disturbances. If, for example, they can be treated as relatively minor incidents which were exaggerated by the mass media then there may be very little to explain. On the other hand, if they were serious and indicate that race relations had reached a particularly low ebb in 1958, then there is a need to explain what brought about the improvement in the city's image.

Burt is one writer who believes that the reports of the disturbances were greatly exaggerated and he contends that Nottingham has always enjoyed harmonious race relations.

> For the general community of Nottingham the chance incident of August 23rd had no real significance. By a number of independent sources, officials of both West Indian and white organisations, I have been told that there is no real conflict between West Indians and whites in Nottingham and that the community remains today a model of harmonious race relations.[6]

This assertion, that the accounts of the disturbances were exaggerated, has been echoed by other writers. For example, Elizabeth Burney and Mark Abrams describe them as the 'so-called race riots' and Mary Grigg refers to them as the 'mis-named race riots'.[7] Whatever their intention, they give the im-

---

[1] The notes to the numbered references appear on pages 229–39.

pression that the disturbances were not especially serious. Yet Wickenden's detailed description of them conveys a quite different picture. He emphasises that they were not entirely unexpected and had been preceded by other incidents. For instance, in 1957, there was an ugly clash between West Indians and whites in the Employment Exchange during which knives were drawn. The first of the 1958 disturbances took place on 23 August. On leaving a pub at closing time a crowd began to argue and brawl and within a few minutes a number of West Indians had stabbed four local people. Another squabble broke out a short distance away and two more people were stabbed. By 11 p.m. a crowd of about 1,500 had gathered and its hostility was directed against any coloured people still on the streets. As a result, the reinforced police force either escorted coloured people home or took them into protective custody. Crowds gathered in anticipation of more trouble the following Saturday. Until 11 p.m. the police succeeded in preventing any further outbreak of violence. Then sections of the estimated 3,000 strong crowd began to attack the police – presumably in retaliation for the protection they had afforded coloured people the week before. Although on this occasion no-one was seriously hurt, large numbers of people were arrested. The following Saturday, at about the same time, after a group of West Indians had been escorted home by the police, a smaller crowd began to attack several houses in which coloured people lived. They broke down a brick wall, used the bricks as missiles, and smashed several windows. The tenants replied by throwing bottles at the crowd. Once again the police acted firmly and the troublemakers were dispersed.[8]

Even if it can be agreed that the disturbances were serious it is still not clear precisely what significance ought to be attached to them. The problem is that there is no way in which one can take the temperature of a race relations situation. It is tempting to talk of a 'rise in racial tension' in much the same way as a 'rise in temperature' and equate an outbreak of violence with a boiling point. Unfortunately the analogy is not helpful. Just as a potential outbreak of violence can be prevented by outside intervention, so violence can erupt as a result of factors extraneous to a race relations situation. Similarly, the presence of a small group may precipitate violence in one city, whereas in another, with perhaps an even greater race problem, there may be no violence because there is no precipitating agent. Furthermore, because the crucial determinant of violence may be a random event or something only indirectly concerned with race relations, an outbreak of violence in itself does not necessarily mean that a city experiencing racial violence has 'worse' race relations than one at peace – or that an episode of violence necessarily indicates a deterioration in race relations in any given city. Clearly it would be unwise to assume that Nottingham now enjoys 'better' race relations without using a more sensitive index than racial violence.

Those who assume that there has been an improvement usually claim that it has stemmed from the city's positive approach to race relations. They draw attention, in particular, to the work of the Commonwealth Citizens Consultative Committee. Davison, for example, wrote in 1964:

> It was in Nottingham that the racial troubles of 1958 first began and it is perhaps not surprising that Nottingham is probably the most active of all the provincial centres in developing a positive approach to race relations. This has been due in no small measure to the drive and initiative shown by the local Council of Social Service (of which the Consultative Committee was part).[9]

In 1967 Mary Grigg concluded that:

> There are no committees in the North as impressive as the Commonwealth Citizens Consultative Committee in Nottingham, which is a good example of how a committee can work effectively without becoming a political bulldozer or shirking the implications of power . . . In a city where mis-named 'race riots' occurred in 1958 the committee has helped to change the city's image of high racial tension to an illustration of steady, successful integration.[10]

And similarly, in its 1967 Annual Report, the National Committee for Commonwealth Immigrants asserted that:

> The Nottingham Commonwealth Citizens Consultative Committee, one of the oldest in the country, continues to be among the leading groups. Because of its early start it was able to anticipate and minimise many of the difficulties such as housing shortage, discrimination in employment, problems of immigrant relations, and youth problems. After so many years of solid work and pioneering activity, the Nottingham Committee . . . may well set an example in this field from which many of the newer committees will benefit.[11]

It is not clear on what grounds the NCCI made this generous evaluation of the Consultative Committee's work. Nor is it clear what is meant by 'minimising the housing shortage or the problems of immigrant relations'. All that is clear is that it is on the basis of such statements as these that the city's current reputation has developed. They have come from a great variety of people. Yet none of the comments have been based on systematically collected evidence. All have relied either on impressionistic observations or, in the case of visitors to the city, the views of a handful of key figures concerned with race relations.

In 1960, less than two years after the disturbances, Burt concluded that Nottingham was a 'model of harmonious relations'.[12] In 1961, during a brief visit, the West Indian High Commissioner declared that 'the situation in Nottingham seems to be as good as in any other provincial city in the country'.[13] In 1964, after an equally brief visit, the Jamaican Deputy High Commissioner said: 'I believe Nottingham is one of the best examples of integration of its kind.'[14] In 1967 came yet another compliment when Mary Grigg made the confident assertion that she could 'feel and see and hear' that race relations in Nottingham were very different from those in the other towns and cities she had visited.[15] However, since racialism can be concealed and racial conflict latent, these short-term visitors ought to have been more cautious in their judgements. On the whole it seems safest to ignore their views except in so far as they help to account for Nottingham's reputation.

But what of the statements made by officials and prominent figures in Nottingham itself? For example, in 1968, the President of the Nottingham and District Trades Council said that 'race relations in industry in Nottingham are extremely good and the envy of other parts of the country'.[16] In similar vein, Nottingham's Principal Youth Employment Officer said, after the PEP Report had demonstrated that employment discrimination was widespread in Britain, and in the year that the Government introduced legislation to curb such discrimination: 'With the same ability coloured youngsters can do just as well as white youngsters in Nottingham.'[17] This view was in line with the local representatives of the CBI and the Chamber of Commerce who, in the same year, had been unwilling to participate in a conference on race relations in local industry on the grounds that there was no employment discrimination in the city and that the findings of the PEP investigation were not relevant to Nottingham.[18] At a centenary celebration of the YMCA in 1970 its General Secretary claimed that Nottingham had set the pace for other cities in helping to integrate immigrants. He added that 'It is one of the characteristics which will always mark Nottingham as a great city.'[19] Following the publication of the first Annual Report of the Race Relations Board, the local newspaper carried as its front page headline: 'Racialism: City Gets Clean Bill – Close Co-operation with Immigrant Groups The Secret'. It continued:

> Although the first report of the Race Relations Board, published today, paints a depressing picture of discrimination practised against coloured people in Britain, the situation in Nottingham appears to be a brighter one.[20]

However, this was not the verdict of the Race Relations Board as the headline implied. Those who read on discovered that it was the verdict of local officials. Almost exactly a year later the newspaper carried a similar headline: 'Race: City Gets a Pat on the Back'. This time it continued:

> Nottingham, one of the two Midland areas selected for a nationwide survey on racial prejudice, emerges from the first results, just published, with 'a particularly good record'.[21]

Those who read on discovered that this was the view of another local figure – Norman Fowler, the then prospective Conservative candidate for Nottingham South. When the report concerned was eventually published it said: 'It is also worth noting that within each borough the pattern of (prejudice) scores was broadly the same for the whole sample.'[22]

It would be wrong to imply that the local newspaper sets out to portray an optimistic picture of race relations in Nottingham. On one occasion it carried a far less optimistic headline and, from time to time, it does include stories of discrimination.[23] But local officials and others in Nottingham do give the impression that they are anxious to promote and protect the city's reputation for tolerance and harmony regardless of the actual situation. Indeed it is fair to say that Nottingham's officially supported public image has been built up by paying scant attention to the views of the ordinary men and women involved in race relations. Thus, whatever reputation it deserves, there is no doubt that its present image rests more on ignorance than knowledge. Those who have subjected it to a closer scrutiny have not found it so convincing. Two journalists, Dilip Hiro and John Heilpern, came to write an article on Nottingham late in 1968 'because they had been told its record was among the most enlightened in the country'. They left 'with the feeling that it had a chance of avoiding trouble, but only if its leaders, commercial and civic, rid themselves of their complacency'.[24] Similarly, after his study of Nottingham's political response to coloured immigration, Katznelson concluded that 'the pre-1958 illusion of harmonious race relations has been restored, but in my view it remains, unfortunately, merely an illusion'.[25]

My own appraisal of Nottingham's race relations comes nearer to the evaluations of Hiro and Heilpern, and Katznelson, than to the others which have been outlined. It has been derived, however, from a closer as well as a more systematic acquaintance with the situation than any of those that have been mentioned. In addition to the findings of a social survey conducted amongst the immigrant and native white populations I have been able to draw upon the information and impressions gained from several years participation in organisations and activities concerned with race relations, and from my contact with many of those people most actively involved in them. Such experience may not impress those who believe that only coloured immigrants and native whites living in the inner city should try to 'tell it like it is'. But at least I can claim to have been nearer to where it is happening than those other academics and commentators who, like me, have been audacious enough to try.

In the course of this book I will argue that Nottingham's reputation for harmonious race relations cannot be sustained and that the optimism which has been expressed by some observers may have risen from misconceptions about the nature of race relations. For example, it is often assumed that the underlying reality of race relations will be clearly reflected in local politics and other, easily observed, features of the situation. Since until recently Nottingham has been without any organised opposition to coloured people, and since its local politicians have never divided along party lines on the racial issue, this assumption very easily leads to the conclusion that the fundamental pattern of race relations is one of harmony. Such a view could be reinforced by reference to the fact that, up till the time of writing, no individual candidate at either a local council or a Parliamentary election has tried to exploit the racial issue for electoral gain and that, from as early as 1955, Nottingham has had a multi-racial voluntary organisation devoted to easing the problems of coloured immigrants. However, it is just as plausible to argue that the factors which have been mentioned help to keep any racial problems which do exist from becoming too obvious and that, instead of reflecting reality, they may serve to obscure it. Without another, independent, source of information about race relations it is impossible to determine which of these competing interpretations is nearest to the truth. Clearly it is necessary to go beyond what may be only superficial features of the situation if an adequate understanding of race relations is to be achieved.

However, other misconceptions about the nature of race relations are reflected in the work of some of those who have made a more considered and academic examination of the position in Nottingham. In a discussion of the part which geographical strategies might be able to play in race relations, Marsh concluded that Nottingham is more likely to accept coloured immigrants in a favourable way than Wolverhampton.[26] What is most pertinent about his analysis is the kind of information which he uses to reach this conclusion. He contends that 'acceptable evidence will have to include some real indication that different kinds of British communities differ from one another in a systematic way in their collective approach to race relations' and suggests that the only single body of data which can provide it is the study of prejudice carried out as part of the Survey of Race Relations. On the basis of this material he concludes that 'Wolverhampton, apparently vigorous in rejecting its coloured immigrants, can be contrasted with Nottingham' and he is then led to ask 'what it is about these towns that produces such a different approach to race relations?'

What in fact Marsh shows is that 31·1 per cent of those interviewed in Wolverhampton gave prejudiced answers to three or four items on a four point prejudice scale, compared with 23·2 per cent in Nottingham. In other words, his contrast between the two towns, his search for an explanation of 'such a different approach to race relations' and his implication that Nottingham is likely to accept a further influx of coloured immigrants more favourably than Wolverhampton are primarily based on a 7·9 per cent difference in the incidence of prejudiced individuals. To be fair, he does emphasise that the difference is statistically significant and does not disappear when factors such as education and class are controlled for – and he also notes the existence of differences of a greater magnitude in the answers given to specific questions. Nevertheless, he does draw unreasonable conclusions about behaviour patterns from relatively small differences in the extent of measured prejudice. In doing so he reveals another common misconception about the nature of race relations: the assumption that, in isolation, expressed attitudes can provide a clear indication of patterns of behaviour. It is true that he examines factors other than prejudicial attitudes in the course of his article and, in particular, notes the possible significance of community stability and integration for patterns of race relations, but he does so only to help account for the difference he has indicated and not in an attempt to find further evidence for it. It is possible that he may be correct in the conclusion he reaches about Wolverhampton and Nottingham – but it certainly cannot be said to follow from the data he presents.

This kind of misconception is particularly important since an assumption of a causal link between attitudes and behaviour underlies much of the work which is undertaken to try to effect an improvement in race relations. Whilst it is not my intention to imply that studies of attitudes are unnecessary in the analysis of race relations, the findings that result need to be interpreted in very close conjunction with other kinds of material.

A further misconception is the assumption that it is possible to develop a good understanding of race relations from an examination of the organisational and political framework within which they occur. The several efforts to evaluate the work of the Consultative Committee seem to have fallen into this trap. Although they vary a great deal in their level of sophistication and sometimes reach quite different conclusions, they share the same organisational and political focus and neglect of the cultural and structural factors at work. Katznelson's study, for example, is searching only when it is directly concerned with the Consultative Committee and the City Council and he uses fairly limited and often impressionistic data about other features of the situation. He is able to point out that there were no coloured councillors or policemen in Nottingham in the period with which he was concerned, that there were no coloured members of school management committees or employees of the Housing Department and that there were very few coloured people in council houses. However, he makes no serious effort to assess the significance of such facts. He is also able to draw on Elizabeth Burney's study of housing in Nottingham – but does so quite uncritically. This is an important point since some of her allegations have been expressly denied by local housing officials. Despite the limitations of his material he feels able to conclude that Nottingham's harmonious race relations are illusory and that the Consultative Committee has served to muffle immigrant protest and divide the coloured population. He also seems willing to rely mainly on the views of a few critics and friends of the Consultative Committee for his conclusion that 'above all, the Committee has insulated the political community from pressure for change in the racial *status quo*'.[27] However sound or unsound such conclusions may be they cannot be wholly derived from the evidence he presents. To reach such conclusions requires material on the coloured communities and on patterns of race relations which cannot be obtained by a close scrutiny of only organisational and political factors. It may be added that, without such information, it is possible to misinterpret the significance of those factors which have been carefully examined.

In pointing to possible misconceptions in the work of Marsh and Katznelson I am not suggesting that their conclusions are necessarily unsound, or that there is not a need for studies of attitudes and the political and organisational aspects of race relations. I am suggesting that they may have gone beyond the limits of their data when reaching some of their conclusions.

What has so far been missing from studies of race relations in Nottingham, and what it is hoped that this investigation will begin to supply, is an appreciation of the role played by cultural and structural factors. It is necessary but far from sufficient to examine attitudes and study organisations and politics. There is a need to show the way in which the cultural preconceptions about coloured people held by native whites, and about Britain and the British held by coloured immigrants, affect the way in which these groups define the situations which confront them. There is also a need to relate such cultural preconceptions to the circumstances which brought the immigrants to Britain. Why did they leave their homes and why did they come to this country rather than anywhere else? Do they intend to make Britain their home or do they intend to return to their country of origin at some future date? It is no less important to know what kinds of positions the immigrants and natives occupy in the fields of housing and employment – and to determine what are the present and likely future characteristics of the housing and employment markets in which they may be competing for desirable but scarce resources. Such considerations must also be related to the general political developments occurring in Britain. The question here is not simply 'What are the stances adopted by the major parties on immigration and race relations?' but rather 'What are the main political problems of the day and how are they likely to impinge upon race relations?' Only if these kinds of elements are investigated will it be possible to say if towns like Nottingham have, or have not, harmonious race relations and, indeed, of what such relations seem to be composed. Similarly, only with an understanding of the role of such factors is speculation on future trends in race relations likely to prove helpful. It may be added that this is also necessary for an evaluation of the likely efficacy of the organisations which exist to try to improve race relations.

In the chapters which follow it will be emphasised that the absence of overt conflict should not be confused with a state of racial harmony. It is the former rather than the latter which exists in Nottingham at present and it is largely the failure to distinguish between them which has led to so much misplaced optimism. It will be suggested that this relative absence of conflict is not the result of any unusual display of tolerance on the part of Nottingham's native white population or the endeavours of the Consultative Committee to ameliorate race relations. It has stemmed partly from the way in which many of the coloured immigrants define their situation in this country. For, despite the disillusionment and discontent which they feel with many aspects of life in Britain, this tends to make them unusually tolerant of conditions which might otherwise provoke a much stronger degree of protest. The relative absence of conflict stems also from what seems to be best described as a fortuitous set of attitudes and circumstances in the fields of housing and employment. This has minimised the amount of direct competition between natives and immigrants and so reduced the chances of overt conflict between them. However, such circumstances are not fixed, and the signs are that they are changing in ways which will increase the likelihood of both competition and conflict.

It is only after the completion of this main part of the study that an attempt will be made to unravel the part which the Consultative Committee has played and can hope to play in the evolution of the city's race relations. It will be followed, in the concluding chapter, with an indication of some of the implications which the analysis has for the formulation of policies on race relations. It will be suggested that existing efforts to improve race relations on a narrow front, and without more general changes in society, will end in failure. Whilst there is no need to wait for a wholesale reorganisation of society before any progress can be made, and whilst there will remain a need for some kinds of specialised agencies, the most effective way to improve race relations in the long term is to bring about changes in other areas of life – such as housing and employment – as part of a general move to improve living conditions for the population as a whole. This must be deliberately directed to those native whites who are the most deprived at present and who, understandably if not correctly, perceive the coloured population as an obstacle in the way of an improvement.

The main influx of coloured immigrants into Nottingham did not begin until the 1950s. At first, West Indians made up the large majority of those who arrived in the city and it was only in the late 1950s and early 1960s that Indians and Pakistanis began to come in substantial numbers. In this respect the movement into Nottingham was fairly typical of the pattern which obtained nationally. At the time of the 1966 Sample Census (which provided the most up to date official figures at the time of writing) there were about 8,500 people in the city who had been born in the 'new' Commonwealth. Since the total population of Nottingham was over 305,000, even allowing for the possibility of some under-enumeration, it is unlikely that coloured Commonwealth immigrants comprised more than 3 per cent of it. The proportion of coloured people was appreciably larger than this because children born in Britain to 'new' Commonwealth born parents were not classified as immigrants – but it is still unlikely that coloured people comprised much more than about 5 per cent of the total. By the early 1970s the coloured section of the population was usually estimated at about 6 per cent. The West Indians probably made up about 56 per cent of it. The remainder were mainly Indians (about 22 per cent) and Pakistanis (about 17 per cent).[a]

If the coloured immigrant population of Nottingham appears to be larger than these figures suggest it is because it is very heavily concentrated in the inner city area. Although, in 1966, many enumeration districts were found to contain a negligible number of coloured immigrants, if any, others contained up to ten times as many as would have been expected had immigrants been uniformly distributed throughout the city. Given that these Census figures do not include the children born in Britain to coloured Commonwealth immigrants, coloured people may have constituted a majority of the population in one or two enumeration districts.

The social survey, which has already been mentioned, was carried out in the part of the inner city which coincided with the boundaries of the Nottingham Central Parliamentary Constituency. It contained, again according to the 1966 Census figures, almost 60 per cent of all those coloured immigrants living in the city as a whole – and an even higher proportion of those living in the inner city. Whilst details of the research methods are included in Appendix 1 it is

[a] In his 1970–1 Annual Report the Organiser for Work with the Commonwealth Immigrant Community (an Officer of the City of Nottingham Education Committee) included the following comments and figures:
There are no official figures of the actual size of the Commonwealth Immigrant population but after consultations and examination of the school returns it is estimated that the immigrant population has, for some time, been between 5 and 6 per cent of the total population of the City, as follows:

	Number	Percentage of immigrant population	Percentage of total population
West Indians	10,000	55·56	3·3
Indians	4,000	22·22	1·3
Pakistanis	3,000	16·66	1·0
Others	1,000	5·56	0·3
	18,000	100·00	5·9

worth noting at this stage that interviews were conducted with samples of adult male immigrants and native whites. In addition, both formal and informal interviews were conducted with immigrant leaders and many other people concerned with race relations in the city.

Although the present study is more encompassing and systematic than earlier investigations it is not offered as a definitive statement on Nottingham's race relations. Much of importance remains uninvestigated. However, I hope that it will provide a basis for a more informed discussion than has previously been possible.

2
The immigrants

This book is about *coloured Commonwealth immigrants*. The emphasis on all three characteristics distinguishes it from those other studies which have focused on *either* the element of 'immigration' *or* the element of 'colour'.[1] Whilst the significance of 'colour' may be growing, the 'immigration' factor has by no means lost its influence on the situation. Moreover, the colonial origin of the immigrants remains of crucial importance.[a] Indeed the present pattern of British race relations began to develop, not with the arrival of the *Empire Windrush* in 1948 as is sometimes supposed, but centuries before with the advent of European colonialism. Only by taking the historical dimension into account, along with the immigrant and racial dimensions, is it possible to begin to understand the contemporary situation.

Most of this chapter is taken up with a consideration of some of the ways in which these three dimensions have affected race relations in Nottingham – or, more precisely, with some of the ways in which they have helped to determine how the immigrants define their situation in this country. The chapter is divided into three sections. As the reasons for migrating and the reasons for the selection of a particular country will play a large part in determining how migrants respond to a new environment, the first section is concerned with why the immigrants left their homes and came to Britain. To answer these questions it is necessary, of course, to do more than recount the reasons given by the immigrants themselves for their migration. Only if such reasons are examined against an appropriate background can they be properly understood. For this reason brief descriptions of the colonial histories and present social and economic structures of the sending societies are included. Because 93 per cent of the West Indians interviewed are from Jamaica, and 95 per cent of the In-

[a] Indeed had there not been a British Empire there would, in all probability, have been no more than a handful of coloured people in Nottingham at the present time. Until 1962 Commonwealth immigration was not controlled and in this respect was fundamentally different from the immigration of aliens. The right of free entry arose as a corollary of British citizenship which, in the days of the Empire, had been granted to all those who, willingly or unwillingly, owed allegiance to the Crown. Once large numbers began to make use of this traditional right of free entry it was withdrawn. Nevertheless, during the period when 88 per cent of those interviewed entered Britain there were no controls.

dians and Pakistanis from either the pre-partition Punjab or Mirpur, they are limited to a consideration of these places.

No less important in determining how a migrant evaluates, and behaves in, the new society is whether he sees it as a temporary or a permanent home. Thus, in the second section, there is a discussion of the fact that most of those interviewed said that they did not intend to settle permanently in Britain. Though I shall argue that these stated intentions to return do not lend weight to Enoch Powell's demand for the introduction of a more substantial voluntary repatriation scheme than that which exists at present, I shall suggest that they are very important to our understanding of how many of those interviewed perceive their place in British society.[2]

Finally, there is an examination of the extent to which those interviewed found Britain as expected. This is of great significance, for all of us respond to situations, at least in part, according to how well they match our expectations. Whether or not the expectations of the immigrants appear reasonable or unreasonable to us is unimportant. For them, they were the obvious yardsticks to use when making their initial evaluations of life in this country.

The Jamaicans

Jamaica became a British possession in 1655. By that time the indigenous population had been completely wiped out and, to satisfy the demand for labour, vast numbers of slaves were brought from Africa to work on the sugar plantations. Today, their descendants remain not only the largest section of Jamaican society but also, in keeping with their heritage, the most underprivileged. It is from this section of Jamaican society that the vast majority of Nottingham's West Indian immigrants have stemmed.

During the early period of British rule, according to Patterson, Jamaica came perilously close to the Hobbesian state of nature.

> It was not just the physical cruelty of the system that made it so perverse, for in that the society was hardly unique. What marks it out is the astonishing neglect and distortion of almost every one of the basic pre-requisites of normal human living. This was a society in which clergymen were the 'most finished debauchees' in the land; in which the institution of marriage was officially condemned among both masters and slaves; in which the family was unthinkable to the vast majority of the population and promiscuity the norm; in which education was seen as an absolute waste of time and teachers shunned like the plague; in which the legal system was quite deliberately a travesty of anything that could be called justice; and in which all forms of refinements, of art, of folkways, were either absent or in a state of total disintegration.[3]

It was at such a massive human cost that Jamaica became, for a time, the world's largest sugar producer. Needless to say, the slaves derived little of value from this period of prosperity. Their lives were brutal and short. Shortly before emancipation the average life span of a negro slave born in Jamaica was a mere twenty-six years.[4] Their tribal cultures were destroyed (although vestigial elements remained) and when emancipation came there was no possibility of them re-establishing the way of life they had enjoyed in Africa.[b] Short of staying with their masters their new freedom was, as Katrin Norris has so aptly described it, 'very much a freedom to starve'.[5] Nevertheless, rather than stay with their masters, a great many of them chose to risk starvation and became subsistence farmers.

The land they occupied was obtained in several ways. Many simply squatted on Crown land; others stayed on with their masters for a time, or earned money by other means, and then bought a piece of land; and some, aided in particular by Baptist missionaries, established 'free' villages on Crown land or abandoned properties. Because of the small size and poor quality of many holdings some of the peasants were obliged to augment their living from the outset by obtaining paid employment from time to time – most usually on a seasonal basis at the time of the sugar crop. For those without land, paid employment was necessary on a more permanent basis and when it was not available they were obliged to 'scuffle' i.e. scrounge from friends and relatives.[6]

Over the next one hundred years the way of life of the peasant class underwent little change. However, it grew from some 300,000 in 1838 to close on 1,000,000 by 1938 and this produced an acute shortage of land.[7] Indeed the supply of land for hill farming was virtually exhausted by 1900.[8] At the time of the 1943 Census almost 70 per cent of Jamaican farms were under five acres in size (43,000 were less than one acre) and 97 per cent of the farms occupied only 39 per cent of the land. In addition, it was the large estates which monopolised the best of it. In general, the peasant holdings were less fertile and often made up of fragments separated by long distances.[9] As a result of this pressure on the land a growing number of families found it impossible to subsist without at least some resort to wage labour. Usually, however, the demand for employment was far in excess of the supply.

[b] 'The British Caribbean culture is one form of Creole culture . . . Its cultural composition mirrors its racial mixture. European and African elements predominate in fairly standard combinations and relationships. The ideal forms of institutional life, such as government, religion, family and kinship, law, property, education, economy, and language are of European derivation: . . . The Creole culture, however, also contains many elements of African and slave derivation which are absent from metropolitan models . . . "African" elements are observable in language, diet, folklore, family and kinship, property, marketing, magic and religion, exchange-labour, economic organisations such as the *susu* or "partners". In music, dress, dancing, and domestic life the African contribution is unmistakeable. Only rarely however do we find African traits persisting in a pure form, more generally they are overlaid with Creole influences or situations, or they are associated with elements of European origin.' M. G. Smith, *The Plural Society in the British West Indies* (Berkeley, University of California Press, 1965), pp. 5 and 6.

At the time of emancipation the Jamaican economy had been almost totally dependent upon the sugar industry. In the 1860s the industry declined – mainly because of the growth of competition and the withdrawal of the tariff advantages which Jamaica had traditionally enjoyed from Britain. It was replaced, to some extent, by the growing of bananas, but this too went into decline when the crop was severely damaged by disease in the 1930s. Fortunately, the decline coincided with a revival in the sugar industry. In more recent years the economy has become more diversified. In 1952 bauxite was discovered in large quantities and has proved a valuable source of income – even if, as Katrin Norris has suggested, the benefits accruing to Jamaica are perhaps less than they ought to be.[10] At the same time an Industrial Development Corporation was established and a modern industrial estate built just outside Kingston. These developments, coupled with the growth of tourism, undoubtedly strengthened the Jamaican economy. But they did not transform it and Jamaica remained a poor country with a predominantly agricultural economy.

In 1943, there were no more than a quarter of a million wage earners in the country and 90 per cent of them earned less than £2 per week.[11] Unemployment stood at 40 per cent. In 1962, as against the 37,000 persons directly employed in industry, there were still 1,000,000 others who lived and depended for their livelihood on the land. The bauxite industry employed no more than 5,000 people and the new industrial estate 4,000 – most of them females. Although the wages earned in the bauxite industry were high, those working in the new industrial estate often earned as little as £2 to £3 per week – an income which might have to support a whole family and perhaps others besides. And yet, whilst these new developments were creating new jobs – albeit on a small scale – the modernisation of the sugar industry was making an estimated 20,000 workers redundant. So as rural poverty pushed more and more from the land the supply of jobs in the urban-industrial areas was, at best, scarcely keeping pace.[12]

It is clear that most adult Jamaicans faced considerable economic hardship in the post-war period. For the generation at school the prospect was no better. At the time that Britain was re-modelling her pattern of secondary education to meet the equal opportunity clause of the 1944 Education Act, most Jamaican children remained destined for an elementary school education. For those who could afford it secondary, and even university, education was available. For the rest, education did not constitute an avenue for economic advancement.[c] Indeed as Smith has observed: 'these (educational) conditions produced

[c]   Although the Jamaican Government initiated a scholarship programme to raise the secondary school population from the 1957 figure of 10,000 to 26,000 by 1967 this still meant that only one child in twenty would receive a secondary school education. See Smith (1965), p. 219.

sufficient frustration to discourage many parents from sending their children to school regularly' – a view confirmed by Moser who, in a study published in 1957, showed that less than a quarter of children attending elementary schools did so for the full eight years.[13]

Although these harsh economic conditions and limited opportunities for advancement do not in themselves constitute a sufficient explanation of Jamaican migration to the United Kingdom, they do form an important part of that explanation. This is readily apparent when we examine some of the characteristics of the Jamaicans interviewed, for only a small minority had the necessary educational qualifications or occupational skills to be assured of even a secure income in Jamaica – quite apart from a standard of living comparable to that enjoyed by most people in this country. All but 4 per cent of those interviewed had been born in villages in rural parishes. Before coming to Britain, however, 19 per cent had been living in Kingston and 4 per cent in other towns. In other words, although 96 per cent were born in rural areas, almost a quarter had already joined in the growing exodus to the urban-industrial areas before coming here. All of those interviewed had received some formal schooling but as many as 70 per cent received only an elementary education and, consistent with Moser's findings, almost half of this group admitted to either not attending school regularly or to leaving school before completing the elementary course. Of the respondents who had remained in the rural villages, 72 per cent had been peasant farmers or farm workers and a further 6 per cent had been fishermen. In the sample as a whole only 8 per cent had been white collar or professional workers. And, although 21 per cent had been engaged in skilled manual work, it is clear from what has been said already about the Jamaican economy that not even these respondents could have been certain of a secure future.

Thus there seems little doubt that the conditions in Jamaica which have been described must account, to a very considerable extent, for migration from Jamaica to the United Kingdom. However, it is important to emphasise that migration from Jamaica in search of work was already a well-established feature of Jamaican life before the movement to Britain began in the 1950s. Large numbers of Jamaicans had worked on the two attempts to build the Panama Canal, in the cultivation of sugar in Cuba and banana growing in Costa Rica and Honduras. Most of the 100,000 West Indians who had become American immigrants before 1924 were Jamaicans and, during the interval between the two World Wars, contract work in the United States was common.[14] So migration – and particularly temporary migration – was nothing new and what demands explanation is not so much why Jamaicans left Jamaica but why they decided to come to Britain and why they came in the post-war period.

Perhaps the most widely accepted answers to these questions are those suggested by Peach. He admits 'that it is difficult to evaluate separately the push and pull factors, since they exist in relation to each other' but still contends that 'the view which sees conditions in the West Indies as the dominant force in the migration is misfounded'. In his opinion the situation in the West Indies merely allowed migration to take place: it did not 'directly stimulate it'.[15] The dynamic, he suggests, came from the demand for labour in the United Kingdom. The evidence he presents in support of his conclusions is intended to show that fluctuations in migration rates were highly correlated with the level of employment vacancies in this country, but not with rates of economic growth, population increase or unemployment trends in the West Indies.

Doubt has been raised about the validity of some of the data used by Peach.[16] But, in any case, his interpretation of it seems questionable. It is not clear what he means by the terms 'push' and 'pull' or what he intends when he notes that conditions in the West Indies were 'permissive' but did not 'cause' the migration to take place.[17] But his emphasis on the 'pull' of Britain gives the impression that the immigrants had a positive desire to come here. Moreover, his stress on the absence of a 'push' and his rejection of the 'causal' significance of circumstances in the West Indies, coupled with his view that such an unfavourable state of affairs merely 'permitted' migration to occur, gives the impression that the immigrants were not at all reluctant to leave their homelands. In other words he conveys an image of a powerful magnet attracting migrants with little or no restraint (or push) at the point of exit.

In one part of his book, however, he uses a metaphor which seems to run contrary to the main thrust of his argument. In evaluating a competing interpretation of the migration which focused on conditions in the West Indies he concedes that it might 'explain the pressure behind the tap, but not its opening and shutting'.[18] This, of course, implies a 'push' much more than a 'permissive' situation and is precisely the kind of position which those he is criticising seem to adopt. The evidence collected in the course of the Nottingham interviews certainly accords more with the conventional explanations of the migration than with Peach's attempted refutation of them. This is in no way to deny the role played by employment vacancies in Britain. But, as Roberts has pointed out, the argument that the expansion of the British economy created jobs to which West Indian and other coloured immigrants were drawn as a replacement population could have been developed without any effort to disprove the conventional view that conditions in the Caribbean were the prime determinants of the migration.[19]

Thus it still seems reasonable to conclude that the main factor bringing about the Jamaican migration was the state of the Jamaican economy: the pressure on the land in the rural areas, the declining number of jobs available in the plantations, the shortage of employment in the urban-industrial areas, as well as the very limited opportunities for advancement via the educational system, all combined to give most Jamaicans little prospect for either security or relative prosperity in the future. To account for the particular migration to Britain in the post-war period must be added Britain's labour shortage. Another extremely important factor was the McCarran-Walters Act. This curbed entry into the United States – a traditional outlet for West Indian migration. Had that avenue not been effectively closed there can be little doubt that Britain would have received far fewer Jamaican and other West Indian immigrants. A third, though far less important factor, was the special significance of Britain in the Jamaican value-system. Stemming from Britain's centuries-long domination of the Island, and the peculiarly strong English influence in the educational system, most Jamaicans feel a strong sense of identity with Britain and often refer to it as 'the mother country'. This is of great importance in other respects and will be considered in more detail below. At this stage, it is sufficient to note that the strong sense of identity with Britain, coupled with the right of free entry which Jamaicans enjoyed until 1962, made this country a logical choice for would-be migrants at a time when we were short of labour and the McCarran–Walters Act had made migration to the United States so difficult.

In the main, these conclusions are confirmed by the statements of those Jamaican migrants who were interviewed in Nottingham. They were asked two questions – the first: 'Could you tell me why you left your home country?' and the second: 'Why did you come to Britain?' By asking two distinct questions it was hoped that it would be possible to distinguish between the factors which 'pushed' the respondents from Jamaica and those which 'pulled', or at least directed them towards Britain rather than any other country.

Table 1 Reasons for leaving West Indies

Reason	%
Economic	54
Travel and experience	46
Further education	1
Other	10
No. respondents	72

As Table 1 shows, a majority of respondents cited clear economic motives in reply to the first question.

Jamaica is a small agricultural country and most of us are farmers – but the price you get for your produce is so small it is hard to make a living.

To get a decent job – good jobs are hard to get in Jamaica.

Well I just felt I'd have a better chance of improving myself if I left Jamaica.

I came away from Jamaica to earn some money.

Well jobs was difficult to get so I wanted to try a new place.

There are so many problems to be a farmer in Jamaica. There is so much disease and pests that overnight your plantation can be all dead. And the winds they do the same. So by harvest you may have nothing to harvest. It is too hard a life.

Well for a job. People broke into my grocery store back home once or twice and robbed the place. So I had to get a job and that was hard back home.

Well I left Jamaica because I saw the advertisements in the 'Gleaner'. I left to better my position. That was the chief reason.

In addition to the 54 per cent who gave explicitly economic reasons, a further 46 per cent gave reasons which suggested that they had left because they wanted to travel and see another part of the world. Some of them, like the following respondent, combined this desire to travel with an economic reason.

Some of my friends was here and wrote and said you could make a good living here. So I came. You see I hadn't had a chance to travel before and see other places.

Others, however, answered the questions solely in terms of their desire to travel.

You see I just felt like a change.

I like to travel.

Well I know I'd find it hard to get an office job here – I had a nice job at home – but I wanted to have the experience.

For a change – a bit of adventure.

These respondents seem to have valued migration for its own sake – a view no doubt fostered by the tradition of travel and migration amongst Jamaicans. But it should not be thought that migration arising from such motives is fundamentally different from that of a more obviously economic character. For both reflect the place of Jamaica, like that of other underdeveloped countries, in the modern world. However underdeveloped Jamaica may be, its population is not unaware of the different kind of life enjoyed elsewhere and no doubt this encourages some to go and see it for themselves.

When asked why they had come to Britain in particular, 78 per cent of those interviewed gave the impression that they had come, not because of any strong positive desire, but simply because Britain was the only country readily available to them.

> Well you see I've been a traveller before. I travelled to America twice. Well I got back and started work and saved a bit of money – I had a little house and I was going to improve it. Then I thought I would go to America again – you see they was recruiting again and I was promised a card. But June was closing and I was still waiting so I thought well I'm going to book my passage to England.

> Why I come here is because it was easier to come here than to any other country.

> At that time I preferred America – but things was too slow.

> I did not prefer England. To be frank I was misguided when I come to England. I was told you could earn £30 here easy. If I had the option to choose I would have gone to America – but I never had no option – 'cos I cannot stay there. I could only go on contract.

> Well you know to go to America you need someone to sponsor you. I know a friend and he come back to Jamaica on holiday – but he had to give his niece the first preference. So I'd have to wait. So I come here where I had cousins.

> I had a chance to go to America once – but I didn't go. And when I wanted to it was easier to come to Britain – and I thought London's streets was paved with gold.

> At the time Britain was the only place you could come to. But it was the 'mother country' as well you see.

Table 2 Reasons for coming to Britain (West Indians)

Reason	%
Entry to preferred country impossible/ Britain only country available	78
Wanted to come to Britain	11
Family and friends here	18
Other	3
No. respondents	72

As Table 2 shows, only 18 per cent said that the fact that they already had friends and relatives in this country influenced their decision to come here. And only 10 per cent (not distinguished separately in the table) gave reasons allied to Britain's place in the Commonwealth – i.e. as the 'mother country'. This is not to say that only 10 per cent of those interviewed felt about Britain in this way. It does suggest, however, that it was not, in itself, a powerful reason for their choice and few respondents gave it as their sole reason. Without doubt the most striking fact revealed by the question is that the large majority of respondents came here for what were essentially negative reasons.

The Indians and Pakistanis

The vast majority of the Indians and Pakistanis in Nottingham come from a relatively small part of the Indian sub-continent. Of the Indians interviewed, 89 per cent had been born in the pre-partition Punjab and as many as 56 per cent had been born in a single district – Jullunder. In the case of the Pakistanis, 64 per cent had been born in Mirpur, an area adjacent to the Punjab, and all the remainder had been born in the Punjab itself.

Although under British rule for about 100 years, until independence in 1947, the people of the Punjab were far less affected by it than were the African slaves who were forcibly introduced into Jamaica. Whereas Jamaica was made up entirely of immigrants, in the Punjab, and indeed India as a whole, the indigenous peoples always comprised the vast majority of the population. And whilst the culture of the African slaves was destroyed as a result of their captivity, that of the various social and religious groupings in the Punjab remained relatively unaffected. So, unlike the Jamaican immigrants who stem from a society which was artificially created in the seventeenth century, the Indians and Pakistanis come from a society with an extremely long history and a rich cultural heritage. Not surprisingly the Indians and Pakistanis do not identify with Britain in the same way as do the descendants of the African slaves. This was made abundantly clear when the respondents were asked: 'Did you feel yourself British before you came to this country?'. In striking contrast to the Jamaicans – 87 per cent of whom replied 'yes' – 98 per cent of the Indians and Pakistanis said 'no'. And whilst many of the Indians and Pakistanis thought the suggestion that they might feel British most amusing, the subject was treated with the utmost seriousness by all of the Jamaicans.

The background of Nottingham's Indian and Pakistani immigrants is, in other respects, not dissimilar from that of the Jamaicans. They too come from countries which are poor and underdeveloped and in the Punjab, as in Jamaica, there is a great shortage of land for farming. Several decades ago the whole of the central Punjab, including Jullunder, was a land of prosperous peasant proprietors.[20] But, as a result of the partition of the Punjab (which took place when India became independent in 1947), a rapidly growing population and the absence of any system of primogeniture amongst the Sikhs, this is no longer the case and there is now an acute land shortage.

As a result of partition several million people were obliged to move from India into Pakistan and vice-versa and, in this exchange of populations, it has been estimated that some 4,000,000 refugees moved into the Eastern Punjab. They took over, for the most part, the smaller and usually poorer holdings of the Muslims who had moved into Pakistan. Such was the resultant pressure on the land that it proved necessary to introduce legislation which fixed a ceiling of thirty acres for each holding.[21]

The two other factors which have been mentioned made the situation even more difficult. Between 1951 and 1961 the population of the post-partition Punjab increased by about 60 per cent to over 20,000,000. With a constant land area of 122,000 sq km, this increased the population density from 103 to 166. In Jullunder, in 1961, the density was as high as 353 – more than twice the density for the state as a whole.[22]

Were the Punjab a highly industrialised state such a high population density would not, in itself, be a particular problem. Neither would it be such a problem if the state were highly urbanised. But in a predominantly agricultural state with over 15,000 villages as against only 130 towns it means that in Jullunder, for instance, about 25 per cent of the holdings are less than one acre in size. Moreover, as the Sikhs who make up the large majority of Indians in Nottingham have no system of primogeniture, this pressure on the land must become more difficult with each successive generation.[23] So, without a curb on population growth (which in any case is a long-term solution), for some, migration into the towns or abroad is the only alternative to starvation.

Alone, this pressure on the land might not have been sufficient to bring about a sizable migration to the United Kingdom. But reinforcing it was the instability created by partition. As has been noted, millions of people were uprooted from their homes and during the period that followed thousands lost their lives. Moreover the movement of refugees accentuated the cleavages between the Sikhs and Hindus within the Eastern Punjab. Consequently, as Peter Marsh has observed:

> The fluid political and social state of the Punjab is a factor which must be noted in any assessment of why people are concerned to pull up roots and start again. If the migrants are those who lost their place in the upheaval of partition their motive for migrating is a very logical one.[24]

Like the Jamaicans, Punjabi Sikhs belong to a social group with a well-established migratory tradition and at least three factors can be mentioned to account for their willingness and ability to move. The first is the geographical location of their homeland which it seems has made them less 'rooted' than other Indian groups.

> The Punjab has borne the brunt and first impact of almost all the major invasions by foreign powers from time immemorial, this having been the traditional route into the sub-continent. The result has been that the people of the Punjab have developed an unusual capacity for adjustment to change, which makes them one of the least 'rooted' communities in India, mentally, culturally, and physically.[25]

Another important factor is the preference given to the Sikhs in recruitment to the British Indian Army after their 'loyalty' during the Indian Mutiny. Nair goes so far as to suggest that 'it would be difficult to find a peasant family in the state from which one or more men have not served in the armed forces and served abroad as a consequence'.[26] Finally, the joint-family system of the Sikhs needs to be mentioned for it has enabled sons or fathers to migrate and yet leave their wives and children in the relative security of their family home.[27]

As a result of these several characteristics the Sikhs seem to have developed what may be termed a 'frontiersman mentality'. They played an important part in the opening up of the Western Punjab towards the close of the nineteenth century and many of them settled on the peasant plots that were subsequently established. Others helped to build the Kenyan–Ugandan railway in the first decade of the twentieth century and some settled there once the work was completed. At about the same time others went to Canada, Australia, California and Fiji. Thus migration was already a well-established feature of the life of Punjabi Sikhs long before the movement to Britain in the post-war period.[28]

Mirpur, like the Eastern Punjab, is poor, underdeveloped and also has a predominantly agricultural economy. In 1964 it was estimated that half of the population was under-employed and that as many as 7,500,000 people were unemployed. According to the former President of Pakistan, Ayub Khan, in a speech to the Royal Institute of International Affairs in 1966, the *per capita* income was as low as £30 per annum. Coupled with this general poverty, the major upheaval involved in the building of the Mangla Dam – which entailed the submerging of 250 Mirpuri villages – added a further incentive to would-be migrants. Rose suggests that Britain was an obvious destination for them for there was a traditional link between it and the district of Mirpur. It seems that in an earlier period the poor quality of Mirpuri land-holdings had resulted, not only in the move to the towns so characteristic of developing countries, but also in many young men joining the Merchant Navy. Later, some of them settled in Britain forming parts of the early coloured settlements in several British ports.[29]

Thus for both groups it seems that rural poverty, general instability and a tradition of migration combined to produce migration to Britain in the post-war period. Other factors were no doubt relevant. It is likely, for instance, that it was the large-scale operations of travel agents, at the time that immigration control was threatened, which enabled migration to reach such high levels in 1961 and the first half of 1962.[30] But, in the main, it was poverty or near poverty, with the additional instability and other factors peculiar to the area, which were the principal determining factors of movement to Britain when we were short of labour and when, by Indian and Pakistani standards, jobs were in abundant supply.

These observations are supported by the data collected in the course of the interviews. Eighty-one per cent of the Indians and 91 per cent of the Pakistanis had been born in rural villages. Prior to coming to Britain, however, 44 per cent of the Indians and 27 per cent of the Pakistanis had been living in towns. Thus sizable minorities in each group had already joined in the movement to the urban areas before coming here. Of those who had completed their education before leaving, 42 per cent had been peasant farmers. This figure, of course, disguises the extent of the connection with the land amongst those interviewed, for many of those who had been wage-earners were the sons of peasant proprietors and had been obliged to seek employment because of the small size of their families' land-holdings. Of the remainder, 19 per cent had owned small businesses and a further 17 per cent had been working as artisans. Only 6 per cent had been white collar workers. This occupational pattern reflects the generally low educational level of the respondents. Only 14 per cent possessed educational or occupational qualifications which might be accorded recognition in Britain.[d] Twenty-seven per cent had received no formal education and the remainder had done no more than complete, or partly complete, the elementary education available. A sizable minority of the Indians interviewed had been affected by partition for, although only 4 per cent had been living in Pakistan prior to leaving, as many as 22 per cent had been born in Pakistan. Fewer Pakistanis seem to have been affected in this way. Though not a single one had been living in India immediately prior to coming to Britain, not more than 9 per cent had been born there.

When asked why they had left their homeland 65 per cent gave straightforward economic reasons (see Table 3).

Table 3 Reasons for leaving India and Pakistan

Reason	Indians %	Pakistanis %	Indians and Pakistanis %
Economic	56	77	65
Travel and experience	37	—	20
Further education	7	9	8
Other	15	14	14
No. respondents	27	22	49

[d] The procedures employed for classifying the educational and occupational qualifications of the respondents are described and discussed in Chapter 5.

There is no industry in our country. Unless we sell our property and our wives' jewellery and come to England we would starve. We send our money home to keep our family in Pakistan. If we could get jobs in Pakistan we would not stay here and be subjected to such humiliation.

To seek employment. I was unemployed in Pakistan.

We were poor. We wanted to work, save money and then return.

It was difficult to support my family on the land I had. I wanted to better my prospects.

Because it is a poor country.

Nobody wants to leave one's country. But the financial situation forced us to leave. We have come here to earn money.

Our family land was small. My own plot was only one acre so it necessary to get a job. But they were very difficult to get. I had to leave for economic reasons.

Thirty-seven per cent of the Indians (but no Pakistanis) gave reasons which, as in the case of some of the Jamaicans, suggested they had left primarily because they wanted to travel and see for themselves the way of life in more affluent, economically powerful, nations.

American pictures have a big effect on the educated Indians. All that pomp and show and money – plenty of girls – put it that way. I thought I'd go abroad for adventure.

To learn about life. I wanted to know the people who had reached such a position that the sun never set on the British Empire.

Finally, like the following respondent, a few gave reasons concerned with partition.

When Pakistan was created we became homeless and migrated to India as refugees. I already had a passport that had been issued during the war. When I found I couldn't settle in India I decided to come to England.

When asked why they had come to Britain (see Table 4) 55 per cent of the Indian and Pakistani respondents (as against 18 per cent of the West Indians) said it was because they already had friends and relatives in this country. This suggests that migration from India and Pakistan was much more of a 'chain migration' than in the case of the Jamaicans whose answers suggested that they came on a much more individualistic basis. The answers of the Indians and Pakistanis lend support to the comments of Rose and his associates who, in *Colour and Citizenship*, wrote:

In the early 1950's pioneer settlers from India and Pakistan who had prospered in British industry began to send for their kinsmen and fellow villagers. It was necessary for the migrant to have some contact or direct sponsor in Britain who could arrange for his housing and employment and in many cases contribute to his fare to Britain.[31]

My brother was here. He helped me to come.

My relatives were already here.

My father lived here for a long time. He had bought the house we live in. So we came here. I craved to come to this country.

My uncle is here since the Second World War. He was foreman and has now been promoted. My brother-in-law has been here since 1952. My father stayed in Malaya. Some members of my family went to Malaya. Others came here.

Some people I knew had come before the War and had made a lot of money and done well – so I thought I would try to come to England and try to do as they had done.

Table 4 Reasons for coming to Britain (Indians and Pakistanis)

Reason	Indians %	Pakistanis %	Indians and Pakistanis %
Entry to preferred country impossible/ Britain only country available	22	32	27
Wanted to come to Britain	18	5	12
Family and friends here	48	64	55
Other	18	5	12
No. respondents	27	22	49

Though only 27 per cent (as against 78 per cent of the Jamaicans) actually indicated that they would have gone elsewhere had the opportunity been available, or that Britain was chosen simply because it was open to them, it is still the case that only 12 per cent said that Britain was a positive choice.

I wanted to go to America but my uncle died so I came here.

America at that time was too difficult. If I could have got a visa to America I would rather have gone there.

I was going to America and I had admission to a college in California. But I came here first for a while and I felt so lonely for home – it was different – all that excitement was gone – I was so homesick. But then I found some business opportunities here and so I decided to stay instead of starting afresh in America.

I could not get to Canada or the United States, so I came to England. England was my last resort. I would even have preferred Australia if I could have got there.

This was the only country I could come to. So I took advantage of the situation.

The reasons given by the Indians, Pakistanis and Jamaicans for leaving make it clear that their migration was voluntary to the extent that they were not forced from their homes in the manner of political or religious refugees. But it seems equally clear that relatively few would have left had the economic conditions at home not been so difficult. There is no reason to suppose, therefore, that migration necessarily meant, or was thought of as, the first step on the way to a new and permanent life in Britain. Indeed, on the contrary, almost all of those interviewed intended to return home eventually.

Migration: temporary or permanent?

There is evidence from several studies that large numbers of coloured immigrants did not intend to settle in Britain when they came here. Philpott, in his article on Montserratian migrants, stated that most of them saw migration as a temporary phase, mainly to gain money, and anticipated returning home sooner or later.[32] Similarly Sheila Patterson in *Dark Strangers* noted:

> Most West Indians do not, at least for some years after their arrival, intend to settle permanently, and many are used to the idea of migrant work and travel.[33]

Other investigators, using quantitative measures, have given more precise estimates of the numbers who intended to settle. Israel found that only 11.5 per cent of those immigrants whom he interviewed in Slough had come to Britain with the intention of settling permanently.[34] Similarly, a study carried out amongst coloured workers in London Transport showed that only 4 per cent of those interviewed had intended to settle.[35] In Bristol the corresponding figure amongst West Indians was found to be 17 per cent.[36] In Nottingham, all coloured respondents were asked: 'When you first came to Britain did you intend to stay here permanently?'. Only 4 per cent said 'yes'. Thus these investigations all indicate, despite minor variations, that the vast majority of coloured people did not see Britain as a place to settle permanently when they first arrived.

Having been in Britain for several years some of those interviewed, in each of these studies, admitted to having changed their minds. In Slough the proportion intent on staying had grown from 11·5 per cent to 20 per cent.[37] In Nottingham, the proportion intent on returning had fallen from 95 per cent to 75 per cent (see Table 5), and in Bristol the corresponding figures amongst West Indians were found to be 66 per cent and 40 per cent.[38] But, though showing a decline in the numbers intent on returning, such figures show equally well that a great many coloured immigrants still do not intend to settle in the country. In Sparkbrook this was found to apply to 56 per cent of the West Indians interviewed.[39] And Davison, in his book *Black British*, reported that in the case of his Jamaican respondents more wished to return home after their second year in Britain than after the first. By the end of the second year 81 per cent of his male respondents and 89 per cent of his female respondents expressed the intention of returning home at some time in the future.[40]

Table 5 Settlement intentions amongst Nottingham respondents

Intention	West Indians %	Indians %	Pakistanis %	All %
To settle	14	33	14	18
To return	78	59	82	75
Don't know	8	7	4	7
No. respondents	72	27	22	121

Obviously no one set of these figures can be used with confidence to indicate how many coloured immigrants intend (or plan, or would like) to return home.[e] The figures vary from area to area and between ethnic groups, and no doubt reflect, to some extent, the way in which questions were put to respondents, the climate of opinion at the time of the interviews and so on. Nevertheless there can be little doubt that on their arrival the vast majority of coloured immigrants did not intend to settle and that this is still the intention of a large if uncertain number.

Until Enoch Powell, in support of his demand for the assisted repatriation of Commonwealth immigrants, asserted that many wished to return home, remarkably little attention was paid to these findings. Indeed, even then, the already published findings cited above were virtually ignored. And Lord

[e]   One cannot assume that the numbers *intending* to return will necessarily be the same as those who are *planning*, or who would merely *like*, to do so. Someone may wish to stay, but at the same time intend, and have plans for, a return. Similarly, someone may wish to return but intend to stay. It follows that an intention to return may exist without someone being able to state when, and how, the intention will be realised. But, to the extent that an intention includes a degree of commitment, it seems to constitute more than an expression of preference or wishful thinking.

Walston, Chairman of the Council of the Institute of Race Relations, in an article entitled 'Repatriation: Why It is Wrong', published in May 1969, showed no awareness of them.

> So far as I know there has been little reliable research among immigrants still in this country as to whether they would like to go home or not.[41]

The results of an Opinion Research Centre poll conducted for the BBC programme Panorama did receive considerable publicity but were summarily dismissed, by most of those involved in the debate on repatriation, as unreliable.[42] And when Dennis Brooks made his findings available, in an article published in September 1969 in the journal *Race Today*, they appeared under the heading: 'Empirical evidence – at long last – on a burning national issue. The unreliability of public opinion polls on this topic is exposed.'[43]

Brooks argued that stated intentions to return should not be treated at their face value. He noted that, although only 10 per cent of those in his sample said they would not go back to their country of origin, it was likely that most of them would remain in Britain. He explained that, for the majority, going back was 'something they aspired to in the indefinite future rather than an event for which they were planning and saving'. He concluded:

> The evidence strongly suggests therefore that whilst many West Indians dream of a return to the Caribbean 'better off' than when they came, the majority of those in public transport at least will not do so. This probably applies also to many in other industries. Their occupational and economic achievements and prospects, coupled with a lack of employment opportunities in their home countries, conspire to keep them here.[44]

Brooks is probably correct in suggesting that many of those who say they will return will not do so. In Nottingham it was found that only one respondent, out of many who did not intend to settle here, had definite plans for a permanent return and, in the course of this section, further evidence will be provided in support of his view. However, this does not mean that we should dismiss the stated intentions of immigrants without further consideration. In terms of the debate on repatriation, it is not unreasonable or surprising that people should be preoccupied with whether or not statements of intent can be used to predict future behaviour. But this is by no means the only issue of relevance. Equally important to students of race relations should be the way and the extent to which an immigrant's intention to return affects his current behaviour. For, even if he is not actively saving for a return, this does not necessarily mean that his behaviour and attitudes are not in other respects profoundly affected by his intention to return.

It is indeed ironic that the one study which dwelt at length on this question was used to prompt the debate on repatriation. In his Eastbourne speech

Powell drew attention to a then recently published article by Stuart Philpott which, amongst other things, noted that most Montserratian migrants in Britain intend to return home. Powell then went on to use this finding to support his demand for the introduction of a policy of repatriation.[45] In writing his article Philpott had hoped to prompt a very different sort of debate. He was concerned with the behaviour of Montserratian migrants in Britain and, in particular, with the extent to which they met the expectations of those left behind. He noted that, just as most studies of Caribbean societies had tended to ignore the important fact that many of the population were working and living abroad, so studies of West Indians in Britain had tended to ignore, or place little emphasis on, the fact that many still maintained very close ties with their countries of origin.

> Studies of West Indians, for example, tend to be either in terms of local
> community isolates . . . or in terms of the processes of accommodation,
> assimilation, or discrimination in the host society. In treating both sending
> society and immigrant organisation as parts of a common analytical framework,
> I hope to provoke interest in the theoretical and methodological refinements
> required to deal adequately with this rather neglected problem.[46]

Perhaps because Montserratians comprise only a small minority of West Indians in this country, Philpott's article has not received much attention from students of race relations. Yet his approach has much to recommend it. He noted that Montserratian migrants come from a migrant-orientated society, i.e. a society in which a significant proportion of the population is involved in seasonal, temporary or permanent out-migration, and learn what is expected of them from an early age.

> These expectations are implicitly taught in the home through the praise of
> migrants who send remittances and through the condemnation of the 'worthless-
> minded' kin who do not 'notice their families'.[47]

By the time the Montserratian goes abroad, he is equipped with a 'migrant ideology' or 'cognitive model' which defines the nature and goals of his migration. This 'conceives migration as a temporary phase, mainly to gain money, which will culminate in a return to the island'.[48] Thus the migrant makes decisions when abroad, not only in terms of their likely short-term consequences, but also in terms of their implications for the more distant future when he will return home. In this way his intention to return acts as a sanction on his behaviour. Philpott found that most Montserratians do meet the expectations of those at home with respect to remittances and also maintain close ties with their fellow immigrants. The ideology of migration acts as an incentive in the perpetuation of the ties which, in turn, help to perpetuate the ideology.

For Montserratian migrants, then, it seems that an intention to return is an important determinant of whom they associate with and how they behave in this country. Of course it cannot be assumed that any migrant who intends to return will share the same migrant ideology as that of the Montserratians – or that their behaviour will be similarly affected. But there is no doubt that the type of ideology held by the Montserratians is far from unique. Indeed the Montserratians are strikingly similar to a migrant type – the sojourner – described by Siu as early as 1952.[49] The sojourner is a migrant who leaves his country of origin not with the intention of settling elsewhere but to do a 'job' which he originally plans to complete in the shortest possible time. He is called a sojourner not because he keeps to his plan, but because however long he stays abroad – often until retirement or death – he continues to think of himself as a temporary resident. He may become very vague about his return and make adjustments which, to an observer, might suggest that he is unlikely to return, but what is important is that he continues to think of himself as an outsider, is content to remain a spectator in many of the affairs of the country in which he resides and maintains ties with his homeland and those others from his home who are also living in his adopted country. His intention to return may be a dream which is unlikely to be realised. But it is a dream, nevertheless, which continues to influence his day to day behaviour.

The Indians, Pakistanis and Jamaicans in Nottingham are, in many important respects, like the Montserratians and sojourners described by Philpott and Siu. They, too, are from migration-oriented societies and, save for 4 per cent, had not come to Britain with the intention of settling permanently. And, when asked why they had come to Britain, 57 per cent of those interviewed said it was because they could not enter the country of their choice or because Britain was the only country open to them. Three-quarters still intended to make a permanent return home and, as Table 6 shows, the intention to stay or return bears

Table 6 Settlement intentions and number of years in Britain

Intention	3–6 years %	7–10 years %	11 or more years %
To settle	21	23	17
To return	79	77	83
No. respondents	19	40	54

no obvious relationship to the length of time spent in this country. Sixty-five per cent said that they tried to keep up to date with events in their country of origin and, moreover, it was found that 73 per cent of those intending to return tried to do this as against 50 per cent of those intending to stay.

Two studies carried out for the Commonwealth Citizens Consultative Committee in Nottingham suggest that most migrants have considerable financial commitments in their country of origin. Amongst the West Indians interviewed, although over 60 per cent had family responsibilities in Britain, almost 90 per cent were still sending financial support to members of their families in the West Indies.[50] In the case of the Indians and Pakistanis, whilst half said that they maintained people in Britain, 85 per cent said that they were completely or partly responsible for the support of relatives in their country of origin.[51]

Migrants who do not intend to settle in their country of residence are likely to be confirmed in their view if they are made to feel unwelcome and insecure. Thus we would expect those migrants who now intend to stay in Britain to be more satisfied, or at least less dissatisfied, with life in this country than those who intend to return. Similarly, we would expect those who intend to stay to be more optimistic, or at least less pessimistic, about their future than those who intend to return. Both of these hypotheses received support from the data collected. Table 7 shows that those intending to stay were less likely to allege that there is discrimination against coloured people in housing and employment and by the police, and also less likely to assert that most English people are unfriendly or hostile towards coloured people.

Table 7 Settlement intentions and allegations of discrimination and unfriendliness

Allegation	Intending to settle %	Intending to return %
Discrimination in employment	77	100
Discrimination in house purchase	68	89
Discrimination in council house allocation	36	59
Discrimination by police	18	30
Most English people unfriendly towards coloured people	9	46
No. respondents	22	91

Table 8 lends support to the second hypothesis. Those who were intending to stay were, in addition to being slightly less ignorant of the existence of the Race Relations Act, more confident that legislation could effectively curb discrimination against coloured people and also much less likely to believe that racial disturbances, of the sort which took place in Nottingham in 1958, might recur.

Table 8 Settlement intentions, anti-discrimination legislation and racial violence

	Intending to settle	Intending to return
Ignorant of Race Relations Act	70	75
Little/no confidence in legislation	20	49
Further racial violence possible	40	86
No. respondents	22	91

However, in addition to supporting the two hypotheses, the findings also raise a fundamental question. Why, if they believe the odds are so stacked against them, do those who say they intend to return not do so? This question is complex and no simple answer can be offered. But several can, at least, be suggested. The first is that there may be a small number who are financially incapable of making a return. For these, Powell's policy of assisted repatriation may have a limited appeal. On the other hand, it is only likely to have an appeal if they consider their position to be near desperate and are unaffected by the other considerations mentioned below. On the whole, it is unlikely that there are more than a handful of migrants who remain here *simply* because they do not have enough money to pay their fares home.

A much more likely answer to the question is that few migrants wish to return home virtually empty-handed. To go home with only a little more, or perhaps even less, money than one set out with is an open admission of defeat. It could involve a loss of face and would almost certainly mean the period spent in Britain, with its attendant humiliation in many cases, had been unprofitable and wasted. Moreover it could place the immigrant at an actual disadvantage on his return: he might, for instance, even find it difficult to get a job. This was the experience of many of those interviewed by Betty Davison in a small study of Jamaicans who had returned home. And, it must be noted, they were immigrants who had been reasonably successful in this country – to the extent that they had not only been able to save enough for their fares but also enough for the cost of settling back into a home in the Island.[52] Most of those interviewed in Nottingham tried, as has been noted, to keep up to date with things in their country of origin. Thus it is most unlikely that they will be unaware of the difficulties they will face on return. For this reason, unless they find life in Britain really intolerable, many will probably stay on till they are sure they are more than adequately prepared for a return – which may be indefinitely.

This leads on to a third possible reason why the migrants tend not to return. The goals of their migration are rarely well-defined. They left, in most cases, not to earn a specific amount of money or to obtain a specific qualification, but to 'better themselves'. Consequently there is not, for most migrants who intend to return, any logical time or set of circumstances when it is obviously appropriate to do so. It is, therefore, not surprising that few of them can give a precise answer when asked how long they intend to stay in this country. The nature of their migration does not allow for such precision. And, of course, the situation is made more difficult if the migrants have brought their wives and dependants to join them. New and complicating factors then have to be taken into account when a return is considered. For example, will the children be able to obtain a comparable education at home?

This uncertainty, which must inevitably surround the decision to return, has been made even more difficult by Britain's immigration laws. When the vast majority of those interviewed entered Britain there were no controls. Commonwealth immigrants were free to return home and then re-enter the country as they wished. Now they have only a short period of grace after which they are obliged to apply, like any other would-be migrant, for an entry voucher. If they return now, and then wish to re-enter Britain, there is absolutely no guarantee that they will be re-admitted. Indeed for those without badly needed skills it is virtually certain that they will be refused re-admission. In his book *West Indian Migration* Ceri Peach suggested that, in the immediate period before the introduction of controls in 1962, large numbers of Commonwealth immigrants who would not otherwise have done so, came here to beat the impending ban. It can be argued that another unforeseen effect of this legislation has been to keep immigrants here who would otherwise have returned. Consistent with this suggestion is the finding that those respondents who intend to return are more often opposed to immigration control than those who intend to stay. Only 38 per cent of the former group, as against 59 per cent of the latter, were in favour of it. Similarly, those intending to stay were much more likely to argue that, whether or not they were in favour of control, it was necessary. This view was expressed by 73 per cent of those intending to stay as against only 47 per cent of those intending to return.

These reasons lend support to Brooks' suggestion that few immigrants will return. But they will remain, in many cases, not because they have a real desire to do so, but because the circumstances in which they find themselves militate against a return. Perhaps the most important obstacle is that the economic conditions which brought most of them to Britain in the first place still obtain. Britain may not be home, its population may not welcome coloured people and there may be discrimination – but jobs and houses are available and life is not yet intolerable.

However unlikely they are to return, the fact remains that 75 per cent of those interviewed still intend to go home. What consequences, other than the maintaining of ties and contact with home, does this have for their behaviour in this country? Two possibilities can be suggested – the first concerning their attitudes towards an accommodation to life in Britain, and the second, their willingness to tolerate unsatisfactory conditions.

If a migrant anticipates returning home he is unlikely to make a very serious effort to seek assimilation into the way of life of the country in which he resides. This is not to say he will not modify his behaviour in many respects. If it proves necessary to adjust in order to make a living or to make life easier, within certain limits he is likely to do so. But this is very different from seeking full participation, and the migrant is likely to continue to think of himself as an outsider. Obviously an intention to return is not the only factor which produces this kind of attitude on the part of migrants. In the case of Indians and Pakistanis, in particular, it probably does no more than reinforce other, more important, factors. Nevertheless, other things being equal, an immigrant with a 'sojourner' as opposed to a 'settler' ideology will be more inclined to remain an outsider.

That Indian and Pakistani migrants see Britain as an alien society and have no wish to be assimilated has been well documented, and probably applies as much to those who intend to stay as to those who intend to return.[53] Unlike the vast majority of Jamaicans, only 2 per cent of the Indians and Pakistanis felt British before coming to this country and when asked: 'Do you feel more British than (Indian or Pakistani) now?', 96 per cent said 'no'. In other words, there was absolutely no indication that they were beginning to identify more strongly with Britain than with India or Pakistan. When asked if they thought the children born and raised in this country to Indian and Pakistani parents would think of themselves as English rather than Indian or Pakistani no more than 41 per cent said 'yes'. Furthermore, only 6 per cent said they thought the parents of such children would not be unhappy should it happen.

> They will think it a disaster. Their children will learn all the bad habits of English children and their parents will be sorry they came here.
>
> They would feel that their children had gone astray.
>
> The parents would feel that they were living in exile. They would feel that coming here had been an 'expensive' affair.
>
> It will happen in only one out of 10,000 cases. It cannot happen. If it did the parents would be most unhappy.

They would feel they had made a big mistake. It would mean their family was on the verge of destruction.

In sharp contrast, it is usually argued that the Jamaicans feel a strong sense of identity with Britain, have a not dissimilar culture and, unlike the Indians and Pakistanis, do not see Britain as an alien society. They already identify with Britain and are willing to be assimilated. In Nottingham, 87 per cent (as against 2 per cent of the Indians and Pakistanis) felt British before coming here. Eighty-nine per cent believed that children born and raised in this country to Jamaican immigrant parents would feel English rather than Jamaican. The corresponding figure for Indians and Pakistanis was 41 per cent. Moreover, 86 per cent of Jamaicans anticipated that the parents of such children would be quite content or even happy should this happen. The corresponding figure for Indians and Pakistanis was 6 per cent.

But, as in the case of the Indians and Pakistanis, there was virtually no in-dication that the Jamaicans were beginning to identify more strongly with Bri-tain than with their homeland. As has been noted, in an important sense the Jamaicans came here already feeling part of this country: Britain was not an alien society – Jamaica was almost part of Britain. It would not, as a result, have been unduly surprising if it had been found that many Jamaicans were, after many years in Britain, now identifying more strongly with it than with Jamaica. This was not found to be the case. Indeed only 7 per cent said that they felt more British than Jamaican. They were matched by 8 per cent who said not only that they felt more Jamaican than British but that they felt less British than when they had arrived. In all 90 per cent identified more strongly with Jamaica than with Britain.

> No, I feel more Jamaican. Before I thought of myself as British but now I think of myself as Jamaican. Now you see we are a nation and anyway when you get here you find that they think that if you are black you cannot be British.

> One hundred per cent Jamaican. I feel more Jamaican now than before I came here.

> No! I'm a Jamaican in every capacity.

> No! From what I'd read I'd thought they'd treat us better.

> Oh no – still Jamaican.

> Yes – but only 'cos I'm here. When I go back I'll be Jamaican again. I'm Jamaican deep inside.

> Well to be honest when I was in Jamaica the teaching we got about Britain gives us she's got a motherly feeling towards us. Now that I'm here its different and I'm proud to be a Jamaican.

Some of these replies, and many others given in the course of the interviews, reflect the considerable disillusionment which most Jamaicans experienced on coming to Britain. To the extent that this has made them question the appropriateness of their identification with Britain it means that they now have more in common with the Indians and Pakistanis than when they arrived. Essentially the same point was made by the authors of *Colour and Citizenship* when they noted:

> ... the danger is growing that they will withdraw into themselves and give up their attempt to approach the English and adjust to their ways. It is becoming clear to them that adjustment has to be all one way. Experience of discrimination and rejection are causing West Indians to question the assumptions which made them the most assimilating of the coloured immigrants. They are being forced to recognise that it is healthier for them to stay with their own kind .. It is possible that now, after many years in Britain, many West Indians may resort to the same defensive avoidance as the Pakistani or Indian who has newly arrived and knows nothing of the country.[54]

And it was this kind of reaction which was evident in the replies of those 13 per cent of Jamaicans who, when asked about the expected pattern of identification of their children, expressed concern that they might feel English.[*f*]

> They'll feel English at first but as they grow up they'll come to think of themselves as Jamaicans. Even now they say things to my kid at school to make her feel like this. The parents will worry in case they get upset about things later.
>
> The parents will not be able to do much about it. You have to learn the hard way.
>
> They'll just accept it but they'll be worried about how this affects the children like when they grow up and start looking for a job and a place to live.
>
> Well I feel sorry for them. I know they is silly. I tries to tell them pretty often that you cannot be British really – not unless your skin is white.
>
> Annoyed – because black people cannot be English. They know this but the children will learn it the hard way.
>
> Those that are sensible will recognise that the children are bound to be conditioned by their environment. But they also know that their kids will get a shock when they leave school and start work – or try to start.

This tendency towards withdrawal amongst Jamaicans is probably due, in the main, to the cool and sometimes hostile reception with which they were received in this country. It is probably reinforced, however, by their intention to return. Respondents intending to return were more disillusioned with life in this country and more apprehensive of the future than those intending to stay,

---

[*f*]　A study of West Indians between the ages of sixteen and twenty-four in London found that two-thirds identified more strongly with the West Indies than with Britain. See D. Stevenson, 'Second Generation West Indians: A Study in Alienation', *Race Today*, vol. 2, no. 8 (August 1970).

and it is likely that this reinforces their intention to return. In the same way the intention to return probably reinforces the tendency towards withdrawal – or at least reduces their interest in seeking assimilation. If Jamaican migrants are to go back they have little to gain from unnecessary exposure to further rebuffs and rejection. They are, as a result, more likely than those who intend to stay to maintain a distance between themselves and members of the indigenous population.

It was noted that though a migrant may not intend to remain in Britain or be seeking assimilation, he will adjust in many ways in order to earn a living or make life easier. It follows that caution must be exercised in the interpretation of such changes. They cannot be assumed, without scrutiny, to be indicative of an intention to remain in Britain, or a positive desire to conform or seek assimilation. It is sometimes tacitly assumed that if a migrant brings his wife to join him, buys a house and joins a trades union then he is consciously conforming to the patterns of the host society and is on the way to being assimilated. Quite apart from the fact that assimilation requires at least acceptance from the indigenous population as well as a degree of conformity from migrants, such an interpretation may be misleading. Though we would expect a 'settler' to conform more than a 'sojourner' we cannot assume that an appearance of conformity indicates the abandonment of a 'sojourner' ideology or a change of reference group.

If, for instance, a migrant decides to send for his wife and family it is possible that this may be because he has decided to settle in Britain and cut his ties with home. But he may have decided to do so for other reasons. Most respondents in Nottingham had been joined by their wives and yet most of them still intend to return. Ninety-eight per cent of married Jamaicans intending to return had been joined by their wives as had 93 per cent of Indians. Only in the case of Pakistanis was there an obvious reluctance on the part of those intent on returning to have their wives join them. Yet even here 47 per cent had been joined by their wives. In the sample as a whole those respondents with their wives in Britain were only slightly less likely to say they intend to return than those without their wives. The respective figures are 73 per cent and 83 per cent.

Why then did those intending to return arrange for their wives to join them? Most probably because they missed them! But in some cases it is likely that wives were brought here in response to changing circumstances beyond the control of the migrants. The introduction of immigration control in 1962, and indeed the threat of control prior to that date, created a difficult situation for those whose wives and dependants were still at home. Could they, for instance, ignore the possibility that future legislation might prevent wives and dependants from joining husbands? Should they then arrange for them to come in case it should prove necessary to stay longer than anticipated? It seems likely that many wives and dependants were brought here, at least in part, as a result of such dilemmas.

The second general consequence which may follow from a migrant's intention to return is that he may find it easier to tolerate unsatisfactory conditions. If a given state of affairs is judged to be temporary – rather than permanent in nature – then it is likely that those affected will take this into account in their evaluation of it. It is equally likely that if the state of affairs is judged to be unsatisfactory, other things being equal, then those who intend to return will be more tolerant of it than those intending to stay. This may help to account, in part, for the relatively little overt protest from coloured immigrants in Britain. For, as we shall show in the next section of this chapter and elsewhere in the book, most of them are dissatisfied with the way they are treated. Certainly the relatively small amount of protest from most coloured people in this country cannot be construed as indicative of only a small amount of discontent.

Expectations and reality

As Table 9 shows, only 11 per cent of those interviewed found this country to be as they anticipated. All respondents were asked: 'Did you find Britain as you expected it?' and 86 per cent said 'no'. However, merely to say that they were surprised is, in most cases, a gross understatement for the follow-up question: 'In what ways was it different?' revealed that many had been profoundly shocked and disillusioned by what they had encountered. In their replies 91 per cent of the West Indians, 62 per cent of the Indians and 57 per cent of the Pakistanis went on to mention prejudice and/or discrimination and, as the following quotations illustrate, the degree of disenchantment was very considerable.

> Well it was hard to get jobs and make money. We was told all lies back home. The discrimination – I was not expecting it here. I was used to it when I had been on contract in America – and in Jamaica it was there too – but I didn't expect it here. Now I know you must expect these things. One of the reasons I prefer America though you see is because there you know just how you stand. No man likes uncertainty.

> To be frank we felt, I think one hundred per cent, that we'd be more welcome here than we was. We never realised that it would be so difficult. Things are better now – but when coming to England first – well it was a big shock. We adored the Royalty you see so much. Oh yes it was so disappointing.

> We didn't expect prejudice at all. We thought England was the home of justice – so we got quite a shock.

> Well at school we's told we's British and England is your mother country so we thought we'd be treated nice here. So you get a shock when you come and they don't like coloureds.

I never knew there was so much colour bar. We treat white men like kings – we don't treat them bad or complain. Oh yes it was a great disappointment. I don't regret the experience but it was a big disappointment.

I didn't expect to find white people sweeping the streets – I didn't expect to find any poverty at all either. I did expect there to be a few nasty guys here but I didn't expect to find real prejudice and discrimination. Because Britain was a democracy these things did come as a bit of a shock and I was very bitter at first. I'm a bit more tolerant now – but I'm still bitter.

I thought the people of Britain would be good and full of affection. Some did treat us well at first but as more and more of us came here they grew less friendly and now most of them are against us.

I was not expecting at all any prejudice or discrimination. As a matter of fact I did not know I was a coloured man until the English told me so. Somebody referred to me as a coloured person on the bus once and that was the first time I knew who I was.

I didn't have any idea how people would feel about us. I knew some English people in India and they was very nice. But when I came here I quickly sensed, you know, that there was something wrong with me.

I expected people to be nice and treat you as equals. Coming here and finding you wasn't wanted was a big shock. It's like a slap in the face.

Well you may think I'm silly but you know when I first came here I didn't think these things was houses. But I didn't like the atmosphere – the people you know – I was really disappointed. I expected them to be quite friendly – but they are not! English people have something against all foreigners but they show it up with colour mostly. But they even dislike their own people if you do not mind me saying so.

In many ways. The missionaries and teachers in Jamaica gave me a very misleading impression of Britain and the British people. Discrimination came as a big shock. We had it in Jamaica but we didn't expect it here.

I was told England was our mother country. But when I came they never want us. They never even hear about us. They think we from Africa!

Other than prejudice and/or discrimination the only surprise mentioned by a substantial number of respondents was the extent to which life in Britain had proved harder than expected. This probably reflects the degree to which they had come to believe that the lives of Europeans with whom they had been in contact at home, or seen in films, were typical of the whole population of countries like Britain.

The rumours that life was easy here were untrue. One has to work very hard to earn a decent living – sometimes seven days a week. The belief that people work eight hours a day is a myth.

I thought life would be easy but I have to do very hard work. I have to get up very early in the morning and come back quite late. I had no idea life would be so hard.

We heard there was a lot of wealth here and everything was automatic. But after working a full day of hard work we have to cook for ourselves. We thought English people were Sahibs but we found them just like common people.

Table 9 Life in Britain compared with expectations

	West Indians %	Indians %	Pakistanis %	All %
Surprised by:				
Prejudice and discrimination	88	48	36	70
Relatively poor living standards	26	30	32	28
Weather	7	4	—	5
English attitudes towards one another	4	4	9	5
Poor quality of housing	4	—	—	2
Other	4	19	9	8
Found Britain as expected	3	14	36	11
No. respondents	72	27	22	121

Table 9 also shows that more of the West Indians had been unfavourably surprised than the Indians and Pakistanis. This is not an unexpected finding. It is predictable from the Jamaicans' strong sense of identity with Britain to which reference has already been made. For this produces high expectations and, at least initially, a greater exposure to the kind of circumstances in which prejudice and discrimination may be encountered.

In order to obtain an unprompted indication of their impressions of English people, respondents were asked an open-ended question: 'What do you think of English people in general?'. Obviously the answers to such a question defy simple classification. Nevertheless, two features stand out very clearly. The first is that only 3 per cent of the sample made thoroughly favourable comments about English people. The second is the large number of West Indians (42 per cent as against only 6 per cent of the Indians and Pakistanis) who complained that the English are unpredictable and hypocritical in their behaviour towards coloured people.

> Some is good – but some is not. But the main trouble with English people is that they don't speak their mind broad enough. That's why I'm more with the Americans – they tell you straight. When an American is not with you he will tell you point blank and then you can keep out of his way. But an English man cannot do that. He may even offer you a cup of tea and not be with you. But some are real nasty in the way they live as well. If they offered me a cup of tea I wouldn't take it.

> The least little trouble they'll turn round suddenly and turn on you and say why don't you go back where you come from. They love to raise Africa. You don't know how to find them.

> They hypocrites.

> Some are good but some are rotten. But the majority you just don't know how you stand with them.

> You people change like the weather. One minute you'll be exchanging hurtful words and the next you'll be saying 'where's your cup'.

> There are some good ones. But most of them I can't understand. One day they're friendly – the next they're not. You don't know how to find them.

> People from the lower classes they're very hostile. But white collar people – whatever they feel they won't show it – they are very careful what they say. But you can still tell what their feelings are.

> Some will talk to you, you know, and then you go round the corner then they would – well I mean you know this is even with their own people – they'll say something funny about you. They're not friendly.

Not surprisingly, most respondents couched their replies in terms of English attitudes towards coloured people. Many seemed quite happy to generalise about English people in this way, although the majority qualified their answers. The following selection indicates the spread of views expressed.

> To me I find plenty of love for them.

> They are people who like to sit and watch you and understand you first. They get to work with you and live with you and then they begin to understand you. But at first they didn't understand so they used to say we're dirty and all that. But gradually they get to know you. And not liking us is not among the 'bigger people' – just the 'lowest' people.

> The British people mind their own business. But with most when you get to know them they will at least try to understand your point even if they don't agree. But some just don't want to understand us. They just don't want us here.

> Well some is not so nice to be honest. They say – 'why don't you go back to your own country?' Some are real nice though. It's just like Jamaicans – there is some good and some bad.

Some of them is very nice but some is no bloody good to you.

Very cold. There is more I would like to say but I won't.

Boy these English people are no good!

Well they have a superiority complex. They used to rule the world and they still feel other people are inferior to them.

The English people are not friendly. They are so cold. I think they are uncertain about themselves. They do not look you straight in the eye. When a man looks you in the eye you have a chance to find his favour. But when he looks down on you – he don't recognise you – you haven't a chance.

They don't like Indians being here. They won't even sit next to you on a bus unless they have to. At least half don't even say thank you when you give them a ticket.

They don't like us – well some are O.K. – but a lot of them are rotten.

Some of them don't give you a chance to prove yourself. They've painted us already – he's a black man and he's no good.

Some of those belonging to good families are quite good. But most don't like us. If you give them something to eat then they are with you. But once it goes down their throat they part away.

If you keep quiet you're all right. But if you don't you've had it.

Despite the shock and disillusionment which figured so much in most of the interviews, very few respondents had recounted their experiences frankly to friends and relatives still in their country of origin. Ninety-five per cent of those interviewed said that they wrote letters or sent messages home, but only 15 per cent gave answers of the following kind when asked what they said about Britain in them.

I write and tell them to try America if they want to. But I tell them that here – if you are coloured – you can only get the job the Englishman doesn't want.

Life is hard and far from easy. Not as easy as it is in India. I tell people the truth – that they should have no illusions about England.

I have told my friends that they would feel better to stay in Pakistan. I tell them that the money is quite good here but nothing else.

The large majority of those who corresponded seemed to have avoided any reference to prejudice, discrimination or similar unpleasant aspects of life in Britain.

Well to be honest I never wrote to anyone much. When I do I just talk about the family – nothing else.

That it is impressive. I only write about the good things.

I don't talk about England in my letters.

Just how I'm keeping.

I never complain. I only say I'm in good health and things like that. I say it's not great but I'm doing all right.

If you believe me I have never mentioned anything about Britain in them letters yet.

I don't write about things like discrimination usually. I did once when someone wrote and said they were coming for a job. So I explained to him the situation. I told him not to come here with high hopes. If you can face these things I said – you come – but if not, stay at home.

Though those who had not written full and frank letters were not asked specifically why they had not done so, some, like the following respondents, did include some indication in their answers.

I tell them it's not bad. You can't tell them it's bad because they'll just write back and say – why are you living there?

Well I don't complain about England in my letters. I just write about family matters and things like that. I wouldn't necessarily recommend anyone to come here. It would depend who they were. If they just wanted education it would be different but if they wanted to settle then I would tell them about the problems. But if you tell the truth they won't always believe you.

If my father were to come here it would really break his heart. To write to my relatives about what Britain is really like would just make them worry. But we have written to our friends. We wouldn't recommend anyone to come here.

We haven't really told them how much we're disappointed. We don't want them to worry. We have told them about the cost of living and housing.

We are earning good money we say. We don't write of our troubles. They would just worry about me if I wrote and told them the truth.

I keep quiet. If they want to come they can come. If I tell them how terrible it is here they will just believe that I'm trying to keep a good thing to myself.

Just family things and the weather. I wouldn't encourage anyone to come – but you know they don't believe us. They think we've got it good and are trying to keep them out.

The main purpose of this chapter has been to try to specify some of the factors which have determined the way in which the immigrant population of Nottingham define their situation in this country. Most of them have tended to perpetuate and strengthen the perhaps inevitable feeling of alienation found amongst members of any migrant group. This is not to say that there are no signs of acculturation or conformity amongst Nottingham's coloured immigrants – nor that some degree of this sense of alienation has not been self-imposed. Nevertheless, most of those interviewed still see themselves very much as outsiders – some even more so than when they arrived. They do so for several reasons. In part it is because most of them came to Britain for negative rather than positive reasons. Though their migration was voluntary, few would have left home had economic conditions not been so difficult. Moreover, many would have preferred to go to other countries had it been possible. They came, in all but a handful of cases, not to settle but to work for a time and then return.[g] Even years later, most of those interviewed still say they do not intend to settle here permanently. A further important factor is that very few have felt welcome in this country. Though the Indians and Pakistanis seem to have been less upset by this than the Jamaicans, it has hardly encouraged them to be more conformist than is necessary. And, in any case, their cultural distinctiveness inevitably brings some degree of separateness. Amongst the Jamaicans, the feelings of rejection have been much more acute. In some cases they have been more than sufficient to overcome the initially strong sense of identity which was felt for Britain. Certainly there were no signs that this sense of identity had been strengthened amongst the Jamaican sample as a whole.

[g] It would be most unfair if I gave the impression that the immigrants came to Britain to take advantage of what was available and then leave, without making any further comment. For they came to take advantage of our labour shortage and not our welfare services. For this reason their migration was very much to our advantage. Whilst it would be absurd to deny that they came here for reasons of self-interest, it is undoubtedly the case that one of the main consequences of their migration was a great alleviation of our labour shortage.

3
Prejudice and the indigenous population

Some of the factors which affect the way in which the immigrant population of Nottingham define their situation in this country were indicated in Chapter 2. For example, most of those interviewed had left their homes for primarily economic reasons, they had come to Britain, in the main, for negative rather than positive reasons and most did not, and still do not, intend to settle here. I also pointed out that the kind of image of Britain held by the immigrants depended, to a very considerable extent, upon the nature of the colonial experience of the countries from which they had come. This chapter is concerned with Nottingham's indigenous population – and in particular with those who live in close proximity to the coloured population in the inner zone of the city. But, like the immigrants, and indeed like most British people, they too bear the marks of Britain's colonial past. Both the positive image of Britain held by most Jamaicans and the negative image of dark skinned peoples held by most British people can be traced to that past. In the same way, the very colonial relationships which gave the immigrants the right to enter Britain freely before 1962 also helped determine the generally unfavourable reception with which they were met.

It is with this generally unfavourable view of coloured people held by the majority of the indigenous population that the first part of the chapter is concerned. But, instead of beginning by presenting the Nottingham findings, I will first discuss those contained in *Colour and Citizenship*.[1] I have adopted this approach for a number of reasons. First, because the *Colour and Citizenship* study of prejudice is the largest of its kind ever conducted in this country.[a] Secondly, because Nottingham was one of the five towns in which interviews took place.[b] And thirdly, because the way in which the findings are presented is very much open to criticism. After suggesting a different way of interpreting

[a] Interviews were conducted in five local government units known to contain relatively large proportions of coloured Commonwealth immigrants. Approximately 500 people were interviewed in each unit. In addition, in order to provide what is described as a 'control' for the intensive surveys in the five boroughs, a national sample was also conducted with 2,250 white adults, but using a more limited range of questions.

[b] The other boroughs were Lambeth, Ealing, Wolverhampton and Bradford.

expressed attitudes towards coloured people there will be a preliminary examination of some of the Nottingham material – not only in terms of the attitudes of those members of the indigenous population who live in the inner zone but also in terms of their social situation. Not all of the characteristics (or the attitudes) of the indigenous population of the inner zone will be described in this chapter. For example, many details will be reserved for the discussions on housing and employment which follow in Chapters 4 and 5. But a general description is included because the significance of attitudes towards coloured people cannot be appreciated properly unless seen in relation to the social context in which they are expressed. I hope the reasons for this view will become clear as the chapter proceeds.

The *Colour and Citizenship* study was carried out as part of the five year Survey of Race Relations in Britain and was designed to measure 'the incidence of colour prejudice in the white population, the demographic characteristics of those who could be described as highly prejudiced, and the social circumstances and the psychological traits which differentiate prejudiced from non-prejudiced people'.[2] Approximately 2,500 white respondents were interviewed. They were drawn from five areas, each of which contains a relatively large proportion of coloured Commonwealth immigrants.

In Nottingham, as in the other four areas, according to Dr Abrams, the author of the study, the majority of the population was found to be tolerant towards coloured people. To use his own words:

> Judging by the statements of some people, one might believe that the great majority of white British people are seething with hostility towards coloured immigrants. One of the projects included in the total research programme of the Survey of Race Relations was a study which shows that this assumption is *entirely false.*[3] (my italics)

Or to use the words of E. J. B. Rose and Nicholas Deakin, the authors of *Colour and Citizenship* in which the results were published:

> The extent of tolerance cannot be stressed too often and is indeed one of the major facts of the actual situation . . . What is needed . . . is not an effort to make people unprejudiced, but rather to remind them that they are unprejudiced.[4]

The precise figures presented in Abrams' report certainly seem, at first glance, to support his conclusions. Thirty-five per cent of those interviewed were found to be 'tolerant', 38 per cent 'tolerant-inclined', 17 per cent 'prejudiced-inclined', and only 10 per cent 'prejudiced'.[c] Moreover, taken at

[c]   Separate figures are not given for the 5 towns but Abrams notes that 'within each borough the pattern of scores was broadly the same as for the whole sample'. Rose (1969), p. 553.

their face value, these findings would seem to augur well for race relations in Nottingham and elsewhere. This was certainly the inference drawn by whoever wrote the *Daily Mirror* editorial of 10 July 1969, the day *Colour and Citizenship* was published:

> The most interesting and encouraging finding in today's impressive report by the Institute of Race Relations is this: only 10 per cent of the people of this country could be described as highly prejudiced about coloured immigrants. They are prejudiced beyond convincing by any argument. That must mean that the vast majority of people – 90 per cent – are ready or can be persuaded to make a success of race relations in Britain.

Similarly, Brian Lapping remarked in *New Society*:

> The most important evidence brought forward to keep politicians on course should be in the chapter by Mark Abrams ... This ought to mean that Powell and those who share his views can be easily contained, that further concessions to their point of view should be unnecessary.[5]

But such conclusions follow only if the findings can be accepted at their face value. It will be argued here that they cannot be accepted in this way and, moreover, that the relationship between race prejudice and the prospect for race relations is far less straightforward than is often supposed.

It is far from clear what Abrams means by the term 'prejudice'. This is not to say that he neglects to define it. On the contrary, the following definition is included in his report:

> Not all negative, unfavourable attitudes towards a group and its individual members necessarily constitute prejudice. The essence of prejudice lies in the fact that the hostility has its origins not in any realistic assessment of the actual behaviour and attributes of the group in question but results rather from processes within the bearer of the hostile attitude.[6]

But there seems very little, if any, correspondence between this formal definition and Abrams' operational measure of prejudice. In his formal definition he stresses that the terms should be used to label only those unfavourable attitudes which have a particular kind of origin, i.e. those which result from processes within the bearer of the hostile attitude. Yet there is no reason to suppose that his prejudice-scale measures only those attitudes and not the others which he states do not constitute prejudice. No claim is made, and there is no evidence to suggest that the scale differentiates between attitudes derived from different sources. His formal definition of prejudice seems to constitute little more than window-dressing.

If Abrams' scale does not measure prejudice as he defines it formally, does it measure prejudice as he defines it operationally? The answer seems to be no. Two general statements are made about the scale. The first, which describes it 'as a device for measuring broad trends in attitudes' is both vague and misleading.[7] That it is vague is self-evident. It is misleading because three of the four items which make up the scale are concerned with only one topic — housing.[d] The second statement is less vague but also misleading. Abrams notes that the scale was constructed 'by selecting those attitudinal questions which provided respondents with an opportunity to express unconditional hostility towards coloured people'.[8] Though not strictly true, it is the case, in three of the four items concerned, that respondents were given the opportunity of rejecting a particular qualification to their otherwise unfavourable point of view concerning the treatment of coloured people. The fourth item is clearly of a very different sort. Respondents were asked to say whether or not they thought themselves superior or inferior to the majority of coloured people in Britain. Those who said 'superior' were then asked: 'Is that because of their skin colour or for some other reason?' This is a very unsatisfactory question for several reasons.[e] But most important, in this respect, is that it cannot be assumed that it is a measure of unconditional *hostility*. It is, to put it at its simplest, possible to judge someone inferior and yet to like or pity them.

If the scale is not a measure of prejudice as it is defined formally, and if it is not even a good measure of prejudice as it is defined operationally, of what, if anything, is it a satisfactory measure? There seems to be one remaining possibility — that it may be a measure of the extent of unfavourable attitudes expressed in the course of the interviews — irrespective of their origin and whether or not they indicate the existence of unconditional hostility. But even this is not the case, for far too little weight was given to most of the items in the questionnaire which tapped unfavourable attitudes towards coloured people. The effect of this was to build in a bias towards the tolerant end of the prejudice–tolerance scale.[9] By adopting weightings no more nor less arbitrary than those employed by Abrams a quite different pattern of prejudice scores can be obtained.

The prejudice–tolerance scale (according to a note in Appendix VII. 3 in *Colour and Citizenship*) was made up of fourteen items. Four of these are 'key'

[d] The three items were about:
1. Whether respondents would have coloured neighbours even if they were professional people.
2. Whether the authorities should refuse housing to coloured tenants even if they had been on the waiting-list the required time.
3. Whether a private landlord should refuse accommodation to coloured tenants even if he knew they would care for his property.

[e] For instance, it would be most surprising if even a self-confessed racialist would attempt to justify his belief in white superiority on grounds of skin colour as such. Yet it appears from Dr Abrams' account of his scoring procedures that only those respondents who said that coloured people were inferior 'because of their skin colour' were scored as prejudiced.

items and the other ten 'supplementary'. An unconditionally prejudiced reply to any one of the four key questions was awarded a score of 15 points. Hence a respondent who gave four such replies was given a score of 60 points. A prejudiced reply on any one of the ten supplementary items was awarded only 1 point. Therefore the maximum obtainable score *seems* to have been 70 points. Whether or not this was definitely the case is not clear. It is even less clear how respondents were actually allocated to the four categories. Towards the beginning of the account of the scaling procedures the 'tolerant' group is defined as those who gave non-hostile replies to the four key questions. It is then added that 'in *each* of the four groups there could, of course, be people who had expressed unfavourable attitudes to coloured people on one or more of the supplementary attitude questions' (my italics). This implies that a respondent classified as 'tolerant' could conceivably have given hostile replies to several, or perhaps even all, of the supplementary items. It also implies that another hypothetical respondent who gave hostile replies to all ten of the supplementary items, but only two of the four key items (i.e. to twelve out of the fourteen) might only have been classified as 'inclined to be prejudiced'. In other words, it seems that the answers to the ten supplementary questions may have made little or no difference to the way in which respondents were classified. This impression is reinforced when further consideration is given to this second hypothetical (but not implausible) respondent. It is explained that those who gave hostile replies to two out of the four key questions (i.e. who obtained 30 points) were allocated to the 'prejudiced-inclined' category and that those who gave three or four hostile replies (i.e. who obtained 45 or more points) were placed in the 'prejudiced' group. Clearly, using only the four key items, our hypothetical respondent's score would be 30 points and he would be described as 'prejudiced-inclined'. If the remaining ten items add anything at all to the scale then it is reasonable to expect it to be clearly shown in this instance for unfavourable replies were given to all ten of the supplementaries. Yet his score, using all fourteen of them, would be only 40 points – 5 points short of the number needed to be classified as 'prejudiced'. Thus there seems to be little doubt that the scale is effectively made up of no more than four questions since the points allocated on the basis of the other ten do not have any effect upon the categories to which respondents are ascribed.

This raises two crucial questions. The first is why the four key items were selected for an additional weighting. The second is why, once having been chosen, they were given such a massive weighting in relation to the other ten supplementary questions. No satisfactory answer has been given to either of these two questions – indeed no answer at all has been given to the second. It is claimed, in answer to the first, that the key items were selected because they gave respondents an opportunity to express unconditional hostility towards coloured people. In fact, as has already been noted, they simply gave the respondents an opportunity to accept a particular qualification to their otherwise unfavourable point of view. Even so, it is hard to see why this should lead to such a disproportionate weighting of the four items. It is difficult to avoid the conclusion that the weighting procedure was arrived at quite arbitrarily.

The effect of the arbitrariness on the picture of the extent of prejudice which emerged from the study can be easily illustrated. Table 10 shows the difference which results when another (no more or less arbitrary) weighting procedure is adopted. The first set of figures represents those which are obtained when

Table 10 Estimates of 'prejudice' amongst Nottingham respondents

	Original weighting %	Modified weighting %
Tolerant	60	23
Tolerant-inclined	27	33
Prejudiced-inclined	9	25
Prejudiced	4	19
No. respondents	455	

Abrams' scaling procedures are used to classify his Nottingham respondents.[f] The second set represents those obtained by modifying the procedures. Only one of the original four key items was retained – that pertaining to the letting of council houses. Those who objected to council houses being given to coloured people even when they had been on the waiting-list for the right length of time were still given 15 prejudice points. The question: 'Suppose there are two workers, one coloured and one white, who do exactly the same work. If one, and only one, had to be declared redundant, should it be the coloured or white worker?' was substituted for an item on private letting. An

[f] A full evaluation of the scale and an exact replication of the procedures demands more information than is given in *Colour and Citizenship*. This is especially necessary since some of the information given appears contradictory. I have asked both Dr Abrams and the Survey of Race Relations for the relevant additional information but have not succeeded in obtaining it. Whilst the Sociology Department at Nottingham University was able to purchase a deck of punch cards on which the information on the Nottingham part of the sample was recorded, as well as the coding frames used for the classification of the raw data, it was not supplied with any material at all on the construction of the prejudice–tolerance scale.

item on whether or not there should be separate immigration requirements for white and coloured immigrants replaced that on the avoidance of coloured neighbours. Finally, the question which asked respondents to state whether or not they considered *themselves* to be superior or inferior to coloured immigrants made way for the question which asked respondents whether or not they believed that the British were superior to Africans and/or Asians. A hostile reply to each of these three new key items was also awarded 15 points. The substitution of these three key items would not have made the prejudice–tolerance scale any less open to criticism. The selection of them was made quite arbitrarily. But to have given them the same weighting that Abrams gave his key items would not have made much, if any, difference to the validity of the prejudice–tolerance scale.

In short, it seems that the figures presented in *Colour and Citizenship* on the extent of prejudice and tolerance in Nottingham and elsewhere are meaningless statistical artefacts. This is not to say that the same applies to the raw data from which the figures are derived. Indeed use will be made of it later in this chapter. However, it does seem that the measure of the extent of prejudice in the five towns ought to be completely disregarded. But what of Abrams' general approach to the problem? Is his formal definition of prejudice acceptable? What is gained by aggregating expressed attitudes and presenting them in the form of a single prejudice score? What, if anything, do such measures tell us about race relations? These are issues of a fundamental kind which demand careful consideration. As has been already mentioned Abrams stresses that 'not all negative unfavourable attitudes towards a group and its individual members necessarily constitute prejudice'. The essence of prejudice he states, 'lies in the fact that the hostility has its origins not in any realistic assessment of the actual behaviour and the attributes of the group in question but results rather from processes within the bearer of the hostile attitude'. Although this is by no means an unusual definition of the term it is only one of many that have been offered by social scientists over the years. Whilst the term 'prejudice' is often limited to those unfavourable attitudes which are a manifestation of basic personality processes, others have adopted quite different usages. Oliver C. Cox is an obvious example. For him prejudice is a 'social attitude propagated among the public by an exploiting class for the purpose of stigmatising some group inferior so that the exploitation of either the group or its resources or both may be justified'.[10]

It is not being suggested that Cox's definition is superior to Abrams'. But it is very obviously different. Moreover the difference is not solely one of terminology. They have not merely chosen to use the word prejudice in different ways by accident. They have done so because they approach the problem with different assumptions. As is so often the case in the social sciences their definitions reflect different theoretical positions. Clearly for Cox prejudice is not a manifestation of basic personality processes but a tool developed by an exploiting class to facilitate exploitation. Prejudice is not the cause of exploitation, it simply facilitates and justifies it. Though Abrams does not make his theoretical position explicit, it is clearly reflected in his definition and very close to that adopted by Ackerman and Jahoda in their study of antisemitism. For them prejudice is something 'which fulfils a specific irrational function for its bearer'. Consequently they stress that 'only when there is evidence that his stereotypes are used as rationalisations for an irrational hostility rooted in his own personality are we talking of prejudice'.[11] Though they show awareness of the arbitrary quality of their definition, they convey the impression that they are analysing the basic or fundamental cause of antisemitism when they study personality factors. In contrast, Cox believes that it is economic forces which are the basic or fundamental determinants of inter-group relations.

Of course, as has already been pointed out, Abrams does not take his own definition particularly seriously. Though he follows the position of Ackerman and Jahoda very closely in offering his formal definition of the term he does not follow their rule for using it, i.e. 'only when there is evidence that (someone's) stereotypes are used as a rationalisation for an irrationality rooted in his own personality are we talking of prejudice'. Abrams talks of prejudice without such evidence. He does not show that the attitudes of the ten per cent whom he labels 'prejudiced' have arisen from 'processes within the bearers of the hostile attitudes'. Though he asserts that the attitudes of this group are 'irrational solutions to personality inadequacies' he does not demonstrate this to be the case.[g]

It cannot be denied that unfavourable attitudes can arise from basic personality processes or that they may fulfil a specific irrational function for those who use them. But they arise in other, no less important ways and can, and do, serve other functions. This can be illustrated by the following simple example. Tom may make unfavourable remarks about Dick for any one or more than

[g] It is true that Dr Abrams made some attempt to measure authoritarianism amongst his respondents and related such findings to those obtained from his prejudice scale. But his authoritarianism scale contained only six items (only four of which were actually used to rate respondents) and he supplies no evidence that such a truncated measure is a reliable and valid index of authoritarianism. In any case, even if we assume it to be adequate, it is still difficult to understand how Dr Abrams felt able to state that the views of the 10 per cent prejudiced are 'irrational solutions to personality inadequacies'. For, even if we leave aside the question of whether or not those who score high on authoritarianism scales necessarily suffer from personality inadequacies, only one third of the ten per cent prejudiced were classified as authoritarians. E. J. B. Rose and associates, *Colour and Citizenship* (London, Oxford University Press, for Institute of Race Relations, 1969), pp. 565 and 588.

one of the following reasons. Because he has been told by his parents that Dick is not a nice boy, because he believes that Dick deprived him of a toffee apple – perhaps because Dick was ahead of him in the queue when the limited supply was given away – or because he, for some deep-seated personality reason, gains satisfaction from saying unfavourable things about Dick. Now whilst it may be important to know why Tom feels the way he does about Dick – especially if we want him to like Dick – it will not be possible to discover why simply by asking him if he thinks he is better than Dick and if he thinks Dick ought not to have a toffee apple next time they are given away – even if he has waited in the queue with the rest. Which is what, in effect, Abrams implies his prejudice–tolerance scale has achieved.

Though perhaps trivial this example does illustrate several important points. In particular, that unfavourable attitudes may be transmitted and learned as a matter of course during socialisation and that they may arise from real or apparent conflicts of interest – as well as from personality processes. It is because unfavourable attitudes can arise in such a variety of ways that I prefer to use the term prejudice in a less narrow way than either Cox or Abrams. As Simpson and Yinger have pointed out, 'the causes of antipathy between groups are cumulative and interactive'.[12] For this reason, and without underestimating the significance of the way in which attitudes have arisen, I prefer to use the term prejudice to refer to all those unfavourable attitudes which involve the prejudgement of groups and members of groups regardless of how they have arisen.

The relative significance of different sources of prejudice towards minorities will vary, of course, from society to society and social situation to social situation. Moreover in any given instance, it will not be possible to disentangle completely the extent to which unfavourable attitudes derive from each of the three sources which have been indicated. Nevertheless, there is considerable evidence that in Britain, at the present time, it is the cultural framework which is the underlying basis for antipathy towards coloured people. Both unfavourable attitudes and a sense of superiority towards coloured people are prevalent amongst the white British population. For instance, Abrams' investigation showed that almost two-thirds of those interviewed considered the British superior to most Africans and Asians. In contrast, only 23 per cent thought the British superior to most Americans. Similarly, he found that at least 60 per cent of those interviewed in each of the five towns thought that coloured immigrants took 'more out of the country than they put into it'. In contrast, only 36 per cent held this view with regard to Greek and Cypriot immigrants to Britain.[13] What is important, however, is not only that these and similar views are prevalent, but that they are held, in a great many instances, by perfectly ordinary men and women, many of whom have never been in close contact with coloured people. In short, it is reasonable to assume that the views held by them must have been culturally transmitted.

There is no need to discuss at length the way in which such views originated. To what extent they derive from the mistaken view of races contained in early attempts by biologists to classify human differences, or as a rationalisation of the brutal treatment meted out to black people during the period of slavery, or as a deliberate attempt to engender in the working class views which would make it difficult for them to see, mirrored in the treatment accorded to black people, their own deprived and exploited condition, are important questions but they need not be discussed here. It is sufficient to note that whatever their origins these views are now firmly embodied in British culture and, to that extent, those who hold them are normal rather than exceptional. Certainly there is no reason why anyone should be surprised by the fact that most British people feel superior towards coloured people. Generations of them grew up in the period when this country ruled over vast areas of the world and hundreds of millions of black people. And they learned, as a result, not only that it was good to be British but that it was unfortunate and a sign of inferiority to be black. Geography lessons at school were a constant reminder of this for large areas of the world's map were coloured red. History lessons recorded the triumphs of the British Army but the treachery of the Indian Mutiny and the barbarity of the 'Black Hole of Calcutta'.[14] On Empire Day children sang 'Land of Hope and Glory' and 'Rule Britannia' and were reminded of Britain's supremacy. And in Sunday School they learned of the daring exploits of white British missionaries who, without a thought for their own lives, took light into the gloom of darkest Africa and the hearts of the black heathen natives who lived there. Children were not taught to hate black people. But they learned that black people were different, that we were their masters and teachers, and that they were naturally subordinate to us.

There is no reason to suppose that either racial stereotypes or this sense of superiority will disappear in the immediate future.[h] Indeed they are still being

[h]   An extremely telling example of the extent to which such a sense of superiority may persist amongst whites (but in a way which would not be revealed by tests of prejudice) can be found in Norman Mailer's fascinating *Miami and the Siege of Chicago* (London, Penguin, 1969), p. 50. He describes his feelings whilst waiting for Rev. Ralph D. Abernathy to turn up for a press conference during the Miami Convention as follows:
    '. . . there was a mental picture of (Abernathy) waking heavily, the woes of race, tension, unfulfilled commitment, skipped promises, and the need for militant effort in the day ahead all staring down into whatever kind of peace had been reached the night before in the stretch before sleep.
    Still it was unduly irritating to have to wait at a press conference, and as the minutes went by and annoyance mounted, the reporter became aware after a while of a curious emotion in himself, for he had not ever felt it consciously

reinforced. The seaside postcard which portrays a white man in a pot sur-
rounded by black and hungry cannibals is perhaps, in itself, innocuous. So
perhaps is the portrayal of black Americans as loyal but rather stupid servants
in old Hollywood films still shown from time to time on British television.
Equally, the following of a documentary on apartheid in South Africa with a
commercial in which black men appear half naked, daubed with war paint and
brandishing spears may seem a little tasteless but not worthy of special mention. Yet each of these images, and many others besides, probably combine to
bolster-up racial stereotypes and feelings of superiority. Statements by
respected public figures and actions by governments may be equally if not more
important in this respect. The control of immigration from the Commonwealth
in 1962, whilst reflecting a widespread public desire, no doubt served in turn to
further convince those who had wanted control that their fears were well
grounded and their demands legitimate. The plea of Enoch Powell for the
repatriation of coloured people; the boast of a Labour Party spokesman during
the 1970 Election Campaign that Britain already had one of the most stringent
immigration control systems in the world; and the introduction of yet more
stringent controls by the Conservative Government no doubt have a similar
effect. For though such actions and statements do not constitute an incitement
to racial hatred they do constitute an important source of legitimacy for unfavourable attitudes and existing hostility. Even the establishment of bodies
like the Community Relations Commission and the Race Relations Board,
symbolising the illegitimacy of hostility and discrimination against coloured
people, by their very existence probably help preserve the feeling that coloured
people *are* different.

In emphasing the extent to which racial stereotypes and feelings of superiority are embodied in our culture I do not wish to suggest that this renders all, or
even most, people positively hostile towards coloured immigrants. But the fact
that they are prevalent does mean that those who hold them are, in an important sense, 'normal' rather than 'abnormal'. Moreover the prevalence of such
stereotypes and feelings does at least constitute an underlying basis for hostility.

So far the discussion has concentrated on only one aspect of Abrams'

before – it was a simple emotion and very unpleasant to him – he was getting
tired of Negroes and their rights. It was a miserable recognition and on many a
count, for if he felt even a hint this way, then what immeasurable tides of rage
must be loose in America itself? . . . Like an advance reconnaissance scout of the
armies of the most quintessential bigotry, one soldier from that alien army flung
himself over the last entrenchment, stood up to die, and posed the question:
"How do you know the Black Man is not Ham, son of Evil? How do you really
know?" and the soldier exploded a defence works in the reporter's brain, and
bitterness towards Negroes flowed forth like the blood of the blown-up dead.'

general approach – his definition of prejudice. We now turn to an equally important element – his presentation of unfavourable attitudes in the form of a prejudice scale. The particular form the scale takes is open to criticism. For instance, no evidence is presented to support the clear implication that it is unidimensional in character – a crucial and standard criterion by which attitude scales are judged. Again, the choice of words used to describe it leaves much to be desired. It will be remembered that it is referred to as a prejudice–tolerance scale and that the four groups distinguished are labelled; 'prejudiced', 'prejudiced-inclined', 'tolerant-inclined' and 'tolerant'. Clearly 'tolerance' is seen as the opposite of 'prejudice'. Yet nowhere is 'tolerance' formally defined. This is especially unfortunate since the confusion which surrounds Dr Abrams' use of the term 'prejudice' makes it difficult to ascertain to precisely what 'tolerance' is intended to be a polar opposite. All that is offered is an operational definition which states that 'tolerant' respondents are those who gave non-hostile replies to all four key questions.[15] In other words 'tolerance' seems to be equated with the absence of hostility. This is a slightly unusual use of the word. An absence of hostility does not necessarily indicate the presence of tolerance. If 'A' positively likes or is quite indifferent to 'B', he is not being tolerant. It is only if 'A' puts up with 'B' despite something about him he does not like that he is being tolerant. Thus to label 35 per cent of the sample as 'tolerant' when unknown proportions of this group may like or be indifferent to coloured people seems to be potentially misleading.

In the abridged version of *Colour and Citizenship*,[16] for which Nicholas Deakin is responsible, several interesting modifications are made to the chapter on racial prejudice. Most striking is the change in terminology adopted. It is noted by Deakin in this way:

> ... there is a slight shift of emphasis in the presentation of the prejudice–tolerance scale which formed part of Dr Abrams analysis; we have chosen on this occasion to consider these findings more from the perspective of the extent of prejudice than in relation to the presence of tolerance.[17]

In plain language this means that Deakin retains Abrams' figures and categories but changes his labels. The terms 'prejudiced', 'prejudiced-inclined', 'tolerant-inclined' and 'tolerant' are abandoned and replaced by either operational definitions or the following terms: 'intensely prejudiced', 'prejudiced', 'mildly prejudiced' and 'no overt prejudice'. The 10 per cent whom Abrams calls 'prejudiced' are called 'intensely prejudiced' by Deakin. The 17 per cent Abrams calls 'prejudiced-inclined' are called 'prejudiced' by Deakin. The 38 per cent called 'tolerant-inclined' by Abrams are called 'mildly-prejudiced' by Deakin. Finally, the remaining 35 per cent whom Abrams calls 'tolerant' are referred to by Deakin as 'showing no overt prejudice'.[18] No doubt the reader will decide for himself whether or not the change of labels involves no more than a 'slight shift of emphasis' as Deakin asserts. I would contend that it most certainly does not and that the new labels give a very different impression from the old. Moreover, as Deakin wrote much of the original version of *Colour and Citizenship*, and is jointly responsible with Rose for Chapter 33 in which Abrams' terms are employed and his findings underwritten, it is to say the least puzzling that the labels should be changed in such a way without a much fuller explanation.[i] But, if nothing else, the change of terms does at least make it abundantly clear how great a degree of arbitrariness has been involved in attaching labels to what seem to be, in any case, more or less arbitrarily determined statistical categories.[j]

This raises a fundamental point which applies whichever set of labels is employed. What does it mean to say that 10 per cent are 'prejudiced' and 17 per cent 'prejudiced-inclined' or, to use the other set of labels, that 10 per cent are 'intensely prejudiced' and 17 per cent 'prejudiced'? What is learned about 'A' when he is said to be more prejudiced than 'B' but less prejudiced than 'C'. Is it, for example, analogous to saying that 'A' is more intelligent than 'B' but less intelligent than 'C' – at least as measured by an intelligence test? In this case something more may be learned about those concerned than their relative performances in intelligence tests. The results may also enable one to predict which of the three is least capable of performing well at school. This is because, despite their very real limitations, intelligence tests seem to be measuring relatively enduring attributes. This is not to suggest that intelligence tests are extremely reliable. Indeed it is partly because of the extent of their unreliability that they have been the subject of so much criticism. But are tests of prejudice even as reliable as tests of intelligence? And do they have as much predictive capacity? A typical answer might be that prejudice is an attitude and as such is an index of a predisposition to behave in a particular way. It would follow that the 10 per cent 'prejudiced' are more likely to behave in a hostile way towards coloured people than the 'prejudiced-inclined' 17 per cent. Yet it is known that

[i]   For instance: 'The degree of tolerance in the population is even higher (than the degree of prejudice). Over one third of all white adults in the sample "expressed views with no trace, or practically no trace, of hostility to coloured people"; nearly two fifths "seemed to be strongly disposed in the direction of tolerance". Together they account for seven out of ten of the sample in the five boroughs with heavy immigrant settlement . . . The findings prompt us to under-score Dr Abrams' basic recommendations that "attempts to improve race relations, while they must not ignore the views of the 10 per cent (prejudiced) minority, should see them for what they are – irrational "solutions" to personality inadequacies which would persist without regard to the policies adopted.' Rose (1969), p. 736.

[j]   Because Dr Abrams wrote the first part of Chapter 28 in *Colour and Citizenship* reference has been made only to him in the criticisms of that part of the chapter. But the responsibilities for any deficiencies in it are presumably shared by those responsible for the book as a whole – i.e. E. J. B. Rose and Nicholas Deakin.

measures of prejudice are not particularly good predictors of behaviour and that whilst not completely fluid, certainly do not remain fixed. In which case the usefulness of traditional measures of prejudice must surely be questioned. What is added to the understanding of race relations by arranging individuals along a uni-dimensional continuum of prejudice?

In fact surprisingly little seems to be added and it is partly for this reason that it has become a virtual commonplace to note that prejudice can exist without discrimination or other forms of hostile or unfriendly behaviour. Though it is possible, of course, that someone with a high IQ may not do well at school, it is at least fairly certain that this will be the fate of someone who has a low IQ. The same does not hold for measures of prejudice. Someone who has recently received a low rating could very well behave in a hostile way. This follows from the fact that his behaviour is a function of much more than his attitudes. Consider the case of a man living in relative comfort who obtains a lowish score on a uni-dimensional prejudice scale. How will he behave given a radical change in his circumstances? Suppose he suddenly and unexpectedly finds that many coloured families are about to move into his previously all-white suburban estate and that the market value of his property drops dramatically – or suppose that he loses his job and is obliged to look for hard-to-find cheap housing in a decaying central city area in which he enters into competition with coloured people for the first time. Will he behave in accordance with his lowish prejudice score? Quite probably not. In which case what was gained by measuring his attitudes on a uni-dimensional scale in the first instance? And, no less important, is there not a danger that a misleading impression might have been given by his lowish prejudice score? This is certainly a possibility if a theory of prejudice is made to do double duty as a predictor of behaviour. McWilliams made a highly pertinent comment in this connection several years ago when he stressed that 'case histories of every German would have failed to explain what happened to the Jews in Germany between 1918 and 1939'.[19] In the same way it is worth reiterating the point made earlier in this chapter – that Abrams' findings might lead some to conclude that the prospect for race relations in Britain is most encouraging. His findings do not necessarily support such a conclusion and this would still be the case were they free of the deficiencies that have been mentioned.[k]

[k]   I do not suggest that Dr Abrams *intended* to produce feelings of complacency. Indeed he has specifically denied this. 'I had hoped that among those who detest prejudice these findings would engender not complacency but rather the courage to fight for their convictions and the confidence that the battle is winnable.' (Letter to *The Listener* 27 November 1969). But, whatever his intention, the point remains that by means of technically unsound procedures Dr Abrams presented a set of 'findings' in an authoritative way and between the covers of an authoritative report which could possibly encourage such complacency.

It remains for me to make my own theoretical position explicit. In Britain, at the present time, most unfavourable attitudes towards coloured people seem to have been culturally transmitted. Though they may well have been reinforced by contact and competition and by personality factors in some cases, the prevalence of unfavourable stereotypes amongst perfectly ordinary men and women, many of whom have never been in close contact with coloured people, provides strong evidence that racial distinctions are built into our cultural definitions. As long as such distinctions are prevalent there can be no solution to the so-called 'colour problem'. This does not mean that open racial conflict is inevitable unless the British become 'colour-blind'. However there can be no guarantee of racial harmony unless racial differences are freed of their current social significance. So long as they are accorded it they must form a potential basis for conflict.

It is inevitable that men will distinguish between members of different cultural, religious and linguistic groups. This is because such differences have an intrinsic social significance. But racial differences have no such intrinsic properties. There is no reason why they should not become as socially insignificant as differences of height, weight and hair colour. On the other hand, the investment of such physical attributes with social significance has very far reaching consequences. It may not be easy, but it is nevertheless possible for a man to change his religion or his language – not so his skin colour. He may be proud of it or ashamed of it but, like it or not, there is nothing that can be done about it. The sons of rich men may become poor and the sons of Jews, Gentile; the sons of radicals may become conservative and ignorant men, wise – but the children of black parents must always remain black. It is this which makes the distinction so invidious.

Obviously the degree to which social significance is attached to the distinction will vary from individual to individual and from social situation to social situation. Indeed for many if not most people, for much if not most of the time, it is probably of no immediate relevance. For instance, few people probably behave differently towards a bus conductor because he is black. It makes little or no difference to their relationship with him. Certainly they would not dream of waiting for another bus in order to avoid contact with him. On the other hand, given only two vacant seats on the bus, one adjacent to a white man and the other a black man, some might consciously choose to sit next to the former rather than the latter. But few would choose to stand rather than sit next to the black man were that the available alternative. In other words, in many circumstances, the distinction between black and white is to all intents and purposes irrelevant. Nevertheless, the initial categorisation into black and white still seems to be the crucial starting point for the understanding of race relations. And, from this point of view, someone who obtains a low score on a prejudice-scale, but who still invests the distinction with some social significance is, in an important sense, similar to someone who obtains a high score. Whereas it is usual to stress the difference between those who obtain high and low scores, it is the similarity which is emphasised here. This is because, given the fundamental distinction between black and white, what it seems most important to determine is in what respects the distinction is perceived to be an important and immediately relevant one to those concerned and in what ways it could come to be seen as relevant. In short, when does it matter that a man is black? Social distance scales are one way of tackling this question. However the very standardisation which is the *raison d'être* for such scales imposes severe limitations on their usefulness. What is needed is not an assessment of relevance and potential relevance in terms of formal and effectively abstract categories, but an assessment in terms which relate in a much more realistic way to the actual social situation of those concerned.

It follows, from what has been said about the importance of the social situation in determining the extent to which attitudes are reflected in behaviour, that the development of race relations may be crucially affected by changes which may not appear immediately relevant to them. Changes in the law controlling the entry of Commonwealth immigrants into Britain, the introduction of laws making racial discrimination illegal and the setting up of bodies like the Community Relations Commission are obviously relevant. Changes in the economic and housing situations are less so. They are areas in which changes take place for reasons which have nothing to do with race relations and in which changes are engineered without any consideration of the effect they may have on race relations. Yet they are undoubtedly of great importance to the development of race relations. Thus, in the long run, it is at least conceivable that Britain's entry into the Common Market and the Conservative Government's Housing Finance Act may prove of greater moment to race relations than decisions on such things as immigration control. Yet it is on solely such considerations as the latter that some students of race relations concentrate their attention.

In summary, patterns of race relations seem to be determined less by the numbers falling into particular prejudiced categories than on whether or not the fundamental categorisation into black and white is prevalent, and the nature of the social situation of those involved. Obviously, how men define their situation may be influenced by the degree to which they are prejudiced. But this is only one of many factors likely to determine how a situation will be defined and there is no reason to suppose that it will necessarily be the most decisive.

That most people in Nottingham consider coloured people different and inferior was firmly established by Abrams' investigation.[*l*] This can be shown in several different ways.[*m*] For instance, respondents were asked: 'Do you think coloured people should be let into Britain to settle on the same basis as other people from abroad or should there be special regulations for coloured people?' Fifty-five per cent said there ought to be special regulations for coloured people. Again, respondents were asked whether or not they considered the British, on the whole, superior or inferior to the majority of people in Europe, Asia, Africa and America. The results are most interesting. The proportion who thought the British superior varied a great deal with the group with which they were compared. Only 24 per cent considered the British superior to the Americans but, rather more, 38 per cent, considered them superior to Europeans. At the other extreme, however, 58 per cent considered the British superior to Asians and 66 per cent thought them superior to Africans. Put another way: 56 per cent thought the majority of Americans to be much the same as the British and 49 per cent made a similar judgement with respect to Europeans. But only 21 per cent thought the majority of Asians the same as the British and the corresponding figure with respect to the Africans was even smaller – namely 17 per cent.

One can only speculate on the reasons for this particular rank order. If only physical criteria are involved it is difficult to explain why Americans are rated above Europeans. On the other hand, if only cultural criteria are involved it is difficult to account for the rating of Asians over Africans. It seems possible that most make an initial distinction on the basis of physical criteria – which would account for the ranking of Asians over Africans, and Americans and Europeans over Asians and Africans – and then employ cultural criteria – which would account for the ranking of Americans over Europeans. But, for whatever reason, it is quite apparent that most of those interviewed consider the British superior to Africans and Asians. The extent to which respondents thought colour a characteristic with social significance is also shown by the answers to the question: 'Do you think colour will ever become unimportant in the way people feel about each other?'. Considering that this question involved speculation not about the immediate future but about whether or not colour would *ever* become unimportant, the answers are particularly striking. In all, 62 per cent said they thought colour would definitely, or probably, remain im-

[*l*]   This is not to say that coloured people are judged inferior *because* of their colour but that colour is used as an index of inferiority and socially significant differences.

[*m*]   The figures which follow are derived from data cards, purchased from Research Services Limited by the Sociology Department at Nottingham University, which contain the information collected from the Nottingham respondents in Dr Abrams' sample.

portant. Only 8 per cent definitely thought that it would eventually become un-important. Thus there can be little doubt that most people in Nottingham make and attach some social significance to the distinction between black and white. Moreover, the figures presented have been offered separately rather than in combination. If they are combined, the proportion who make the distinction is seen to be much larger than the separate figures might suggest. For instance, 46 per cent of those who did not say there ought to be special immigration regulations for coloured people did say that the British were superior to most Asians and Africans. Thus 80 per cent of the Nottingham sample said that there ought to be special entry regulations for coloured people and/or that the British are superior to most Asians and Africans.

Of course it is inter-play between the attitudes and circumstances of those who live in the inner zone of the city which is of most interest in this study. Thus, in the remainder of the chapter, some of the general characteristics of the people who live there will be noted before a more detailed examination of the inter-play within the fields of housing and employment is presented in Chapters 4 and 5.

Whereas all of the coloured people interviewed were immigrants, most of the white respondents had been born in Nottingham or its immediate environs. Though white aliens were excluded from the sample, all those born in other parts of Great Britain were included. Yet as many as 73 per cent had been born in or around Nottingham and 70 per cent had lived all of their life in the city. In further contrast to the coloured respondents, only 2 per cent of whom were over sixty at the time of the interviews, 25 per cent of the white sample were over sixty – and as many as 17 per cent were of pensionable age. Taken together these findings are particularly important. On one hand is a sample of highly visible immigrants only half of whom had lived in Nottingham for more

Table 11 Period of life spent in Nottingham

	Native whites %	Coloured immigrants %
All life	70	—
More than 25 years	13	—
15–24 years	7	10
5–14 years	13	81
Less than 5 years	4	9
No. respondents	124	121

Table 12 **Age structure of samples**

	Native whites %	Coloured immigrants %
21–9 years	15	8
30–9 years	21	37
40–9 years	19	38
50–9 years	19	14
60+ years	25	2
No. respondents	124	121

Table 13 **Social class composition of English sample**

Social class	Employed %	Retired %	All %
1	1	—	1
2	4	4	4
3a	8	17	10
3b	40	30	38
4	31	26	30
5	17	22	18
No. respondents	101	23	124

Categories are derived from Registrar General's
'Classification of Occupations'.
3a represents non-manual workers.
3b represents manual workers.
Figures in 'Employed' column include 2 sick and 4
unemployed respondents.

than ten years at the time of the interviews and only 10 per cent of whom had lived there for more than fifteen. On the other, in very sharp contrast, is a largely home-grown white sample 94 per cent of whom had lived in Nottingham for more than ten years and 86 per cent of whom had lived there for more than fifteen. It is therefore hardly surprising, as the next two chapters will show, that many of the white respondents feel they have a prior claim on jobs and houses.

Of those white respondents who were currently employed at the time of the interviews 88 per cent were manual workers and as many as 48 per cent of them were unskilled or semi-skilled. In the white sample as a whole, 86 per cent had been, or were, in manual jobs and 48 per cent of them in unskilled or semi-skilled work. This occupational pattern closely accords with the educational qualifications of the sample. Eighty-four per cent had attended either elementary or secondary modern schools and 71 per cent were without any formal qualifications.

In the vast majority of cases those interviewed were earning less than the national average. As Table 14 shows, of the currently employed, 37 per cent were earning, on average and before deductions, £15 or less per week. Seventy-four per cent earned £21 or less. These figures, moreover, include overtime earnings. Fifty-six per cent had a basic weekly income, before deductions, of £15 or less and 85 per cent £21 or less. The basic wage of those who usually worked overtime was, in 74 per cent of cases, £15 or less. In only 4 per cent of cases were those who worked overtime earning more than a £21 basic. Clearly most of those who worked overtime were doing so to boost a low basic wage. Without overtime pay 85 per cent of the sample would have had weekly earnings of less than £21. That these figures represent earnings *before deductions* should not be overlooked. By the time National Insurance contributions and Income Tax are taken into account, they are appreciably smaller.

Table 14 Earnings, before deductions, of currently employed white respondents

	Basic wage %	Earnings %
£10–15	56	37
£16–21	29	36
£22 or more	15	26
No. respondents	86	86

Of the 95 white respondents who were currently employed, nine preferred not to give details of their earnings. However, an examination of the jobs of this small group indicates that it is most unlikely that their exclusion will have made any noticeable difference to the distribution of earnings shown in the table.

One way in which these findings can be put into perspective is to compare them to national average figures for 1968, the year in which the interviews were conducted. In that year, according to official sources, the average weekly earnings for full-time male manual workers over the age of twenty-one were £23. The average earnings of those in the sample who belonged to this category were £18.11 – almost £5 less than the national average. The small number of non-manual workers in the sample fared no better. The average weekly earnings for male administrative, technical and clerical employees in the same year were £29.75. The average earnings of the small number of the respondents who belonged to this category were £22.07 – not far from £8 less than the national average. Indeed their average earnings were almost £1 less than the national average for manual workers.[20]

No attempt was made to determine the size of the pensions or other income of retired respondents. But there is no doubt that most were dependent on state pensions and perhaps supplementary benefits – augmented in some cases by small savings and the help of relatives. The net result was that in most cases they were living near, if not actually below, the poverty line.

It does not seem necessary to include any further details at this stage to support the general categorisation of the social situation of those members of the indigenous population who live in Nottingham's inner zone. They obviously constitute, in comparison with most of those who live in the countries from which the immigrants have come, a relatively affluent group. One could show, for instance, that their life expectancy is longer, their housing conditions superior and their real incomes much larger. However, in comparison with the indigenous population of this country as a whole, they constitute a deprived and underprivileged minority. Though in international terms they may be relatively well-off, in national terms they are relatively poor. So though the immigrants have come from poor countries to what is a relatively rich one, they are living alongside the very section of the white population who, in terms of relative poverty and insecurity, are most like them. Most of those interviewed belong to the group my Nottingham colleagues Coates and Silburn have termed 'the forgotten Englishmen' in their book on poverty.[21] They are not in danger of starving, but neither do they enjoy, or have much prospect of enjoying, the secure and comfortable existence which so many of the immigrants believed typical of everyone in this country. They subsist, by national standards, on low wages or mean pensions, and this is the main reason why they live in the inner zone. There they live what is effectively a different kind of life from that which is taken for granted by so many of their fellow countrymen who live in the pleasant suburbs that ring the city. It is those in the inner zone who suffer most from Britain's inability or unwillingness to spend sufficient of its national income on the replacement or improvement of slum property, from high and seemingly ever rising prices and from the loss of dignity and self-respect which so often accompanies material deprivation. They comprise, in short, one of the most vulnerable sections of the indigenous population and, in many respects, those most likely to feel threatened by highly visible competitors for scarce resources. The immigrants have come here, in the main, in an attempt to escape from the cycle of poverty and insecurity endemic in their own societies. They have come as victims and casualties of their own economic systems and the world's economy. In the inner zone of the city, however, they have joined another group of whom many can reasonably be described as victims and casualties. In this respect at least they have a great deal in common with their white neighbours.

In this chapter an alternative approach to the study of English attitudes towards coloured people, to the by no means unusual or unorthodox one adopted by Dr Abrams in his report for the Institute of Race Relations, has been proposed. I have argued that the study of race relations is not much illuminated by the use of scales to divide up populations in terms of the degree to which they are 'prejudiced' (even when the scales are technically less suspect than that used in *Colour and Citizenship*) or with the establishment of simple correlations between levels of prejudice arrived at in this way and such standard variables as age, sex, and socio-economic status. What seems to be more useful is a consideration of specific attitudes and only then if they are related to the circumstances, as well as demographic characteristics, of those who have expressed them.

Attitudes about how appropriate it is for coloured people to have equal access to various kinds of housing, for example, should not be submerged along with other views in a single prejudice score. In that way useful insights may be lost. And, even then, it may not help much if such attitudes are correlated with demographic characteristics in a more or less mechanical fashion.[n] To begin to understand the relevance of attitudes to behaviour there

[n] One of the recommendations contained in *Colour and Citizenship* warrants a mention at this point. The authors seem to assume that the negative correlation found between length of education and degree of prejudice must be causal in nature and that, as a result, the extension of the school leaving-age would bring about a reduction in prejudice. The possibility that the correlation might reflect more about the kind of people who have stayed on longer at school in the past and their circumstances, rather than the beneficial effect of longer schooling in itself is not considered. 'The findings concerning the effects of education suggest that an increase in the educational level of the population would reduce the amount of prejudice, other things being equal. Even a single year's further education beyond the present school leaving-age of fifteen would have a valuable return in decreased levels of prejudice. Even if there were no other compelling reasons, this in itself would constitute the strongest argument for raising the school leaving-age. The more education the population receives, the more this effect is likely to be felt. The most tolerant group of all, in the national study, were those who had been educated beyond the age of eighteen; while these comprised only 4 per cent of the population the majority are still under forty years old. The continued and further expansion of higher education at all levels would, on this evidence, be associated with a valuable reduction in prejudice.' Rose (1969), p. 738.

is also a need to know something of the circumstances of those who express them. For instance, what sort of housing conditions do they enjoy? How satisfied are they with such conditions? Are there any factors likely to bring about important changes in such conditions in the future? Will they be for the better or for the worse? Only by taking such matters into account can the significance of attitudes for behaviour and social relationships be appreciated. Unfortunately, when Abrams did venture in this direction his analysis did not go very far.[o]

As yet, of course, the analysis in this book has not gone far in this direction. But the remarks towards the end of the chapter have, I hope, served as something of an introduction to the distinguishing characteristics and circumstances of the white respondents. And it ought already to be apparent that replies from them may differ greatly in their significance from similarly-worded ones from people in very different circumstances. In the next chapter we shall look more closely at, amongst other things, attitudes on housing, how these relate to housing circumstances and, consequently, what significance they may have for patterns of race relations.

[o]   See, for instance, Dr Abrams' discussion of the relationship between patterns of housing tenure and attitudes on housing. Rose (1969), p. 579.

4
Race relations and housing

Nottingham's present housing problems have their origins in the eighteenth century. Before that the town seems to have been relatively free from them. In 1684 Celia Fiennes described it as 'the neatest town' she had seen and, forty years later, in a similar vein, it was judged by Daniel Defoe to be 'one of the most pleasant and beautiful towns in England'.[1] There does not seem to have been any particular housing shortage nor even any clear demarcation of residential areas according to the social standing of the inhabitants. By the middle of the eighteenth century 'the town consisted of not more than 2,000 houses containing 10,000 people'. Moreover, 'most houses had stretches of gardens and many had orchards'.[2]

Unfortunately, this seemingly happy state of affairs did not survive the population explosion of the late eighteenth century and the rapid development of industrialisation. Indeed, according to the Second Report of the Health of Towns Commission, by 1845 the slums and overcrowding in Nottingham were worse than those of any other industrial town.[3] Much of this deterioration has been attributed to the political deadlock which prevented the complete enclosure of the common fields before 1845.[4] Although there was an almost six-fold increase in the population between 1750 and 1850 the town's boundaries remained virtually unchanged. Developments beyond the open fields, in places like Hyson Green and New Lenton, provided only marginal relief and the first half of the nineteenth century was characterised by a rapid inflation in land values, extreme overcrowding and a significant decline in the quality of many of the new dwellings erected. As Chapman has recently reiterated:

> Thousands of houses were erected by greedy speculators who studied, not the convenience and health of those obliged to take them, but how they might best secure 20 per cent on their outlay.[5]

A survey, carried out by an *ad hoc* Board of Health set up when cholera threatened in 1831, showed that of the 11,000 dwellings in the town 7,000 to 8,000 were 'constructed back-to-back, having no means of through ventilation and generally without other than a common convenience to several dwellings'.[6]

Boundary extensions were eventually incorporated in the 1845 Nottingham

Enclosure Act. Minimum housing standards were also specified and, for the time, the Act was undoubtedly a fairly progressive piece of legislation. Not only was the building of more back-to-backs prohibited, but each new house was to have its own 'privy', be provided with a garden or yard of not less than 30 sq ft, have three distinct bedrooms and walls at least two bricks thick. Of course private developers could not be obliged to provide houses of this standard for all those who needed them and the number, quality and location of those built on the newly available land was determined not by any criterion of social need but by the profit motive. Consequently, in the period 1851–6 for example, most of the 2,100 houses built were far beyond the means of those most in need of them. Moreover, even when specifically working-class dwellings were erected, the Act was no guarantee against developers cutting corners. It was reported in 1852 that the 'only approach to cheap houses on the newly enclosed lands are some ... in the Meadows ... which adopt the back-to-back system, but obviate all its objections'. And, at the end of 1860, the Sanitary Committee reported that there were about 500 dwellings in the Meadows 'quite destitute of drainage'.[7] As the Nottingham Journal observed in 1856, 'the problem has yet to be solved of providing ... such a description of dwelling as should supply the need of a very numerous class of persons of less adequate means'.[8] It is worth noting that, more than a century later, this self-same problem of low wages still faces those who attempt to improve the housing conditions of today's slum dwellers.

In the main, in this post-enclosure period, where sites were pleasantly located and, as a result, high prices obtainable (as in the case of those on the undulating land overlooking the protected open spaces of the Arboretum and Forest), mainly large and expensive houses were built. On the less pleasant sites suitable only for the labouring classes (such as the Meadows which was subject to flooding and immediately adjacent to the industrial development which had followed the opening of the canal and railway), the new houses were small and cheap. They did improve, it is true, on the appalling back-to-backs which had been built in the earlier, pre-enclosure period. But they were sadly lacking when compared to those middle-class properties being built at the same time.

The pattern of housing which had emerged by the last quarter of the nineteenth century can still be recognised today. To the north of the old town stood Sherwood and Mapperley where the houses were large, well-appointed and expensive. To the west was the Park – originally an area of private parkland owned by the Duke of Newcastle which had been turned into a high class residential district following the Reform Bill riots of 1831 during which the Duke's own residence had been destroyed. To the south was the Meadows where, as has already been mentioned, poor quality, terraced, working-class cottages had been built on the enclosed common land. Similar blocks of houses were to be found to the north-east in St Anns. Then, finally, there were the back-to-backs in the old town itself.

Another piece of legislation enacted in 1877 brought the parishes of Sneinton, Lenton, Radford, Basford and Bulwell within Nottingham's boundaries. From these industrial suburbs the town inherited a further stock of working-class housing. However it does seem that most of it was at least an improvement on the back-to-back property in the old town.[a] Moreover, though the population increased by over 80 per cent to 157,000 as a result of the boundary extension, the town's area was increased by over 500 per cent.

By the end of the First World War the population had grown to over a quarter of a million and there had been a further expansion of the housing stock. Nevertheless, the overall residential pattern of the city remained relatively unchanged and there was still a shortage of adequate housing. The 1921 Census showed there to be 63,621 families in the city but only 61,876 structurally separate dwellings – a larger deficit than that which had been observed in 1911. And, although some slum clearance had taken place, a Report of the Housing Committee in 1919 designated 3,814 houses as being in 'unhealthy areas' requiring demolition, as well as drawing attention to the existence of a further 3,012 houses elsewhere which could not be made fit for human habitation. Moreover, many of the other, less obviously decrepit, houses still fell far below the standards taken for granted by most British people today. For example, as late as 1919, over half of all dwellings in the city were still dependent on pail closets for their sewage disposal.

Until this date almost all houses in England had been built by private enterprise and the vast majority of families had rented their accommodation from private landlords. From 1919 this pattern of provision began to undergo fundamental change. As T. H. Marshall has pointed out, 'the War gave to the housing question a new urgency'.[9] The men at the Front had been promised 'homes for heroes' and it would hardly have been politic to free rents from the controls which had been introduced during the War in an effort to prevent exploitation. On the other hand, without freeing them from control, it was most unlikely that private firms would be willing to build anything like enough houses to meet the shortage. The Government of the day responded to this dilemma, in a relatively radical way, by introducing subsidies to local authorities. In the future they were to build houses themselves and, when necessary, let them at uneconomic rents. Most of the loss incurred would then be made good by the Exchequer.

[a]   Indeed, according to Chapman, 'in general the new districts were developed as "handsome villages" delightfully placed round the periphery of the "green belt" formed by the open fields'. S. D. Chapman (ed.), *The History of Working-Class Housing* (London, David and Charles, 1971), p. 146.

N

Map 1 City of Nottingham

In Nottingham, between 1919 and 1940, 66 per cent of all new houses were built and let by the Corporation with the aid of government subsidies. Between 1945 and 1964 the proportion was 75 per cent. Most were intended to supplement existing stock rather than replace slum property. For this reason, and because of the shortage of land within the main body of the city, most of the building took the form of distinct low-density estates around the city's boundaries. Only as recently as 1960, when Nottingham's first multi-storey block was completed in Denman Street, was a real start made on slum clearance.

Accompanying the development of council housing since the First World War has been a growth in owner-occupation. Whereas in 1914 only about 10 per cent of the 8 million dwellings in Britain were owner-occupied, today this form of tenure applies to over half of the 17 million dwellings.[10] Within the city of Nottingham itself, the trend towards owner-occupation has been comparatively small. This is because much of the growth has taken place in suburbs outside the city's boundaries. Nevertheless, according to the 1966 Sample Census, 26 per cent of the dwellings in the city were in owner-occupation; a marked change from the situation at the end of the First World War.

The growth of council housing and owner-occupation has brought about both a proportionate and an absolute decline in the size of the privately rented sector of the housing market. In 1914, 90 per cent of dwellings in England and Wales were rented from private landlords. Today only about 20 per cent come into this category. In Nottingham, in 1961, 36,904 dwellings were privately rented and they comprised about 39 per cent of the total housing stock. By 1966, although there were nearly 1,000 more dwellings in the city, the total number rented from private landlords had fallen by nearly 4,000 to 33,020 and they comprised only about 35 per cent of the total stock.[b] Evidence of a different sort was provided by a study of Nottingham landlords carried out in 1967. When interviewed, it was found that they then owned 40 per cent fewer dwellings than at the end of the Second World War.[11] To some extent this decline can be attributed to the existence of rent controls. For, although small fortunes can still be made, landlordism is less lucrative than in the past. Many of today's landlords own only one or two dwellings and in some cases the rents they obtain only barely cover the cost of proper maintenance. Slum clearance is another important factor. It has diminished the large stock of mainly nineteenth century property which has been rented rather than owner-occupied since its erection, but which shows no signs of being replaced.

The changes that have been mentioned have fundamentally altered the character of Britain's housing problem. This is correctly pointed out by the

[b] In Britain as a whole the number of privately rented houses fell from about 4,500,000 to about 3,500,000 in the period 1957–64. *The Housing Programme 1965–70*, Cmnd. 2838 (HMSO, 1965).

Conservative Government in the first sentence of their White Paper *Fair Deal for Housing*: 'Over the last fifty years the housing problem has been transformed.' But, as it equally correctly continues, 'it has not been solved . . . millions of our fellow citizens still face acute housing problems. There are nearly two million slums. There are another two million homes without such essentials as bathrooms or indoor sanitation. There are still many tenants who find the cost of their home a hardship. There are still people with no home at all.'[12]

The essence of the problem in Nottingham is not so much homelessness as housing quality.[c] Thousands of families still live in substandard accommodation. This no one would deny. But, because there is no agreed definition of what constitutes substandard housing, one cannot be so categoric about how many families suffer in this way. The position taken here is that the Conservative Government have pointed to an acceptable definition in their White Paper. Not to have the exclusive use of what they describe as 'such essentials' as a bathroom, indoor lavatory and hot water tap is a clear indication of substandard housing.[d] By that standard, in 1966, nearly 41 per cent, i.e. over 40,000 of Nottingham's households were inadequately accommodated. Obviously such households were not spread uniformly throughout the city. In Clifton ward, for example, which is dominated by a post-war council estate, only 2 per cent of households lacked the exclusive use of these three basic amenities. But in Bridge ward, which includes the Meadows, 87 per cent were without them.

So at no time over the past two hundred years has Nottingham been free of a severe housing problem. It is amongst today's victims of the problem that most of the city's coloured immigrants are to be found. In 1966 only 2·8 per cent of the city's population had been born in the countries of the 'new' Commonwealth.[e] But, as Map 2 illustrates, they were heavily concentrated in certain areas. And, as Table 15 shows, the areas were those which contained the largest proportion of substandard housing.

In the research area (which contained nearly 60 per cent of the city's 'new' Commonwealth born population) 69 per cent of households were without the

---

[c]   At the time of the 1966 Census there were 102,170 households in the city and 98,540 dwellings. Most multi-occupation was to be found in the sphere of furnished accommodation.

[d]   In fact, the exclusive use of these three basic amenities are only three out of fourteen conditions making for a 'satisfactory dwelling' according to the Central Housing Advisory Committee. See *Our Older Homes* (HMSO, 1966), pp. 13–14.

[e]   This is not to say that only 2·8 per cent of the population were 'coloured'. The figure may include a small number of white persons born in the 'new' Commonwealth. More important, the figure does not include those children born in Britain to 'new' Commonwealth born parents. In 1966 probably about 4–5 per cent of the population were 'coloured'.

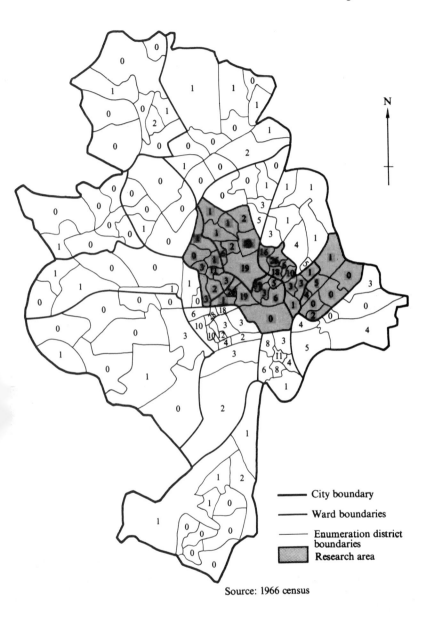

Source: 1966 census

Map 2 Percentages of persons born in 'new' Commonwealth

Table 15 Housing quality and the 'new' Commonwealth born population

	Proportion in enumeration districts born in 'new' Commonwealth	
	More than average %	Less than average %
Households with exclusive use of hot tap, w.c. and bath	28·4	72·4
Households without exclusive use of hot tap, w.c. and bath	71·6	27·6
No. households	102,170	

exclusive use of a hot water tap, indoor lavatory and bath. Many of the houses had been built without them. Others, though now old and deteriorating, were originally built to much higher specifications. Because most of them are now multi-occupied and because structural alterations are rare, toilets and bathrooms must be shared and kitchens improvised. Almost invariably the effect of this is even faster deterioration. For planning purposes the Corporation's Housing Department divides houses into five categories and, at the time when the study was made, almost all the houses in the research area belonged to one or other of the following three:

1. Property known to be unfit (presumably for human habitation).

2. Substandard and sometimes unfit houses which, with very high expenditure, could be improved to a reasonable standard. (Generally it is considered that such a high level of expenditure cannot be justified).

3. Solid houses, many without modern amenities, but forming potential improvement property.[13]

In Chapter 3 it was suggested that race relations could be crucially affected by the housing situation. To date, the most systematic examination of the relationship between them is to be found in the work of Rex and Moore and it will be profitable to discuss the Nottingham data against the background of their analysis.[14]

They begin with the assertion that 'in modern industrial societies the structure of social relationships is determined by a pattern of conflicting interests set

up by the differential control by different groups of men of material facilities'.[15]
However, they do not consider that the conflicts which arise over housing are
simply a reflection of the class struggle in industry. They note that 'among
those who share the same relation to the means of production there may be
considerable difference in ease of access to housing' and that 'a class struggle
between groups differentially placed with regard to the means of housing . . .
may at local level be as acute as the class struggle in industry'.[16] This position,
they suggest, is in accord with that set out by Weber in his essay 'Class, Status,
Party'.

> In saying this we follow Max Weber who saw that the class struggle was apt to
> emerge whenever people in a market situation enjoyed differential access to
> property and that such class struggles might therefore arise not merely around
> the use of the means of industrial production, but around the control of domestic
> property.[17]

The fact that more than a market principle is at work in the way in which
houses are distributed in Britain necessitates no more than a minor change in
Weber's perspective.

> We need only qualify this slightly to include groups differentially placed with
> regard to a system of bureaucratic allocation to arrive at a notion of 'housing
> classes' which is extremely useful in analysing urban structures and processes.[18]

The basic process underlying urban social interaction is, according to Rex
and Moore, competition for the scarce and desirable houses of suburbia. For,
of the various types of accommodation available in a typical city, it is these
which are judged most desirable 'according to the status values of British
society'.[19]

> All participate in a socio-cultural system in which the middle class way of life
> enjoys high prestige and in which the move to the suburbs is a built in
> aspiration.[20]

> There will, of course, be some deviants, romantics and intellectuals who actually
> prefer living in the inner zone, but the persistent outward movement which takes
> place justifies us in saying and positing as central to our model that suburban
> housing is a scarce and desired resource. Given that this is so, I suggest that the
> basic process underlying urban social interaction is competition for scarce and
> desired types of housing.[21]

> The model we have posited assumes the existence of . . . an aspiration to
> relatively detached family life amongst all groups.[22]

Because of this wide agreement on the desirability of particular kinds of
housing, its scarcity and the relative independence of the class struggle for
houses from the class struggle in industry, Rex and Moore suggest that it is
useful to distinguish the following 'housing classes':

1. The outright owners of large houses in desirable areas.
2. Mortgage payers who 'own' whole houses in desirable areas.
3. Council tenants in council-built houses.
4. Council tenants in slum houses awaiting demolition.
5. Tenants of private house-owners, usually in the inner ring.
6. House-owners who must take lodgers to meet loan repayments.
7. Lodgers in rooms.[23]

Though the most obvious gulf is between those who occupy desirable houses (classes 1, 2 and 3) and those who do not (classes 4, 5, 6 and 7), there are many reasons why the latter are unlikely to become a single, organised, self-conscious group. For example, those close to achieving the appropriate qualifications for either a mortgage (or its equivalent) or a council tenancy are likely to consider that the existing mechanisms for obtaining suburban housing are legitimate. It is also unlikely because other conflicts exist between members of the four disadvantaged classes. The most important of these, say Rex and Moore, is that between lodging-house landlords and tenants on the one hand and their ward neighbours and the city authorities on the other. But, in addition, there are those between landlords and tenants and between members of different ethnic groups.

The situation of the coloured immigrant is different from that of the indigenous inhabitant of the zone of transition in one vital respect. In attempting to enter the suburban way of life he is likely to encounter some form of discrimination. Moreover, because the terraced cottages in the inner zone contain a relatively static native population, the immigrant has little option other than to become either a lodging-house landlord or a lodging-house tenant. His particularly disadvantaged position in the housing market does not earn him the sympathy of the native whites. On the contrary, in addition to the hostility arising from cultural and personality factors, the immigrant becomes 'defined as a man who overcrowds and destroys good houses and it is his position in the housing market which defines his situation for the native'.[24]

Most of the organisations which operate in the inner zone, whatever their avowed aims, are directly or indirectly involved in the complex conflict situation which has been described. However, the great variety of organisations which exist and the fact that they all fulfil several functions, has the effect of blurring and muting rather than sharpening the conflicts. Nevertheless, Rex stresses, the conflicts remain.

> The essence of the situation is still that there are a number of ethnic groups engaged in conflict over the allocation of housing, and though their conflict may not be carried through to the point of violence, it remains the centre of the overall interaction system. It is always possible in such a situation that if there were a

crisis organisations would become functionally and ethnically specialised and that the lines of conflict would be more sharply drawn.[25]

Rex and Moore's theoretical model has been subjected to a number of criticisms since its introduction in 1967.[26] Some, unfortunately, seem to have been based upon a misreading of it. For example, Richmond's attempt to demonstrate that certain socio-psychological variables are more important determinants of the attitudes expressed by native whites towards coloured immigrants than their position in the housing market is an attempt to refute a position that was never adopted by Rex and Moore.[27] Indeed, as attitudes towards coloured people are culturally transmitted to a very considerable extent, it would be surprising if any neat correspondence were to be found. The acquisition of attitudes in this way means that not dissimilar views are likely to be found amongst people in different housing situations. More generally, it means that the conventional exercise of correlating expressed attitudes with standard demographic variables such as age and sex is unlikely to be particularly rewarding. Having noted this, it must nevertheless be emphasised that the housing or more general social situation of a native white may be of crucial significance in determining whether or not attitudes find expression in particular forms of social action. The position adopted here with regard to Rex and Moore's work is that their basic approach is extremely useful, although their model does have a number of particular weaknesses.

Their contention that most urban dwellers in Britain are in competition for the scarce houses of suburbia and that this is the basic process underlying urban social interaction requires close examination. There are at least two possible ways in which it can be interpreted. The most obvious is that competition arises because most people *want* to live in the suburbs rather than in the inner city. The survey evidence reported in *Race, Community and Conflict* does not, however, support this interpretation. For whilst it is true that the vast majority of English respondents did say that they would not live in Sparkbrook if they had a choice, the evidence, as it is presented, only confirms that about one quarter said that they would like to live in the suburbs.[28] In the case of the immigrants, not even a majority expressed a desire to leave Sparkbrook. The respective figures for the Irish, West Indian and Pakistani respondents are 37 per cent,[29] 50 per cent,[30] and 36 per cent.[31]

Asking respondents where they would like to live 'if they had a choice' raises difficult problems of interpretation. As Lambert and Filkin have pointed out, where choice is institutionally constrained, respondents may well respond to questions having already scaled down their aspirations to what appears to them to be possible.[32] Thus it is quite feasible that some of Rex and Moore's respondents may have answered in terms of what they could reasonably hope for rather than what they really wanted. Nevertheless, the fact remains that the

Sparkbrook findings do not support this first interpretation of Rex and Moore's contention that most urban dwellers are in competition for suburban housing.

The second possible interpretation is that those who live in the inner zone and wish to improve their housing conditions must be in competition for suburban property because it is, as a rule, only through such property that an improvement can be obtained. In other words, competition for suburban housing is an inevitable product of the constraints which are built into the housing market. Seen in this way, the failure to find support in terms of stated preferences would not constitute a problem to the theory. Though this interpretation is not found in such an explicit form in *Race, Community and Conflict*, it comes close to a point made by Rex in a subsequent article. In discussing the difficulty of interpreting stated preferences for housing he writes:

> What we have to do is give an account of the constraints which we as
> sociologists know to exist in the world and an account of the immigrants' perception of the world before going on to discover what 'choices' are made.[33]

In the immediate post-war period such an interpretation might have been acceptable for then most new building was in suburban areas. More recently there has been a significant amount of slum clearance in most towns and it is now possible to obtain council-built property in the inner city area. Increasingly then, an improvement will not necessarily require a move to the suburbs. This is not to say that there will not continue to be a great deal of competition for suburban property. But it is still the case that this second interpretation of Rex and Moore's assertion is also unacceptable.

Before turning to an examination of the Nottingham material on housing preferences as it relates to competition for scarce housing resources, it is worth considering Rex's most recent remarks on the relevance of survey data. He points out, as an example, 'that we do not learn anything at all decisive when we learn from a survey that a certain percentage of Pakistani immigrants do not "want" council houses. What we learn is that they gave a particular answer to a questionnaire.' 'Unfortunately', he adds, 'sociologists have a fatal fascination with the study of individual preferences because they are easily amenable to investigation by survey.'[34] What he does not make clear, however, is why he and Moore asked questions of this sort in their own survey and what status they attach to the answers they received. It can be agreed that statements of individual preferences need to be interpreted in terms of the context in which they are expressed and that they are too often treated at their face value. But this does not account for their reporting and then effectively ignoring such findings.

In Nottingham all respondents were asked: 'Are you happy with the area you live in or would you like to move to another one?' Almost half of the natives (47 per cent) and over two thirds of the immigrants (70 per cent) said that they were happy where they were. Such findings are of interest for at least two reasons. First, because they suggest that many people may be happy, or not particularly unhappy, living in the inner zone. And, secondly, because they suggest (as did the Sparkbrook findings) that immigrants may be less often unhappy with life in the inner zone than the natives.[*f*]

Those respondents who expressed a desire to live elsewhere were asked what it was about life in the inner zone that they did not like. Though there was considerable variation in the answers, almost all were about either the kind of people who lived in the area or its physical characteristics. Of the English respondents who were dissatisfied, about two-thirds (68 per cent) complained about the characteristics of the residents of the inner zone. In about half of these instances, specific references were made to coloured immigrants.

> There's too many coloureds round here . . . No – nothing else. This area's known as the jungle.

> It's dropped one hundred per cent since the coloureds came. We can't sell our house because the property's dropped so much in value. This is a terrible street – we're scared stiff. There's good and bad in everybody and they're the same – but the ones round here are really dirty. They keep late nights and have parties all night. It makes you sick.

In the other half, no particular complaints were made about coloured immigrants and, in several instances, they were specifically excluded from criticism.

> It's not safe to leave my wife in at night by herself – women have been attacked round here if they go outside for anything. You can't even go to the phone – women that is.

> It's deteriorated. It's a general area for people who can't afford better and that pulls it down. It's not the coloured's we object to.

Of the smaller number of immigrants who expressed dissatisfaction with the area, somewhat fewer (46 per cent) complained about the kind of people who lived there.

> It's too crowded – and another thing the kids on this street are terrorising our little girl. As soon as she walk out they bang her. And the parents are just the same. Just the other day one of those women (the respondent pointed to her from the window) threatened to slap my little girl. We have to have the police in the street – there's always quarrelling. If you leave anything outside it's gone – even the doormat! The neighbourhood it's alright – but the people that live here they're no good.

[*f*]   Some of the reasons why immigrants find life in the inner zone has advantages were noted by Elizabeth Burney after she carried out a 'straw poll' in Nottingham. Elizabeth Burney, *Housing on Trial* (London, Oxford University Press, for Institute of Race Relations, 1967), p. 211.

> The people here are not educated. They are jealous that I am doing my own business. The neighbours do not like a black man doing business.

In addition to the complaints about the inhabitants of the area, 41 per cent of those English respondents who were unhappy mentioned its physical characteristics.

> It's a bloody deathtrap that's why! People come down the hill too quickly and cut across the other road. There's been some bad accidents – we've been witnesses.

> It's bad for the children. You see we're right on the main road and there's nowhere for them to play.

A similar proportion of the immigrants who were dissatisfied mentioned such factors.

> It's dirty. The roadsweeper hardly ever comes – probably because the blacks live here now!

> Well – before it was not too bad – but now they have that Bingo at the end of the street. But the area's not too bad. If I just lived in another street it would be alright.

These findings suggest that although dissatisfaction with various aspects of life in the inner zone is widespread, by no means all of those who live there are dissatisfied. Moreover, the answers given by some of those who did express dissatisfaction were very specific. That is they stated, more or less explicitly, that they would be happy if only some particular drawback could be removed. The respondent cited above, who did not like having a Bingo hall at the end of his street, is one such person. There is, of course, more than survey evidence available to support the view that some people do not mind, and indeed may prefer, the inner zone to elsewhere. For instance, the inhabitants of the first part of the St Anns area scheduled for demolition under the Council's slum clearance scheme petitioned the Corporation to improve their houses but not to demolish them.[35] More recently, a petition was submitted to the Corporation requesting that a block of 250 houses in the Meadows should be improved rather than demolished.[36] The arguments used have been summed up by Ray Gosling, Secretary of the St Anns Tenants and Residents Association.

> It is impossible to modify, adapt or repair the whole of the existing fabric in these rings of decay that encircle our town centres. But within any given development area this condition is not total: always there is the odd good street, the several scattered fine houses – and always there are people of spirit . . . We intend to show . . . that it is economically possible and humanly desirable to take the very bad out now, patch for the present the not so bad, improve the reasonable, preserve the good.[37]

In addition to questions concerning satisfaction with the area, all respondents were asked if they were satisfied with their housing conditions. Although in this case rather fewer expressed satisfaction, dissatisfaction was still far from universal. Indeed, as many as 45 per cent of the immigrants and 35 per cent of the natives said they were satisfied. As the following quotations indicate, most of those who were unhappy complained that their houses were, in one way or another, physically inadequate.

> The house is very damp. We've tried all sorts of things but it's no good – it still comes through.

> There's no bath or hot water and you've got to go outside to the toilet.

> It's in a bad condition but we can't get any repairs done. The toilet's outside and there's no bath. There's not even a coal house – and we've got to pay the rates on top of the rent.

> Well it's awfully cold you see in winter. You can feel the draught coming in through the roof. I've only got a paraffin heater and you can't have that on when you sleep – and with this rheumatism it's very bad.

But again, as in the case of dissatisfaction with the area, some complaints were very specific.

> Because there's no passage. That's the main trouble – otherwise I'm satisfied. I've had a bathroom put in and there are electric points in every room. But the front door leads straight into the living room and so if you put down a carpet in this room it's worn through in three months.

The pattern of satisfaction and dissatisfaction which emerges when the answers to these two questions are examined together is quite complex. Only 37 per cent of the natives and 24 per cent of the immigrants expressed dissatisfaction with both their housing conditions and with the area. Those who said that they were satisfied with both were not much less numerous – the respective figures for the natives and immigrants being 23 per cent and 40 per cent. Then there were those respondents who expressed satisfaction with the area but not their housing and those who expressed satisfaction with their housing but not the area. Amongst the natives, 12 per cent came into the former category as did 30 per cent of the immigrants. In the latter category were a further 12 per cent of the natives and 5 per cent of the immigrants. If the nature of dissatisfaction (and satisfaction) were also to be taken into account the pattern would then become exceedingly complex.

To say that someone is satisfied with his house or the area in which he lives does not necessarily mean that an improvement would not be welcomed. But a sense of satisfaction is usually indicative of an acceptance of the *status quo*. At its simplest, one would not expect a man who is satisfied with his house and the area in which it is situated to be as concerned about the activities of others as someone who is dissatisfied and actively seeking an improvement. Thus the degree of expressed satisfaction with life in the inner zone and the complexity of the pattern of dissatisfaction must have serious implications for Rex and Moore's assertions about the nature of conflict over housing. It will be remembered that they suggested that almost all were in competition for the scarce houses of suburbia. The findings in Nottingham suggest that some do not seem to be competing for any kind of housing and that not all the others are competing for the same kind of housing. Whether those living in the inner city *ought* to feel satisfied with what many of us would judge to be thoroughly unsatisfactory conditions is not an unimportant question. But here we are less concerned with *objective* deprivation than with how *felt* deprivation may affect race relations. From this point of view the most significant implication of these findings is that very often native and immigrant may not be in competition with each other over housing. The fact that 40 per cent of the immigrants expressed satisfaction with both the area and their house and that only 24 per cent were unhappy with both cannot be ignored.

Even when natives and immigrants are actively competing for the same scarce resources it should not be thought that conflict between them is inevitable. If competitors consider each other to be legitimate competitors in terms of some formal or informal rules, then the consequences are likely to be different from those which arise in a situation in which one or more of the competitors judges the competition to be illegitimate in some way. To lose in the first instance might be unfortunate but acceptable. To lose in the second may be quite unacceptable. When members of the native population compete with each other for housing the competition is usually considered legitimate. But if, for instance, it became known that someone who was well able to buy himself an expensive property had been allocated a council house, then there might be an outcry. Clearly it is a matter of some importance to establish whether or not the native population consider coloured immigrants to be legitimate competitors for those scarce housing resources which are at stake. It is also a matter of importance to establish the extent to which the immigrants consider the competition in which they are engaged is fair or unfair – but this is something which will be examined later in the chapter.

All English respondents were asked whether or not immigrants ought to be treated in the same way as English people in the matter of house purchase. As many as 81 per cent considered that they should and no more than 15 per cent thought that English people ought to receive priority. As the following quotations illustrate, most of those favouring equal treatment gave very similar reasons for their view.

> Everybody's entitled to buy their own house if they want to.

> If they've got the money let them spend it. Wish I'd got the money.

Their money is the same as ours.

If they've got the money certainly.

They make a lot of money so they can afford them and that's alright.

They've got the same right if they've got the money.

If they can pay why shouldn't they have the same chance?

It's just part of life. A property owner's not interested in who pays for the house so long as he has the money.

If they've earned the money they should be allowed to buy the houses as it means they've had to work.

In contrast, when asked whether or not equal treatment ought to obtain in the allocation of council houses, 61 per cent were in favour of giving English people priority and only 30 per cent were in favour of equality of treatment. Once again, most of the reasons given by the majority in defence of their view took the same basic form. This would suggest that they reflect commonly held assumptions amongst those interviewed rather than individually arrived at arguments.

Because we're English and this is England.

It's our bloody country so we should get first chance.

If a man's fought for his country he should be able to get the advantages he's fought for.

Because we're the ones that have been paying the taxes for years. We've contributed more to the country than the immigrants have.

This is our place isn't it?

We're born here – it's our right.

Why should they come here and get all these council houses? They get a damn sight more than most of us get.

Because the English fought to keep out the invaders and all both governments have done since is to open the doors to them all.

England's a small country. It's overpopulated and we've fought two wars to keep our country English so we should have priority.

I've been born and bred here and I can't even go on the list. They just come here and go straight into them. The council even suggested my wife and children should go into Nazareth House while I found a bigger house.

We're born and bred English. They can't just come here and take houses the English have been waiting for for years.

It's our country. The coloured people round here are very nice – they're no trouble at all. But it is our country.

It is interesting to speculate on why it is that so many of those who consider coloured people to be legitimate competitors in the private house-purchasing market do not feel the same way about the allocation of council houses. It may well be that, unless there is a good reason to adopt a contrary position, they tend to endorse the existing order of things. At present it is market mechanisms which play the dominant role in the field of house purchase. If more of those concerned were to be in the market to buy their own houses, and their self-interest more directly involved, they might find more fault with existing arrangements. But, as was pointed out in the last chapter, 86 per cent of those interviewed were manual workers and earning, on average, including overtime and before deductions, only just over £18 per week at the time – £5 less than the national average for manual workers. Clearly they were not in a position to *buy* an improvement in their housing conditions. And this is precisely why the allocation of council housing is so important to them. In any case, bureaucratic selection rather than the market mechanism already determines who is to be allocated a house and who is not. What, therefore, could be more obvious than discriminating in favour of those who by virtue of their English nationality have an *a priori* case for preferential treatment?

One extremely important fact about the housing situation in Nottingham which is not anticipated by Rex and Moore's model is the widespread extent of owner-occupation amongst coloured immigrants. This may be because the model is too heavily based on the particular characteristics of the Sparkbrook area in which their research was conducted. But, having suggested this, it is important to note that Rex and Moore do not make it clear how much of their model is intended to apply to areas other than Sparkbrook. For instance, in Rex's essay 'The Sociology of a Zone of Transition' the following quotation can be found.

> What is needed is an account in terms of the action frame of reference which explains particular kinds of land use and building use in terms of the action-orientation of typical residents. What follows is an attempt to do this on the basis of research experience in Birmingham. The theory which emerges may in part be generalisable but clearly *where important variables in the historical situation differ in other cities other models may have to be developed.*[38] (my italics)

But, only a few pages later in the same essay, Rex adds:

> It should be noted that considerable variations in this pattern of housing-class conflict would follow from differences in the economic, political and cultural situation in different individual countries. *Such differences as these, however, call for modification of the basic model which we have elaborated, not for its rejection.*[39] (my italics)

And, whilst the suburban aspiration is clearly intended to characterise other areas,[g] Rex is anxious to point out that other cities in England and elsewhere may have different histories and other forms of housing stock and tenure as well as other groups in a state of conflict.[40]

At least two further housing classes must be added to Rex and Moore's list if it is to be adequate to deal with the situation which exists in Nottingham's inner city.[h] They are:

8. The owners of large houses in the inner ring who do not take lodgers.
9. The owners of smaller houses in the inner ring who do not take lodgers.

Why these were not included in Rex and Moore's list is not altogether clear. They were aware of the importance of class 9 in other cities, but implied that it was more or less non-existent in Birmingham.

> In northern cities these immigrants found small back-to-back cottages for sale at £400–£500. But there were no such houses in Birmingham.[41]

On the other hand there seems to be some doubt as to whether or not such houses were as conspicuously absent in Birmingham as they suggest. Valerie Karn, in a critical examination of some of Rex and Moore's statistics, noted that, according to the 1961 Census, as many as 60 per cent of Indian and Pakistani and 39 per cent of West Indian heads of households were owner-occupiers. She also drew attention to their rather inclusive definition of a lodging-house and a statistical error which may have caused them to overestimate the proportion of immigrant families in lodging-houses.[42] But, however adequate or inadequate the list of housing classes may have been for Sparkbrook, it certainly needs to be supplemented for Nottingham. The extent to which this is so is made abundantly clear by the figures given below in Table 16.

As many as 59 per cent of the immigrants interviewed in Nottingham belonged to one or other of these two additional classes. That is, they were owner-occupiers of large or small houses and did not take in lodgers or let any part of their accommodation. Unfortunately, when data was collected, no dis-

[g]   He notes, for example, that 'in many countries the suburban trend may not have the same cultural importance *which it has in England . . .*' (my italics). J. Rex, 'The Sociology of a Zone of Transition', in R. E. Pahl, *Readings in Urban Sociology* (London, Pergamon, 1968), p. 216.

[h]   In order to avoid confusion I have continued to use the term 'class' in the manner adopted by Rex and Moore. But I am not convinced that their usage is as Weber intended. He did note that such things as 'ownership of domestic buildings' could bring about further differentiation of the class situation. However, he was primarily concerned with how the ownership of such property could be exploited for gain, or serve as a source of power. Rex and Moore's list of housing 'classes' is essentially a list of levels in a given housing-status hierarchy, and those who belong to their various 'classes' are often in different market situations.

tinction was drawn between classes 5 and 7. For this reason it is not possible to say how many respondents were private tenants of whole houses as distinct from parts of houses. Even so, no more than 23 per cent of the immigrants came into this combined category and only a further 9 per cent belonged to class 6, i.e. house-owners who take in lodgers. Thus something less than 32 per cent must have been lodging-house landlords and tenants and, whether or not Miss Karn's criticisms are accepted, this is a markedly different situation from that found in Sparkbrook.

The very different pattern of tenure found amongst the immigrants as compared to that found amongst the natives is shown in Table 16. As many as 68 per cent of the former already owned or were in the process of buying their own house. In contrast only 16 per cent of the natives were owner-occupiers. And, whereas as many as 83 per cent of the natives rented their accommodation (62 per cent from private landlords), no more than 31 per cent of the immigrants were tenants. The figures in the third and fourth columns of the Table are included to show the very close correspondence between the survey findings and those of the 1966 Sample Census. They certainly imply that the survey findings cannot be explained away by a sampling error or any similar factor.

Table 16 Patterns of housing tenure

Types of tenure[a]	Native whites %	Coloured immigrants %	All[b] %	Sample census %
Council tenants (4)[c]	14	8	13	14
Tenants of whole houses and lodgers in rooms (5 and 7)	62	23	57	56
House owners with lodgers (6)	2	9	22	26
House owners without lodgers (8 and 9)	14	59		
Other	8	1	7	4
No. respondents	124	121	245	7,947

[a] Figures in brackets indicate type of housing class.
[b] The figures in this column have been calculated by an appropriate re-weighting of the figures in the first two columns.
[c] At the time of the 1966 Census and the research interviews almost all of these were in slum houses awaiting demolition.

These findings on patterns of housing tenure, and those others which have so far been presented in this chapter, help to explain why it is that Nottingham's severe housing problem has not produced particular antagonism between native and immigrant. Many of those who live in objectively substandard housing do not seem to be particularly dissatisfied with it. This is not to say that they might not be willing to accept a modern suburban dwelling if offered one. But they do seem to be content to settle for a lot less. This is not an altogether unexpected finding. The inner zone is not entirely without advantages. Moreover, as Runciman has demonstrated with regard to earnings, those who are objectively deprived often have very limited horizons.[43] It has also been noted that those who are dissatisfied with life in the inner zone are dissatisfied for a variety of reasons and that this almost certainly has the effect of reducing the amount of direct competition between immigrant and native for housing. Finally, and related to this, it has been shown that most immigrants have either elected or been obliged to buy their own houses and that this is a practice which the vast majority of the indigenous population of the inner zone seem to find acceptable.

Several important matters remain to be examined. What difficulties face those immigrants who do not wish to remain in their present accommodation and want to buy a house in the suburbs or obtain the tenancy of a council-built house? Are they treated in the same way as other prospective purchasers or would-be council tenants, or do they find themselves at a disadvantage? And, regardless of the realities of the situation, how do immigrants *believe* they are treated? Such matters will become even more important in the future than they are today. Then far fewer coloured people will be content to remain in the kind of accommodation they occupy at present. First generation immigrants are almost invariably more tolerant of poor living conditions than their children. Moreover, as was pointed out in Chapter 2 the still widespread intention to return home amongst the immigrants may have the effect of raising an already high tolerance threshold. As more immigrants become reconciled to remaining in Britain, and more of their children begin to look for their own accommodation, the desire to escape from the inner city will almost certainly increase.

When asked whether or not coloured immigrants had the same chance of buying their own houses as other people, or if they found it more difficult, as many as 84 per cent of the immigrants said that they found it more difficult. Though highly significant in itself this finding does not constitute proof of discrimination. There were just as many English respondents who believed that immigrants had at least an equal chance of buying their own houses as there were immigrants who believed that they had greater difficulty, and there are many estate agents and others concerned with the sale of houses in Nottingham who would deny that there is any discrimination against coloured people.[44] Indeed some would argue that the very extensiveness of home ownership amongst immigrants lends clear support to this view. It is not easy to determine which of these two opposing viewpoints is closer to the truth. It can be conceded that immigrants may make charges of discrimination as a result of misunderstandings. On the other hand, if an estate agent does make a habit of discriminating against coloured people he is hardly likely to admit it openly – especially since the introduction of the 1968 Race Relations Act. It is also possible that a relatively junior member of an agency may be responsible for acts of discrimination unknown to, and against the wishes of, his superior. And, of course, the extent of home ownership amongst immigrants does not necessarily mean that special problems have not had to be overcome or that they would not have had to be overcome if a more exclusive property had been involved. Clearly the results of some form of 'objective' testing of discrimination are needed to settle the disagreement. Unfortunately no such testing has yet been undertaken in Nottingham. However, it was incorporated into the 1967 PEP investigation of racial discrimination and, as the results of the study did not reveal any variations between the six towns involved, they are well worth summarising at this point.[45]

Forty-two tests were conducted with seven estate agents in each of six towns.[46] Three matched testers were used; a West Indian, a Hungarian and an Englishman. They visited each of the agents on either the same day or within a short period of time, and asked for a list of properties within a particular price range, and for details of mortgages and the down-payments required. Discrimination was observed amongst 27 of the 42 agents. In four instances the West Indian was offered fewer addresses than the other two applicants and, in another, both he and the Hungarian were offered fewer than the Englishman. In three cases the West Indian was told that there were no suitable properties available, although lists were given to the other two, and in a further instance he was given a different list of properties. In nine cases he was told that it would not be possible for him to obtain a mortgage or was offered less advantageous terms than the other applicants. Finally nine agencies asked either the Englishman or the Hungarian, or both, to leave their addresses, but did not extend the same invitation to the West Indian. Following the tests, twenty of the discriminating agents were interviewed (the other seven refused) and confirmed what the tests had shown: that coloured people were denied access to some desirable housing; that they were less likely to obtain a mortgage; and that even if a mortgage were granted it would probably require a larger than usual deposit and/or a higher than average rate of interest.

As the following quotations illustrate, the complaints made by the immigrants interviewed in Nottingham are consistent with the findings of PEP's situational tests and, in the absence of any evidence to suggest that the situation may have been different in Nottingham from that in the other six towns studied, this must enhance the standing of their statements. Those who alleged that coloured people did not find it so easy to buy their own houses were asked in what ways it was more difficult. Sixty-two per cent said that they had greater difficulty in obtaining mortgages; 40 per cent said that coloured people found it more difficult to buy good houses in good areas; 25 per cent alleged that higher deposits were demanded from them; 19 per cent suggested that coloured people were obliged to pay higher prices; and 17 per cent claimed that they were charged higher interest rates.

> There is a big difficulty getting the mortgage. Sometimes they say 'this is the interest – if you want the house this is what you have to pay'. So to get the house you have to pay more interest than the English people. If they don't want to give you the house they say lot of interest – so high that you cannot take it.

> Well we've just been turned down on a house in St Anns Well Road area. We got the mortgage through; paid the surveyor's fee and then I sent my wife into the estate agent and he say, 'The owner is refusing to sell it to you because you're coloured'. So of course I went and gave him a lot of lip and the owner apologised and promised to pay what time I had lost at work – but I refused. Anyway we didn't get it. But you see it's usually the estate agents – they're terribly prejudiced. I think the estate agents are worse than the people. And where someone is willing to sell you a house you go to the estate agent he says he has already got someone for it. And then you go back to the person and say this – and they say they don't know about it.

> We get charged more interest but of course often they just won't sell them to us – that is very widespread. There are a lot of firms who like to deal with immigrants – they say, 'We are serving them' – but of course they are also exploiting them by charging higher interest rates.

> Every firm you deal with you have to pay a higher deposit. Even with the money you get turned down in many areas – especially good ones.

> In 1958 I went to buy a house and was told it was already sold – yet they kept advertising it for six weeks. On another occasion I was looking at a house and was told it was £1,750 yet it was later sold to a white man for £1,500.

> I am paying a high rate for my mortgage. I am paying 18½ per cent interest. The mortgage is the first difficulty. Secondly, when you go to look at the house, if the neighbours see you they try to stop you buying it. One of my friends wanted a house in West Bridgford priced at £3,000. The owner accepted and he put down a deposit. Then he got a letter to say the man had changed his mind. The lady next door who had seen him bought it herself and a little later sold it to a white man.

> Well I don't know if it's true but I'm told some houses on the agent's list have got white marks on and some black. But we've been to lots of houses for sale and when they see you they just say no.

> Discrimination – they will turn you down when they find out you are coloured. Or they increase the price of the deposit if you are coloured. You have to put 40–60 per cent down. I have to put 50 per cent down for my house. Some building societies will just not give mortgages to coloured people. As beggars

can't be choosers we have to go to the ones like the ___ ___ Building Society who take advantage of you. You have to pay 8 to 16 per cent if you are coloured. _____ , the Estate Agents, put you in contact with the ___ ___ . One house I wanted cost £800 and I went to _____ who asked to see the house. Like a daft fool I took him and he bought it for £750 cash and then resold it for more straight away. I was like a child I could not do anything.

Well I know a neighbour who was moving and she told me that a number of neighbours had pleaded with her not to sell the house to a coloured person. Again, when we tried to get a house in Wollaton one of my firm's partners contacted the agents who were the firm's clients but it was still no good. One of the reasons English people feel this way is because many coloured people live in poor, dirty and overcrowded houses – it's just a vicious circle.

The PEP tests were made before the 1968 Race Relations Act came into force. What effect it has had on discrimination is not clear. Although a recent study has shown that employment discrimination still exists, there has not been any comparable follow-up study in the field of housing. What is apparent is that the Board's Conciliation Committees have received comparatively few complaints. But, for several reasons, this may not be indicative of an effective ending of discrimination. The PEP report made it clear that immigrants are often unaware that they have been the victims of discrimination and the introduction of the Act has not altered this situation in any way.[47] It may also be that some immigrants do not know that the Act exists. Although at the time that the interview schedule was drawn up the 1968 Act had not yet come into force, it is worth noting that as many as 70 per cent of the immigrant respondents did not know of the existence of the 1965 Act – and less than 2 per cent knew how to make a complaint. Despite the greater publicity given to the 1968 legislation it is still possible that many are not familiar with its provisions. No less important is that a victim of discrimination has little incentive to make a complaint under the present terms and workings of the Act.[48] Only a small minority of complaints are upheld. The procedures are often very protracted and even when an allegation is confirmed there is no guarantee that any material settlement will result. Indeed, because there is no provision for the suspension of a sale pending an enquiry, there is a strong probability that the house in question will no longer be on the market. In other words, whatever the outcome, the victim will almost certainly remain a loser.

There is at least one further and very important reason why the small number of complaints should not be assumed to be a sign that discrimination is a thing of the past. The PEP tests were more a measure of 'potential' rather than 'actual' discrimination. And, as their report pointed out 'the majority of the immigrants do not expose themselves to possible discrimination by looking for accommodation on the open market'.[49] In other words, the extent of latent discrimination may be large even though the amount of actual discrimination is small. Certainly coloured people in Nottingham have not yet made a major assault on the suburban housing market. In a memorandum submitted by the Nottingham and District Estate Agents' Association to the Select Committee on Race Relations and Immigration in 1971, it was pointed out that the type of house bought by immigrants was usually in the price range £1,000–£2,000 and 'in fact, doesn't often exceed the latter figure'. The exceptions, it was added, who were beginning to buy normal suburban properties, were 'the better educated immigrants', i.e. doctors, dentists and other professional people.[50] When questioned on the scale of this outward movement Mr Dodson, the Treasurer of the Association replied: 'It is going very slowly I would say. It is noticeable now from, say, five years ago. Then you rarely got any enquiry for a £5,000 or £6,000 house from coloured people but now you do – three, four or five times a year.'

Those coloured immigrants who buy cheap houses often obtain loans from finance companies rather than building societies or the local authority. Very often this means that they are obliged to pay very high rates of interest. The problem facing them was set out by the Assistant Secretary to the Nottingham Building Society in the course of his evidence to the Select Committee.

> I think the problem is that when they try the normal financers – the building societies or the local authority – and for various reasons cannot get finance there, they are forced into the hands of the usurers who will charge them anything they can. By the time they get into their hands the usurers know they cannot get finance elsewhere and they can charge exorbitant rates of interest.

When asked what sort of interest rate they might be charged he replied: 'I would say 15 per cent to 20 per cent.'[51]

The organisation most closely concerned with the problems facing coloured people in the sphere of housing is Nottingham's Fair Housing Group. Set up in 1968 with a grant from the Gulbenkian Foundation, it has established close links with the City Council, Estate Agents and Building Societies and by February 1971 had dealt with over 800 enquiries. On the basis of this experience they commented as follows in their evidence to the Select Committee on Race Relations and Immigration.

> We regret to state that discrimination still continues to appear in various forms when an immigrant intends to purchase a house in one of the suburban areas of the city. The discrimination practised in this field is so subtle that even the Race Relations Act has become powerless to prevent it.[52]

So, although it is not possible to produce *conclusive* evidence of widespread discrimination against coloured people, there can be little doubt that some does take place. Moreover, there is good reason to suppose that there may be very considerable latent discrimination. If, and when, large numbers of immigrants do attempt to leave the inner city they are likely to encounter one or more of the kinds of obstacles that have been mentioned. Moreover, as the majority undoubtedly anticipate discrimination, it may be that failure to obtain a property for quite innocent reasons may still produce allegations of discrimination. The significance of this possibility should not be underestimated. For, as Thomas observed many years ago, 'If men define situations as real they are real in their consequences.'[53]

It was noted earlier in the chapter that one of the most striking changes in the housing situation in recent years has been the increasingly important role played by public housing. By 1970, Nottingham Corporation owned 41 per cent of the city's total stock. Over the next decade the proportion is expected to rise to over 50 per cent.[54] Yet at the time of the investigation, only a tiny proportion of coloured families were living in council houses. The 1966 Census showed that there were very few coloured people in suburban council estates and no more than 8 per cent of those interviewed were living in council-owned property in the inner city. There are several factors involved in this under-representation. Most of the suburban estates were built before the major influx of immigrants and contain a fairly stable population. As a result, those on the waiting-list must wait for up to five years for a vacancy. Obviously insufficient time has elapsed for the city's coloured population to be proportionately represented in this type of housing. It is also probable that immigrants may be under-represented on the waiting-list. Some of those interviewed were ignorant of the council house system and others made it plain that they had no desire to live in a council house. Whether those who are on the list receive their due share of allocations is not known. Although the Housing Department has kept a record of the ethnic origin of those allocated houses since 1968, no record is kept of the ethnic origin of those on the waiting-list. As a result, it is not possible to determine if coloured immigrants are re-housed to the same extent as members of the native population. The explanation offered by the Director of Housing for this odd procedure (that a substantial number of those on the list are eventually removed – because, for instance, they find their own accommodation) is hardly satisfactory.[55] Most would agree that the only case for keeping such a record of ethnic or racial origin is that it can be used as a check on the fairness of the Housing Department's procedures – and even this is not judged a sufficiently good reason by the leaders of some of the city's immigrant organisations.[56] To keep records which do not allow such a check to be made is only likely to engender even more suspicion than that which exists at present.

The inadequacy of the statistics is particularly disconcerting in the light of an allegation made by Elizabeth Burney in her book *Housing on Trial*. Writing in 1967 she suggested that one reason 'for the absence of coloured people on council estates (in Nottingham) is a deliberate policy of housing them in old terraced houses acquired especially for the purpose'. 'This policy was launched', she asserts, 'just as some immigrants began to wake up to the possibilities of the council waiting-list and has been expanding ever since.'[57] There is no doubt that many coloured families were offered and did accept such substandard houses. Whether it happened in the way suggested by Miss Burney is less certain. She offered no evidence in support of her charge and it has been expressly denied by the Corporation. In his evidence to the Select Committee the Housing Director stated:

> We are accused from time to time of putting immigrant families into this type of accommodation (i.e. substandard). In fact, they have a free choice of selecting not only the type of accommodation they want but the estate in which they wish to live. If they are prepared to wait the necessary time for a new house – and again I stress that this is the waiting-list I am dealing with – then they can wait like any other member on the list for that period of time.[58]

Many of those interviewed shared Miss Burney's view of the situation rather than the Corporation's. Immigrant respondents were asked: 'Do you think immigrants have as much chance of getting council houses as anyone else or do you think they find it more difficult?' Only 12 per cent considered they had the same chance. And, whilst as many as one third did not feel able to judge either way, a majority of 54 per cent thought immigrants found it more difficult. These were then asked in what ways it was more difficult. Forty-one per cent said the coloured people were only allocated old houses in poor areas.

> You would have to change the colour of your skin to get a council house in a nice area.

> Well, what I've heard is that they re house white people in the modern ones and put coloured people in the old ones.

> I don't know how they work it but it's actually out of the question for a coloured man to live on a nice new estate – Clifton for instance – there's no-one on it. Maybe if he's got a white wife – but you can get the substandard ones alright.

A further 42 per cent went even further in their criticisms of the council treatment of coloured people.

> The only people that get them are guinea pigs – just to pretend there's no prejudice.

> They do register our names but we're ignored when the houses are allocated. If some immigrants do get them it's just to hoodwink people.

> Even if our name is registered they do not let us have our turn. They say that we cannot keep them clean so they try their best not to let us have them.

There were also several respondents who claimed that it was more difficult to get onto the council waiting-list. Yet, unlike some other local housing authorities, Nottingham has never included a period of residence as a condition of registration. Provided an applicant lives within the city's boundaries, is over the age of eighteen and can meet two conditions, he will be put on the waiting-list. The conditions, however, are very stringent and it is probably this which has caused some immigrants to believe that they are unfairly treated. Earnings must not be more than £25 per week (£20 at the time of the interviews) and an applicant is excluded if he is living in 'self-contained' accommodation. As a result of this latter condition there are thousands of low-income families in obviously substandard yet 'self-contained' accommodation who are not even able to join the queue for council houses. Indeed the requirement is so important that the main waiting-list has become officially known as the 'lodgers waiting-list'. Those who benefit most are young married couples living with parents or in rooms. For the aged, those in severe overcrowding and 'special' (e.g. medical) cases there are separate lists. But even when these are taken into account there is clearly little correspondence between the number of families registered for council housing and the number who are in need of it. The 1966 Census indicated that about 40,000 households did not have the exclusive use of a hot water tap, bath and inside toilet. Yet in the same year there were less than 5,000 names on Nottingham's council house waiting-list.[59]

For those excluded from the list there remains the possibility of being included in a slum clearance programme. But, as Table 17 shows, compared to many other authorities Nottingham's slum clearance record is poor. It is against this background that the present slum clearance drive must be evaluated. 'The Corporation has', as Silburn points out, 'belatedly set itself a target which other authorities established for themselves some years ago.'[60] And it seems that even this only came about after 'some prodding from the Ministry of Housing and Local Government'.[61]

Two major schemes are now underway. The first, in St Anns, began in the winter of 1969 and the eleventh and final phase is scheduled for completion in the Autumn of 1976. The second, in the Meadows, began in the summer of 1972 and the fifth and final phase is scheduled for completion in the summer of 1980. For a town the size of Nottingham these are very large projects. Before the start of redevelopment St Anns had a population of about 30,000 and those parts of the Meadows scheduled for demolition had a population of 14,500. Together they housed some 15 per cent of the total population and redeveloping them is inevitably having repercussions throughout the city. By the time the St Anns scheme is complete the number of dwellings will have been reduced from about 10,000 to 3,500.[62] In the Meadows the reduction will be from about 5,000 to just over 2,000.[63] Assuming one household per dwelling this means that close on 10,000 families may be displaced. Many will be re-housed by the Council in developments elsewhere in the city involving little or no slum clearance, or in existing houses which fall vacant. But there will be others who have to make their own arrangements.

Table 17 Nottingham's slum clearance performance

	Unfit houses in 1965	Average annual demolition rate	Number of years to complete
Manchester	54,700	2,960	18
Birmingham	40,915	2,397	17
Sheffield	28,500	1,395	20
Leeds	17,220	2,728	6
Hull	16,000	814	20
Bradford	14,693	1,167	13
Nottingham	12,525	454	28
Leicester	9,000	647	14

This table is constructed from information contained in Table 1 of *Our Older Homes*, A Report of the Central Housing Advisory Committee (HMSO, 1966).

Column 1 represents the estimated number of unfit houses in 1965.

Column 2 is the annual demolition rate for the period 1961–5.

Column 3 is the time it would take to clear the unfit houses if the same rate of demolition were to continue.

One small group will consist of those who lose possession of their houses before Compulsory Purchase Orders are placed on them. The landlords of houses in good condition are awarded compensation in relation to the prices their houses would fetch on the open market. As sitting tenants reduce market value it is in the financial interests of property owners to get rid of them and sell with vacant possession whenever possible. However, only those living in a dwelling at the time an Order is made have a right to be re-housed. Should a family leave or be evicted before then, that right is forfeit. How many families have been, or will be, affected in this way it is impossible to say. But Nottingham's Fair Housing Group have come across several cases.[64] It is also known that quite large numbers have been affected elsewhere.[65]

Those who choose not to be re-housed by the Council will be much more numerous. There will be a few who do not want to live in council houses and others who are unwilling to accept any of the dwellings offered them when it is their turn to be re-housed. But the greatest difficulty is likely to arise over those families who cannot afford the increase in rent which will be involved in moving to council-built accommodation. At the time of writing it is not known what the new rents will be after the so-called 'fair-rents' principle is applied to them under the Conservative Government's new policies for housing finance. But in a large number of cases they will be many times what is paid at present – even if help is sought under the rent-rebate scheme. This will create a real dilemma for many of the low-income families in the clearance areas – especially since moving to a new house will involve much more additional expense than the rent increase. There will be new curtains to buy, central heating bills to pay, perhaps increased fares to work and numerous other small yet still significant items of expenditure. In a time of rapid inflation like the present, the situation of low-income families is unusually difficult – not only because they have such limited means but also because it is so difficult for them to plan ahead. An unexpected price rise which one housewife may hardly notice can ruin another's carefully planned budget. It is not surprising that many such families will choose to find other inferior, but inexpensive, accommodation when they are uprooted.

There are already clear signs of this kind of movement.[66] Moreover, immigrant families figure very prominently amongst those involved in this retreat before the bulldozer. Of the 415 coloured immigrant families uprooted during the St Anns redevelopment in the period 1968–72, 62 per cent of the West Indians and 84 per cent of the Indians and Pakistanis remained in the central city area. Furthermore, as many as 33 per cent of the West Indians and 69 per cent of the Indians and Pakistanis moved to old property in the central city area. In short, 41 per cent of all the immigrant families who left their homes in this phase of slum clearance moved into other slum housing elsewhere in the city.[67] Such findings are not altogether unexpected. Indians and Pakistanis, in particular, place some emphasis on home ownership and seem to prefer to live close to their relatives and friends. There is a tendency for the basic earnings of immigrants to be smaller than those of native workers – and very often money is sent to needy relatives in the country of origin. In addition, for those who remain determined to return home, the extra cost of better housing may not appear a worthwhile investment.

Those who do decide to search for old but cheap property, whether immigrant or native, will find the situation increasingly difficult as clearance continues. As the demand for cheap property increases, the supply will be decreasing. This could have serious implications for race relations. To date there has been a relatively ample supply of cheap housing and this, along with the other factors mentioned above, has had the effect of reducing the amount of direct competition between native and immigrant. As the supply diminishes the potential for competition and conflict is increased – especially since there is also a possibility that the re-housing of coloured families in St Anns and the

Meadows will produce resentment on the part of some of those native families in the uncleared areas still without any hope of obtaining a council house. Although the issue is too complex to be examined here, these problems do lend support to those who argue that Nottingham, in common with other authorities, should improve rather than demolish existing properties much more than they do at present.

In this chapter an attempt has been made to show something of the relationship between housing and race relations in Nottingham. Despite the severe housing problem which exists and the fact that social significance is undoubtedly attached to the distinction between themselves and coloured immigrants by most native whites, there does not appear to have been much open conflict over housing. But it seems that it is the complex and fortuitous set of attitudes and circumstances that has been outlined, rather than any unusual display of tolerance on the part of Nottingham's indigenous population, that has been responsible for this situation.

Whether or not a situation of severe housing shortage will produce particular antagonism between black and white depends upon several factors. The first is the extent of dissatisfaction felt by those living in objectively substandard housing conditions. In this instance it has been noted that many of those living in such circumstances seem content to tolerate them. It has also been noted that those who express dissatisfaction do so for a variety of reasons and that, amongst other things, this may have had the effect of reducing the amount of direct competition over housing between black and white. It is the extent of this direct competition for the same scarce housing resources which is the second factor. The evidence which has been presented suggests that it has been minimised, not only by the pattern of satisfaction and dissatisfaction which exists, but also by the fact that most immigrants have bought their own houses from the previously plentiful supply of cheap properties available. In doing so they have not been involved in any marked competition with the native population. The third factor is the extent to which the whites consider the coloured immigrants to be legitimate or illegitimate competitors for those scarce housing resources which are at stake. The findings show that most of the native whites did not resent coloured people buying their own houses and so this too has probably reduced the potential for conflict between them. The final factor is the extent to which the natives and immigrants are able to obtain the kind of housing they require. So far the presence of the immigrants has made little impact on the prospects of the whites although, as was pointed out towards the end of the chapter, this situation is changing rapidly.

The effect of the other factors mentioned is also likely to increase in the future. The extent of dissatisfaction amongst all groups who remain in poor housing is likely to grow. The increasing shortage of cheap properties, and the dependence of yet more people on council accommodation, can only increase the amount of competition between the groups. Again, many of the white population seem likely to resent council property being allocated to coloured people. For these several reasons the prospect of open conflict over housing seems to be increasing rather than decreasing. Clearly it would be a mistake simply to assume that the present drive to improve housing conditions is likely to increase the likelihood of racial harmony. Indeed, implicit in what has been said is the view that the relative indolence of the Corporation in the past may have contributed to the relative absence of housing conflict.

In addition to conflict over cheap housing, there could also be problems as more and more coloured families move into previously all-white or predominantly all-white districts. However, a majority of 57 per cent of those interviewed said that they did not mind coloured people living in their area and 41 per cent said that they would not mind having a coloured neighbour. In other words, at least in the inner zone, a very substantial minority of English people seem to have become reconciled to the presence of coloured families. Similarly, there have been relatively few objections when coloured families have moved into previously all-white or predominantly all-white council estates. It is true that in one now well-known case a prospective neighbour threatened to burn down the house next door if a coloured family moved into it, and that in a study of 47 coloured families on such estates some 20 per cent reported various kinds of difficulties.[68] Nevertheless, considering that many hundreds of coloured families have now been placed in modern houses by the Council, the number of serious incidents has been very small. It seems that in conditions of good housing there may be much better prospects for harmonious race relations. In private estates, where residents often feel that their house values are endangered, the white residents may be less passive. But, as so few coloured people have moved into private suburban housing, there has been little opportunity for any such hostility to show itself. Of course, the way in which English people are likely to respond to new developments is no more significant to race relations than how much discrimination will continue to limit the housing opportunities available to coloured people. And this involves, not only the direct discrimination in housing which has been discussed above, but also that arising indirectly from discrimination in the field of employment – one of the topics to be discussed in the following chapter.

5
Race relations and employment

Most of the adult male Commonwealth immigrants now living in Britain have settled in areas with a demand for labour. But, unlike the rest of the overseas-born population, the main coloured groups seem to have been disproportionately drawn towards those places where the demand has been moderate rather than high.[1] According to Peach this is because they have acted as a replacement population for regions which have failed to attract a sufficiently large white labour force to meet their needs. He distinguishes between three types of region. The first comprises those which have had little or no demand for labour and a net outward migration balance. These have been avoided by the vast majority of coloured immigrants. The second consists of those which have had a high demand for labour but a high net inward migration balance. These contain only moderate proportions of coloured people. The third type comprises those areas of demand which have either failed to attract sufficient internal migration or experienced a net outward migration balance and it is in these that the immigrants constitute the highest proportion of the population.[2] Peach is also able to show, in support of his hypothesis, that West Indian migrants (with whom he was primarily concerned) were most concentrated in industries which had not increased their relative share of the work-force between 1951 and 1961 and, as he points out, this very often reflects an *uncompetitive* demand for labour.[3] Moreover, the fact that some immigrants are in growth industries does not seriously undermine his argument since very often they are working in the least attractive sections of them. Further support comes from the finding that whereas the population as a whole has shown a tendency to move away from large towns, the immigrants have settled most often in large decreasing towns and least often in those which are smaller but increasing.[4] In short, Peach suggests that in the main they have moved in as a replacement population to the 'decreasing urban cores of expanding industrial regions'.[5]

Other kinds of evidence on the employment of coloured workers point in the same direction. Peter Wright, for example, on the basis of interviews and a questionnaire survey of managers, found a general unwillingness to employ coloured workers except when adequate alternative sources of labour were unavailable.[6] Furthermore he noted that 'the coloured workers tended to obtain the jobs which white workers valued least – foundry workers in Major Castings Ltd., the "menial tasks" in the Quality Steel Co., the labouring jobs which the white workers "steered away from" in the Sovereign Steel Works and so on'.[7] Indeed, after noting that many firms had first sought foreign white workers as substitutes for native workers he suggested that 'at least initially the coloured worker does not automatically get the job the Englishmen won't take: he may only get those which foreign workers do not want either'.[8]

The movement into Nottingham corresponds fairly well with the pattern described by Peach. The city is part of what the *East Midlands Study* describes as a 'comparatively under-populated enclave in the great arc of conurbations formed by London, Birmingham, Lancashire and West Yorkshire'.[9] The region consists of the administrative counties of Derbyshire (except the north-western corner), Leicestershire, Lincolnshire (the Parts of Holland and the Parts of Kesteven), Northamptonshire, Rutland and Nottinghamshire, together with the county boroughs of Derby, Leicester, Lincoln, Northampton and Nottingham. With a population of about 3,250,000 it is one of the least crowded regions of the country. Its population density in 1965 was well under 700 per square mile, whereas that of the adjacent West Midlands was nearly 1,000 and that of the South-East nearly 1,600.[10] On the whole the Region is fairly prosperous and it has a long record of low rates of unemployment. Whilst unemployment figures for the East Midlands are not available for most past periods, data is available for the larger North Midlands Standard Region and, as Table 18 shows, the unemployment rate has been consistently below the national average.[11] In 1965, the year of the *East Midlands Study*, there was a strong and increasing demand for labour in the region. Even so, as that Report noted, the excess of vacancies over unemployment was, overall, less than half what it had been in 1955 and the demand for men in particular was still well below the average for the period 1952–65.[12] Clearly, during the period when Commonwealth immigration was at its height, the East Midlands was a region with a fairly high demand for labour. Yet it was not very successful in attracting workers from elsewhere in the United Kingdom and, of a total migratory gain of 80,000 in the period 1951–64, no more than 10,000 were workers from other parts of the country.[13]

Nottingham's own unemployment record, whilst not quite so good as that of the East Midlands as a whole, still compares very favourably with the situation nationally. This is due in large measure to the fact that the city now contains a great variety of industries. Yet, until as recently as World War I, it was very heavily dependent on clothing and textiles. Its association with these two industries goes back to the late sixteenth century when the Reverend William Lee of nearby Calverton invented the stocking-frame. Although for some time the

Table 18 Male unemployment rates in Nottingham, East Midlands and Great Britain, 1952–72[a]

Year	East Midlands[b] %	Nottingham %	Great Britain %
1952	0·6	1·3	1·6
1953	0·8	1·1	2·1
1954	0·6	1·0	1·8
1955	0·6	0·8	1·4
1956	0·5	0·8	1·2
1957	1·0	1·2	1·9
1958	1·4	1·5	2·0
1959	2·2	2·7	3·2
1960	1·6	2·2	2·4
1961	1·2	1·9	2·1
1962	1·5	2·3	2·4
1963	3·8	4·4	4·6
1964	1·5	2·5	2·6
1965	1·0	1·9	1·9
1966	1·0	2·2	1·8
1967	2·5	3·3	3·3
1968	2·7	3·6	3·5
1969	2·8	3·6	3·4
1970	3·3	3·9	3·7
1971	3·6	4·4	4·1
1972	5·0	5·7	5·8

[a] Figures represent percentage unemployed in January of each year.
[b] Figures 1952–62 for N. Midlands, 1962–65 for Midlands and 1966–72 for E. Midlands.

new craft of framework knitting was centred on London, by the early eighteenth century it had gravitated back towards the East Midlands and many thousands worked in their own homes on hired frames. Nottingham's famous lace, on which the town was to become especially reliant, also began its life on a stocking-frame. And, even though it was Heathcoat's bobbin net machine which finally supplanted hand lace-making, the connection with framework knitting is still strong for he (as well as other developers) originally trained as a framesmith. But perhaps the most significant influence exerted by the local hosiery industry was the encouragement it gave to mechanical spinning.[14] At first horse capstans and then water provided the power. The big breakthrough, however, came with the application of the rotary steam engine and it was a few miles away at Papplewick in 1785 that the world's first power mill was established. The key figure in the development was Richard Arkwright whose real claim to fame lies, despite his usual portrayal merely as an inventor, in his organisation of cotton spinning in factories.[15] Although a native of Lancashire, it was in the Nottingham area and with Nottingham capital that he began the transference of the industry to the sources of labour supply in the towns.

By 1861, as many as 75 per cent of those employed in Nottingham's characteristic industries were in textiles or clothing.[a] Whilst over the next fifty years the proportion fell to 60 per cent, during the same period no less than 40 per cent became dependent on lace alone.[16] Had there continued to be such a heavy reliance on this single industry there would almost certainly have been a severe economic recession in the town in the 1920s, for few industries can have suffered such a dramatic reversal in their fortunes. It was brought about by a virtual revolution in fashions. Whereas in the past there had always been changes in the styles and purposes for which lace was used, following World War I there was a 'veritable revulsion' from the material itself.[17] Fortunately, the decline of lace was offset by other developments. The hosiery industry began to expand again and by 1931 there were nearly twice as many hosiery workers in the city as there had been before the war. Garment making, or 'making up' as it is known locally, also grew in importance as ready-made clothing became increasingly popular with the advent of chain and departmental stores. But, even more significant, was the development of other industries. In 1883 Boots Cash Chemists was established; followed, five years later, by the Boots Pure Drug Company. In 1877 John Players was founded and about the same time Frank Bowden set up the Raleigh Cycle Company. All three firms proved to be in growth industries. Moreover, they were particularly well adapted to the difficult economic situation of the inter-war years which favoured those firms which produced consumer goods for the home market. This is not to say that Nottingham survived the inter-war years unscathed. But, with the exception of the lace trade, the unemployment it suffered was cyclical rather than structural. Even mining, which produced so much structural unemployment in other areas, proved to be an asset to Nottingham in the 1930s.[18]

Today, 'Nottingham is remarkable for the variety of its industries and its well balanced economic structure.'[19] The once all-important textile industry shares the stage with several others and, with the exception of textile finishing, employs more women than men. In 1966 it provided jobs for no more than 12·6 per cent of the labour force and 60 per cent of them were filled by women.

[a]   i.e. with the exclusion of those industries and services which are found in all large towns.

The clothing industry, which supplied 5·2 per cent of the jobs available, is even more dominated by women and in the same year no more than 17 per cent of its employees were men. A similar pattern exists in the tobacco industry where 60 per cent of the 7,000 jobs were occupied by women. But, in the manufacture of engineering and electrical goods, in which 10·5 per cent of the labour force were involved, men outnumbered women by as much as 4 to 1.[20] This sector has grown considerably since World War II and it has been suggested that its development epitomises the remarkable capacity for adaptation which has characterised Nottingham's economic growth.[21] Between the Wars the city prospered mainly as a result of the production of consumer goods for the home market. More recently, the local structure has adapted itself to meet the increased emphasis on the production of capital goods for both the home and export markets. To a great extent this has been achieved, as in the inter-war period, by the expansion of existing firms rather than the introduction of new ones.

Although several studies have provided information on the occupational background and level of skill of the Commonwealth immigrants who have come to areas like Nottingham in search of work, no clear-cut or complete picture has emerged. Indeed, in the case of the West Indian immigrants, about whom there is most information, the picture is positively confusing. On the basis of data obtained from a random sample of the case histories of immigrants interviewed by the Migrant Services Division of the West Indies Commission in London, Ruth Glass concluded that the great majority of West Indians had been black-coated and skilled workers at home.[22] In contrast, in the *Civil Service Argus* of February 1955, it was suggested that as many as 65 per cent of West Indian immigrants were unskilled.[23] Other studies have produced findings markedly different from both of these.[24] The discrepancies arise from the different ways in which samples were obtained, from the fact that the studies were conducted at different times, and because some studies were concerned with the West Indies as a whole whilst others concentrated on particular islands. But, whatever the reason for the confused picture, the fact remains that there is no established yardstick against which to measure the extent to which the occupational background of the Nottingham sample is typical.

An additional reason for caution in presenting data on the occupational background and level of skill of the Nottingham sample is that a number of writers have suggested that the degree of skill claimed by immigrants cannot always be accepted at face value. Richmond, for example, has noted that many of the skilled technicians recruited in Jamaica during World War II turned out to be far less skilled than they had claimed. Davison even abandoned his attempt to obtain data on the occupational background of a sample of Jamaicans because of such difficulties.

> A man would claim to be a 'painter' or a 'mechanic' simply because, in some remote past, he had held a brush or a spanner in his hand or even watched someone handling these implements. Without some simple trade testing scheme, the attempt to register occupation simply on the word of the respondent seems a somewhat futile exercise when it is borne in mind that for the sake of prestige, to say nothing of future employment prospects, it is a human reaction to exaggerate attained skill.[25]

The problem, however, is not simply that a man may be tempted to exaggerate his level of skill or degree of experience. It is difficult to apply a notion of skill developed in one society to another, perhaps more developed, country. A man may very reasonably describe himself as skilled and yet equally reasonably be judged only semi-skilled by someone in another country. Even in Britain, with a relatively formal apprenticeship system, there is a great deal of variation in both the content and quality of training. A youth who 'serves his time' in one firm may not develop particular skills to anything like the same extent as his counterpart elsewhere. As a result he could appear poorly trained in the eyes of other employers. The problem is obviously greater when the training takes place in another country – especially if it is a technologically less advanced one such as Jamaica which does not have a formal apprenticeship system.[26] This does not mean that a British apprenticeship is necessarily superior to a Jamaican. Indeed it could be that the use of relatively sophisticated equipment may result in the inadequate mastering of some basic skills without which a British trained person would find it difficult to hold down an equivalent job in Jamaica. But it does mean that caution must be exercised when making statements about the extent to which the immigrants are or are not skilled.

Of those interviewed in Nottingham about 11 per cent had emigrated on completing their education and had not been employed in their country of origin. Of the remaining 89 per cent, about half had been connected with agriculture – most often as peasant farmers. But, amongst the West Indians, there were some who had been employed on estates or plantations and others who had farmed a small plot in addition to doing other work. The next largest group comprised those who had been doing what may be loosely described as skilled manual work. Another 7 per cent had been small entrepreneurs and no more than 8 per cent had been in white collar or professional employment.

There is no obvious way in which to categorise the educational experience of the sample and the scheme adopted is necessarily crude. An initial distinction was made between those who had some form of educational qualification and those who had not. The former were then divided into those whose qualifications were such that they were virtually certain to be accorded recognition in this country and those whose qualifications might well be treated with a degree of suspicion by English employers. Though this is not a conventional way of classifying qualifications and involves a considerable amount of guesswork, it does have the merit of reflecting the realities of the situation with which immigrants are faced. The remainder were divided into those who had completed the basic education available to them, those who had partly completed it and those who had received no formal schooling. The answers given did not convey any signs of the exaggeration which might have been expected on the basis of the experiences of Richmond and Davison. Only a quarter of the respondents claimed any qualifications and almost 40 per cent said they had received no formal education or not completed the basic education available to them. It was judged that the vast majority of those with qualifications might encounter problems of recognition. These included, for example, those who had completed apprenticeships of an informal kind and others with further educational qualifications with which most people in Britain would be unfamiliar. Although the kind of classification employed does not really lend itself to cross-national comparison, it does seem that the West Indians in the sample are, on the whole, better educated than the Indians and Pakistanis. All those without formal schooling are Indians or Pakistanis and 31 per cent of the West Indians, as against 14 per cent of the Indians and Pakistanis, claim to possess some form of qualification. On the other hand, the small group of highly qualified respondents with qualifications almost certain to be recognised in Britain is composed only of Indians and Pakistanis.

The modesty of the immigrants' claims to qualifications was matched by the realism of their employment aspirations. Whatever the validity of Beetham's controversial claim that many coloured school-leavers have unrealistic job aspirations, there was no evidence of this amongst the immigrants interviewed in Nottingham.[27] In answer to the question: 'What kind of job did you want when you came to Britain?', 53 per cent said that they had not been thinking of any particular kind of job. Those who had were also asked: 'Did you expect to get such a job or were you just hoping you would?'. Three-quarters had come with firm expectations and as many as 60 per cent of them had obtained the kind of job they wanted. In contrast, no more than 15 per cent of those who had only been hopeful had succeeded. In short, most of those interviewed made no claims to any particular marketable skills and most did not come to Britain in search of any particular kind of job. Most of those who had come with firm expectations had been sucessful, whereas those with less firm expectations had rarely been successful.

It has been argued that most of Nottingham's coloured immigrants came here in search of work. To this extent their migration has proved worthwhile for, despite the deteriorating employment situation at the time of the interviews, only 3 per cent of the sample were out of work. Moreover, as many as 58 per cent had experienced no unemployment since obtaining their first job in this country. As Table 19 shows, the peak years of unemployment amongst Nottingham's coloured immigrants were 1961 and 1962 when immigration was at

Table 19 Adult male unemployment in Nottingham, 1959–71[28]

Year	Total number unemployed	West Indians % of total unemployed	Indians and Pakistanis % of total unemployed
1959	2,268	3·4	2·0
1960	1,778	4·8	1·0
1961	2,744	4·8	1·5
1962	2,397	8·7	5·6
1963	3,210	4·9	3·2
1964	2,016	4·0	3·1
1965	1,453	4·1	1·7
1966	2,269	3·4	1·2
1967	3,482	3·3	1·5
1968	3,666	2·4	1·2
1969	3,648	1·8	0·7
1970	3,928	2·0	0·9
1971	4,555	2·3	1·3

Figures are averages of numbers unemployed at four dates in each year. Until 1965, 'total number unemployed' included those 'temporarily stopped'. For this reason the proportion who are immigrants is slightly underestimated.

its height. Since then the extent of unemployment amongst the coloured population has shown a fairly steady decline. But it is still not known if coloured people are over-represented or under-represented amongst the unemployed. Although the Department of Employment and Productivity records the ethnic origin of those unemployed, the relative proportions of each ethnic group in the work-force is not known.[29] Consequently it is not possible to calculate rates of unemployment. All that can be said on the basis of the available data is that fluctuations in the overall number of unemployed are not matched by corresponding fluctuations amongst the immigrant groups and that it is, as yet, impossible to determine why this is the case.

What is not in doubt is that coloured immigrants are over-represented in some fields of employment and very much under-represented in others. Table 20 shows the distribution of Nottingham's male workers in the Registrar

Table 20 Distribution of male immigrants in Nottingham industry, 1966

Industry	West Indians %	Indians %	Pakistanis %	All coloured immigrants %	All males %
Agriculture, forestry, fishing	—	—	—	—	0·1
Mining, quarrying	13·9	4·5	2·4	10·4	1·8
Food, drink, tobacco	1·4	1·5	—	1·3	5·0
Chemicals and allied industries	1·0	—	2·4	1·0	2·1
Metal manufacture	15·9	4·5	—	11·4	0·6
Engineering and electrical goods	10·6	11·9	24·4	12·7	8·9
Shipbuilding, marine engineering	—	—	—	—	0·1
Vehicles	6·7	—	2·4	4·7	4·7
Metal goods not specified elsewhere	1·0	—	4·9	1·3	1·2
Textiles	5·3	17·9	17·1	9·5	8·2
Leather, leather goods, fur	0·5	—	—	0·3	0·3
Clothing and footwear	—	—	—	—	1·2
Bricks, pottery, glass, cement, etc.	3·8	9·0	2·4	4·7	0·6
Timber, furniture, etc.	2·4	1·5	—	1·9	2·0
Paper, printing, publishing	—	—	14·6	1·9	3·3
Other manufacturing industries	—	—	—	—	0·5
Construction	11·5	4·5	—	8·5	10·1
Gas, electricity, water	0·5	1·5	—	0·6	3·2
Transport and communications	9·1	25·4	17·1	13·6	8·9
Distributive trades	2·4	7·5	7·3	4·1	14·0
Insurance, banking, finance	0·5	—	—	0·3	2·7
Professional and scientific services	2·9	3·0	—	2·5	6·7
Miscellaneous services	2·4	3·0	—	2·2	8·2
Public administration and defence	8·2	4·5	4·9	7·0	5·5

General's 24 industrial categories at the time of the 1966 Census.[30] Whereas native white workers are to be found in all 24 categories, West Indians are found only in 19, Indians in no more than 14 and Pakistanis in as few as 11. There are probably several factors responsible for this particular distribution pattern amongst the immigrant groups. It may be due in part to the fact that Indian and Pakistani migration lagged behind the West Indian and so the figures may represent slightly different stages of the immigration process. However, it is much more likely to be due to the greater communication problem faced by the Asians which, in addition to making some employers reluctant to employ them, also encourages voluntary concentration. There is, in addition, a much greater cohesion amongst Indians and Pakistanis than West Indians. These suggested explanations are consistent with the findings of two studies of employment carried out by the Nottingham Commonwealth Citizens Consultative Committee. Whereas only 20 per cent of the West Indians said that they had found their jobs through relatives and friends already at the firm in question, this was the means used by as many as 56 per cent of the Indians and Pakistanis. Conversely, whereas 52 per cent of the West Indians had approached their employer directly and without the help of friends, relatives or the Employment Exchange, this had been done by only 17 per cent of the Indians and Pakistanis.[31]

The West Indians are most clearly over-represented in mining, quarrying and metal manufacturing; the Indians in textiles, transport and brick, pottery, glass and cement making; and the Pakistanis in textiles, transport, paper, printing and publishing, and the manufacture of engineering and electrical goods. All three immigrant groups (but particularly the Pakistanis) are conspicuously under-represented in the public services of gas, electricity and water; insurance, banking and finance; the distributive trades; professional and scientific services and the food, drink and tobacco industries. To what extent these instances of under-representation result from discrimination, unsuitable or inadequate qualifications, a failure to apply for jobs or highly stable labour forces is not readily apparent. But it is obviously an important matter to which we will return.

Table 21 shows that all but 5 per cent of the immigrant sample were in manual jobs at the time of the interviews. Moreover, almost three-quarters of them were doing either unskilled or semi-skilled work. This pattern obtained almost identically for all three immigrant groups; the only marked difference being that the handful of those in non-manual occupations included no West Indians. Compared to the sample of white natives living in the same area, the immigrants were not only more likely to be doing manual work but also more likely to be in unskilled manual work. Almost three times as many English respondents belonged to social classes 1, 2, and 3a and nearly twice as many to class 3b. In contrast, more than twice as many immigrants were in social class 5. This low level of occupational achievement amongst the immigrants is not markedly out of step with the skill levels they claimed for themselves. Certainly the proportion in non-manual and skilled manual jobs is as high as could be reasonably expected. However, this does not mean that degrees of responsibility or rates of pay are necessarily in accord with experience and/or qualifications. Moreover, it is not clear why so many of the immigrants are in unskilled work. It is true that the proportion of immigrants in semi-skilled work is the same as that for the white natives. But very often only a minimal degree of training is required to enter the semi-skilled status category and an initial lack of skill is far from being an unsurmountable obstacle. For this reason it would

Table 21 Distribution in Registrar General's social classes[a]

Social class[b]	Native whites %	West Indians %	Indians and Pakistanis %
1, 2 and 3a	13	—	10
3b	40	25	18
4	31	35	33
5	17	40	39
No. respondents	101	72	49

[a] Excluding those respondents who were retired at the time of the interviews.

[b] 3a (non-manual workers)
3b (manual workers).

not have been surprising if immigrants had been found to be over-represented amongst the semi-skilled as well as the unskilled. That they are not would seem to be consistent with Wright's conclusion – namely that coloured immigrants tend to be employed in unattractive jobs for which it is difficult to recruit white native labour. It must also be remembered that had the samples been representative of the city as a whole, rather than the inner city area, then the occupational gap between the immigrants and natives would have been even greater. This is because within any given occupational level coloured people are more likely to live in the inner city area than English people. Thus the immigrant sample corresponds much more closely to a microcosm of the whole coloured community than does the native sample, to the white community.

It has been argued that most of the immigrants left home in search of work and came to Nottingham because of the town's labour shortage. To the extent that they have found jobs, and the labour shortage has thereby been reduced, the process of immigration would seem to have been mutually beneficial. Whilst the jobs they have obtained have usually been of a fairly menial kind this does not seem to have involved any great loss of status for the majority – or proved out of step with their expectations or ambitions. At the same time, it is just such jobs which those who had employed them had previously found it most difficult to fill. Clearly the curbing of coloured Commonwealth immigration was not the action of 'rational economic man'. This is very evident in the fact that a rise in the rate of alien immigration accompanied the fall in the rate of Commonwealth immigration.[b] It may be true that most white natives felt threatened by the influx of coloured workers and favoured immigration control, but there certainly does not seem to have been any sound basis for their seeing the immigrants as an *economic* threat. Their entry may have involved an increase in the competition for such scarce resources as housing but, except perhaps in so far as a reduction in the labour shortage might have marginally weakened the bargaining position of white native workers, the arrival of the immigrants can hardly be construed as constituting any threat to the economic security of the indigenous population. In places like Nottingham jobs have been readily available and those offered to the immigrants have been, in any case, very often those which the indigenous workers did not want. Where there has been a job shortage, immigrants have not been much in evidence. In short, in the employment sphere, apart perhaps from the novelty of working alongside coloured people, there has been little reason for anything other than a response of relative indifference from most white native workers.

This has not always been the case. Indeed several instances of racial violence in Britain have arisen out of feelings of economic insecurity engendered by the employment of coloured immigrants in times of high unemployment. The violence which took place in Cardiff in 1919 is perhaps the clearest example. Most of the coloured people in the town were seamen or ex-seamen, and during the War, when there was no shortage of work, their presence was tolerated – especially since their chances of promotion above the rank of boiler-man, donkey-man or able-seaman were very slender. With the post-war contraction in the shipping industry and demobilisation, which brought about a very substantial increase in the level of unemployment, the white native workers became less tolerant. Their fear that coloured workers constituted unfair com-

[b]   Between 1963 and 1967 the number of work vouchers issued to non-white immigrants fell from 28,678 to 4,721. During the same period the number of work permits issued to aliens increased from 39,963 to 45,867. *Observer,* 13 October 1968.

petition was not altogether unfounded. So long as a coloured man was signed on in a non-British port he could be paid at a lower rate than any seaman, native or otherwise, signed on at a British Port. This both increased the native seamen's resentment of the non-Europeans and also encouraged the latter to settle in Britain in the hope of obtaining the better pay and conditions that would then apply − so exacerbating the situation yet further. Coloured men, Little explains, 'were looked on by white unions not as a section of the same labouring class striving for a livelihood on exactly the same basis as any other Union member, but as the representatives of an altogether different competitive category, which directly or indirectly was responsible for keeping white seamen out of work'.[32]

On 10 June 1919, a precipitating brawl between a small group of coloureds and whites set off a disturbance involving an estimated 2,000 people in which pistols as well as sticks and stones were used. In its efforts to get at coloured people the white mob attacked a number of shops, one of which was completely demolished. Two houses were extensively damaged and another was set on fire. Fifteen people were admitted to hospital and one died shortly afterwards. Similar incidents continued for a few days and did not end until the mob was eventually overawed by a reinforced police force and two lorry loads of soldiers in full fighting kit. A similar pattern of events occurred in other ports where coloured people lived. On Tyneside the trouble was again precipitated by a minor incident − in this case a dispute about signing on a ship's crew. A severe outbreak of violence followed and eventually a detachment of sailors was called in to help police break up the disturbances.[33]

There were further incidents on Tyneside in 1930 and 1931. The first was the culmination of many demonstrations by white seamen during the previous four months when unemployment amongst them was exceptionally high. When the Shipping Federation decided to take on Arab seamen, 1,500 men assembled on the quayside, stood before Board of Trade officials and attempted to prevent the Arabs signing on. Knives, razors, sticks and even lumps of coal were used in the ensuing violence and a number of people were injured. In 1931, a further outbreak of violence erupted over the employment of coloured firemen and again several people were injured.[34]

Although such incidents serve to illustrate the potential for racial violence which exists during periods of high unemployment, it would obviously be a mistake to assume that violence is likely whenever unemployment is high. Indeed, unless the unemployed members of the indigenous population are in direct competition with, and living in close proximity to, the coloured workers − and unless the situation is or can easily be conceived of in racial terms − then violence is unlikely. The present unemployment situation in Britain does not have these characteristics. Nevertheless, so long as native workers do not see coloured workers as ordinary members of the work force, it is not difficult to envisage circumstances in which the current pattern of tolerance might give way to more open hostility.

That many workers still distinguish between coloured immigrants and other members of the work-force is not in doubt. For example, 67 per cent of those interviewed in Nottingham said that the English ought to be given priority over coloured immigrants so far as jobs were concerned. When asked why they felt this, almost all justified their view by asserting, in one way or another, that preferential treatment was one of their rights as Englishmen. The prevalence of this essentially Burkean notion helps to explain why it is that Enoch Powell's views on race relations have found so much resonance amongst the English working class.

> It is obvious – those whose country it is should get first choice.

> Because I'm English. I'm not prejudiced. It's just an Englishman's right.

> Because I live here. The West Indies isn't England it it? We didn't ask them over.

> It's England isn't it? I'm Alf Garnett. He said that when God made this earth he allotted a little bit to everybody. I've got no intention of going to India.

> It's our country. I know some blacks are born here but I still think the Englishmen should have priority.

> It's obvious – we belong here – they don't.

This attitude persists despite the fact that coloured immigrant workers seem to follow whatever is the normal pattern of trades union membership at their place of work.[c] Indeed, amongst those interviewed in Nottingham, trades union membership was more common amongst the immigrants than the white native workers. Whereas as many as 58 per cent of the natives were not and never had been union members, this was true of no more than 36 per cent of the immigrants. Moreover, whereas 54 per cent of those English respondents who were or had been members said that they had joined because it was compulsory, this held for only 34 per cent of the immigrants: the remaining 66 per cent had joined of their own accord.

Given the prevalence of this attitude, and despite the willingness of immigrant workers to conform to unionisation patterns, further open hostility from white workers cannot be ruled out. And, as Carole Blair and others have noted, the provisions of the 1972 Immigration Act make it more likely.[35] Most coloured Commonwealth immigrants now entering Britain belong to the

---

[c]   In some instances immigrants have shown a greater willingness to unionise than white workers. Peter Marsh, *The Anatomy of a Strike* (Institute of Race Relations Special Research Series, 1967).

category known as 'non-patrials'. This means that they have no automatic right to enter the United Kingdom and can do so only if given leave by the Secretary of State at the Home Office. If admitted for a limited period, the terms of admission can be altered at any time and should the Secretary of State deem their continued stay in Britain 'not conducive to the public good' they can be deported. Moreover, to obtain patrial status and so acquire the right to remain in Britain permanently a Commonwealth citizen now has to satisfy the Secretary of State that he is of 'good character'. Obviously those who are anxious to remain in Britain will take care to stay out of trouble and might, for example, be reluctant to become involved in industrial disputes or risk antagonising their employers in other ways. In tense situations such understandable reluctance might look very different to native workers and be strongly resented by them.

Although there is a possibility of resentment arising in this way, resentment on the part of the immigrants is more likely. Indeed the part of the interview which dealt with employment was very often dominated by expressions of resentment. This is particularly significant for, as has already been noted, most of the immigrants had fairly realistic as well as modest job aspirations. Most often, in fact, the resentment stemmed not from personal job dissatisfaction but the conviction that racial discrimination was widespread. Even so, in contrast to the pattern of replies obtained on satisfaction with housing, there were more complaints about jobs in the immigrant sample than in the white native sample. More precisely, there were more complaints from the West Indians.[d] Whereas 74 per cent of the English respondents were satisfied, as were 72 per cent of the Asians, this applied to 51 per cent of the West Indians. There were also differences in the kind of dissatisfaction expressed by the members of the respective ethnic groups. As Table 22 shows the English respondents were more likely to complain about their level of remuneration than either the West Indians or Asians. The immigrants, on the other hand, and particularly the West Indians, were more likely to complain about poor working conditions. The Indians and Pakistanis were distinguished by the small proportion of them who complained about the boring nature of their work and the large proportion who claimed to be trained for, or capable of, better work. Respondents who were unhappy with their jobs were also asked about the sort of job they thought they should have and their chances of obtaining it. Though the numbers in these sub-samples are very small it is worth noting that the immigrants were

[d] Wright also found that West Indians were more often dissatisfied with their jobs than Indians and Pakistanis. Peter L. Wright, *The Coloured Worker in British Industry* (London, Oxford University Press, for Institute of Race Relations, 1968), pp. 150–2.

more pessimistic than the native respondents and that the reason they cited most often for their poor prospects was racial discrimination.

Table 22 Reasons for job dissatisfaction

Reason	Native whites %	West Indians %	Indians and Pakistanis %
Insufficient money	46	32	23
Boring work	21	24	8
Poor working conditions	8	32	15
Capable of better work	29	32	61
No. respondents	24	34	13

The extent to which the immigrants believe in the existence of racial discrimination was made clear when they were asked: 'Do you think that immigrants have the same chance of getting jobs as English people *with the same qualifications*?' As many as 95 per cent said 'no'. These were then asked why they thought they had less chance and 91 per cent said it was because they were coloured.

Because of colour – I *know* it is colour.

It's colour. It seems as if they just see people that are black as something bad.

Just because we're coloured – they just don't like us.

Colour – they don't think we're as good as they are.

They don't tell you straight but it is because of the pigments of your skin. But they don't tell you straight – they just tell you there is no vacancy. Provided the white man is there he will get the priority. I understand that to an extent but why should a European come before a Jamaican? They was not born here either.

Definitely colour – it's our skin – definitely.

Colour prejudice – but to be fair it happens in more countries than Britain.

Well they are the host community so you have to expect it. It's not surprising they should look after themselves first. But it's not fair that a man should be treated so because his skin is a different colour.

Colour prejudice – that's all it is.

It's the colour of the skin – they think that coloureds are inferior to them.

The coloured respondents were also asked if they thought there were any particular kinds of jobs which immigrants had more difficulty in getting than English people with the same qualifications. As many as 96 per cent said 'yes' and the sort most often specified were supervisory (72 per cent) and clerical (51 per cent). Also mentioned, but much less often, were jobs involving face to face contact with the public, skilled technical work and jobs in the police force.

> Any good job – like a job that is more important or pays good money. The better jobs they give to the English people.

> Foreman – they feel the coloured man's not capable of it.

> Foreman – you'll never get that job – it's out of the question.

> Well the jobs you get most is labouring jobs – office jobs is impossible. If a coloured man gets to be a charge-hand – and one or two have mind you – well they don't get no further.

> Any white collar job – it's difficult to get any white collar job. Supervisory, technical or even semi-technical – we have great difficulty in getting jobs like these.

> Good jobs – if you get a job it will be the kind of job you don't want – a very hard job or a very poor one.

> More or less any kind of job that requires training. They don't think your qualifications can be good enough.

> Office jobs – and skilled work. I know plenty chaps they don't really do their trade. Lots of the Jamaicans over here are tradesmen – tailors, shoemakers, carpenters and the rest – bricklayer and all these. Most people think you can only do labouring work and such like. So they have to stick themselves into anything. And foremen – nobody got jobs as foremen here. Even in the pit I'm working in there are coloureds there that have 'overmen' papers but they won't employ them as 'overmen'.

> White collar jobs and any good job. There is a wrong feeling that the coloured man should be subservient all the days of his life. In London I don't know but in Nottingham and Derby you ain't got a chance.

Those respondents who had not already mentioned personal experience of discrimination in reply to the two above-mentioned questions were also asked: 'Do you think you yourself have ever been discriminated against when looking for a job or when you have been in line for promotion?'. Taking the three answers together it was found that only 28 per cent believed that they had never been the victims of employment discrimination. Moreover, several respondents were reluctant to make an allegation even though they seemed fairly certain it had occurred. This is reflected in the relatively large number of respondents classified as 'don't knows' (19 per cent), for those who said that they might have experienced discrimination, but were not certain, were placed in this category. All told, as many as 53 per cent claimed to have been subject to discrimination and the following quotations give some indication of the kind of allegations that were made.

> In the short time I was unemployed I had plenty of instances. They would say that the vacancy was filled and yet they would still advertise the job. They didn't even bother to interview me or find out about the level of my qualifications.

> Just last week a firm advertised for joiners. I rang up and they confirmed the jobs were still available. But when I get there they say the advertisement was a mistake. They took my name and said they would write next time they had a vacancy. Then they advertised again but did not write to me. That sort of thing has happened to me a lot.

> I tried for a job as a sales rep. and I had all the qualifications but at the final stage I was rejected and told that their customers might not like a coloured man calling on them. When I asked them: 'Am I fit for the job?' they said 'Oh yes'!

> Many times. Once I had a job with _____ _____ . It was a dirty job but I liked it. To be a stoker you had to get three months training. Well, what made me leave there is because by then I was 'spare-man' and I know my job and whenever the head stoker wasn't there I had to take his place. When he left there was nobody entitled to the job except me so I applied to get it. But there was a fella came six months after me – he was Irish or Scottish I think – they gave him the job. *So I had to show him how to do it*! But after I had to do this – before about ten minutes were up – I got up and went and gave my notice to leave. I couldn't get away with that at all. Worse than that the Shift Engineer took me into the Chief Engineer's office to see if it was alright to leave in such a short time. He wasn't in at the time so I sat down in an ordinary little chair to wait. When he came in he said to me – '*You don't sit down in this office!*' So I get up. Every word I say is true – that was my first experience – and *they're* supposed to be intelligent people.

> There was a job for an assistant catering officer going at the _____ _____ . I applied for it and was short-listed. The man who got the job had worked under me in the past and was still only an assistant cook whereas I was a head cook and had my City and Guild qualifications. I can state very frankly that this racial discrimination does exist.

> Several times. I remember once I went for a job at _____ _____ _____ . You know their shopfitting department. I'm sure I could have done the job. I was told by an Englishman who was working there that it would be a good job. So I went to see this Personnel Officer. He said: 'Well – we are wanting joiners – but it's high class work.' So I said 'I can do high class work'. He says: 'I'm sorry I don't think you are suitable.' So I said: 'How do you know?' and he said: 'I don't think you're skilled.' It was just as I tell you – he just didn't want to give me a chance.

> I left my job in the city and the Exchange tell me there is a job going at a biscuit factory. Well I go along there and there's only white fellas working there. And they tell me they haven't got no job. But when I go back to the Exchange they tell me there was still a vacancy there. So it must have been me being coloured why they wouldn't give me the job.

From time to time allegations such as these have found a more public expression. For example, Mr Kandola, President of Nottingham's Indian Welfare Association, in a speech made in February 1967, complained that racial discrimination was preventing coloured school leavers from obtaining jobs commensurate with their ability. He also noted that there were no coloured milkmen, postmen, traffic wardens or policemen in Nottingham and that although as many as one-third of the City Transport's work force were coloured none were employed at the staff level. In addition, he noted that another bus company seemed to be totally opposed to the employment of coloured people. In subsequent statements Mr Kandola repeated his charge against the Transport Department and also noted the difficulties faced by Nottingham's coloured taxi-drivers, none of whom had been able to obtain full insurance cover. In April 1968, Mr Atwal, General Secretary of the Indian Workers Association in Nottingham, accused the Corporation's Education Committee of discriminating against coloured teachers. And, although this particular charge has been officially denied, as have some of the allegations made by Mr Kandola, there is little doubt that most coloured people remain convinced that racial discrimination is widespread.

The immigrants' belief in the existence of employment discrimination was shared by as many as 42 per cent of the native white sample. But more (49 per cent) considered that coloured immigrants had at least as much chance of getting jobs as Englishmen with the same qualifications and there are other, more influential, members of the local English population who agree with them. Towards the end of 1967 the Employment Sub-Committee of the Nottingham Commonwealth Citizens Consultative Committee attempted to organise a seminar for trades unions and management on 'Race Relations in Nottingham Industry'. Similar meetings, modelled on the important national conference held earlier in the year under the auspices of the National Committee for Commonwealth Immigrants, had already taken place elsewhere in the country. Representatives of the CBI and Chamber of Commerce were, however, strongly opposed to the idea. They argued that the holding of such a conference would incite racial feelings rather than allay them and that there was no racial discrimination in the employment field in Nottingham. Though the employers' representatives were aware of the findings of the PEP report on racial discrimination they did not feel that its findings were relevant to the situation in Nottingham. The conference did not take place.[36] In May 1968, the Nottingham Evening Post published a special supplement for school-leavers. Under a headline *Colour Makes No Difference Here* one of the articles claimed:

> The colour of your skin is no drawback if you are a school leaver looking for a job in Nottingham. 'With the same ability coloured youngsters can do just as

well as white youngsters' says Mr Spencely, Nottingham's principal youth employment officer. A coloured girl looking for an office job may take a little longer to place, but if she is capable of doing the job the youth employment service can place her. But a limited command of English can prove a drawback to some immigrant children when they leave school. 'When coloured youngsters are unemployed it is usually because of limited ability due to limited communication' explained Mr Spencely.

Whilst these differing viewpoints are important in their own right, and must be taken into account in any attempt to explain the behaviour of those concerned, more objective evidence is needed to determine whether or not racial discrimination is widespread. Unfortunately such evidence is in short supply. Although the East Midlands Conciliation Committee of the Race Relations Board, which is based in Nottingham, has dealt with cases of racial discrimination in employment since the introduction of the 1968 legislation, there are many reasons why the small number of cases brought to its attention cannot be treated as an indication of the extent of discrimination.[e] Immigrants may not always know when they have been discriminated against. They may be unaware that the Race Relations Act exists or be ignorant of the complaints procedure. Or, even if aware of the discrimination and the complaints procedure, they may choose not to register a complaint. The Conciliation Committee certainly acknowledges this and indeed it commented as follows in its 1971–2 Annual Report.

> In the Committee's view the fall in the number of complaints is in no way a reflection of the level of discrimination, and is a considerable cause for concern, the more so as during the year a greater effort was made to increase the awareness of minorities of their rights under the Act ... While the Committee consider that the Act has made an impact on many in a position to discriminate, they are of the opinion that discrimination remains extensive especially in the private housing sector and in some fields of employment.[37]

The Conciliation Committee is concerned with actual discrimination. This is particularly important since many immigrants are known to avoid potentially discriminatory situations. As a result, there may be a great deal of latent discrimination and yet little *actual* discrimination. Whilst to date there has been no comprehensive testing of the extent of this latent discrimination the one limited study which has been conducted does suggest that it is fairly widespread.[38] Four types of employment were investigated in Nottingham and a number of other towns. The jobs concerned were sales and marketing; accounting and office management; electrical engineering and secretarial work. The technique used was simple but ingenious. Carefully prepared and convin-

[e]   In 1970–71 there were 38 allegations of discrimination in the field of employment. A further 4 cases were dealt with by the appropriate industrial machinery. In 1971–72 the number of allegations dealt with by the Committee fell to 19 but the number dealt with by the industrial machinery increased to 12.

cing applications bearing the names of fictitious individuals were sent in reply to advertised vacancies. They were carefully matched except for minor details (to increase their apparent authenticity) but contained clues to indicate the country of origin of the applicant.

The test of discrimination used in the study was whether or not applicants were invited for interview or sent an application form. As Jowell and Prescott-Clarke emphasise, this 'is a particularly decisive and absolute form of discrimination: the employer is (deliberately) denying himself the opportunity of even considering an applicant whose qualifications appear to be suitable; and the disadvantaged applicant is denied the chance even of competing with other applicants, whether or not his qualifications are better than theirs'.[39] And, of course, it is quite possible that discrimination might still be met by an applicant who overcomes this initial hurdle. In other words, the study must be assumed to have underestimated the real extent of latent discrimination in recruitment to these sorts of jobs.

The results revealed virtually no difference in the degree of discrimination between either the four areas studied or the four job types which were covered. The most successful of the immigrant applicants were the Australians. Indeed their success rate of 78 per cent was just as good as that of the white British applicants. The Asian applicants, with a success rate of only 35 per cent, met by far the most discrimination. The West Indians and Cypriots, both with a score of 69 per cent, did markedly better than the Asians but less well than the Australians. Other controls built into the study made it possible to discover that immigrants who completed all their secondary education in Britain did not encounter significantly less discrimination than more recent arrivals and that those immigrants who had higher qualifications than their white counterparts were not treated significantly differently from those with equal qualifications. One particularly important conclusion of the study was that 'in none of the cases of discrimination found, could a complaint feasibly have been made under the Race Relations Act by the disadvantaged applicant: he or she would simply never have known that discrimination was taking place. All refusals were (predictably) polite, benevolent and often charming: e.g. "We would like to wish you every success in obtaining the type of position for which your qualifications fit you." No doubt Asian immigrants in particular will have to face the fact that their country of origin is frequently the only significant qualification taken into account.'[40]

Thus there can be little doubt that, whatever the extent of actual discrimination in Nottingham at the present time, there is a great potential for discrimination. Should increasing numbers of coloured children qualify for the kind of white collar jobs investigated in the study and meet actual discrimination, it will inevitably lead to disappointment and bitterness. The only certain way to prevent such a reaction is to introduce measures effective enough to eliminate all employment discrimination. However, even this will not help if young coloured people do not have qualifications commensurate with their abilities.

Over the past twenty years large numbers of West Indian, Indian and Pakistani children have come to Nottingham to join their parents. Whilst most of those coloured children now entering the schools have been born in Britain, the large majority of those who have already left school (as well as many of those still at school) were born overseas.[*f*] Very often they came late in their school careers. In the case of the Indians and Pakistanis they came with little or no knowledge of English. In the case of the West Indians they came with what educationalists have increasingly come to recognise as a form of English very different from our own. So, even at this simplest of levels, immigrant children have been at a considerable educational disadvantage compared with their English counterparts.[41] When one also takes into account that at the same time that they were beginning school in this country they were often having to establish personal relationships with a parent (or parents) with whom they had had little contact; that their own culture and pattern of education was usually very different from that encountered in our schools; and that they were settling in those areas least well endowed with educational facilities and services, it is obvious that very great help was needed to ensure that they had anything like the same opportunity to do as well as English children of comparable ability.

There is little doubt that Nottingham's former Director of Education, Mr George Jackson, was fully aware of such difficulties. Indeed, writing in the Institute of Race Relations Newsletter in 1966 he emphasised:

> Too often the education of these children is considered solely in terms of ability in English. In practice. learning English is only one of the major difficulties facing them. . . . English is only the tool of communication; much more important for the teacher is the child's pool of ideas and understanding of natural and scientific phenomena. The teacher has to build up for the young child a new background of information and frequently a new set of values. . . . The immigrant child needs special care, both for his social and educational needs, for quite a long time.

He continued by stressing that 'it is easy to underestimate the pupils' difficulties in adapting themselves to a new country and to a very different educational approach, in which there is less "lecturing" and more "pupil participation",' and warned that 'there is a tendency on the part of some boys and girls to aquiesce in a state of educational retardation'.[42]

[*f*]   In 1966 Nottingham's Director of Education wrote: 'A significant change is, however, beginning to take effect in that in the next two years many of the coloured children entering the schools will have been born in this country.' George Jackson, 'The Education of Immigrant Children in Nottingham', *Institute of Race Relations Newsletter* (February 1966).

Given this appraisal of the difficulties facing immigrant children it might be expected that Nottingham's provision of 'special care' for them would be of a high standard. Mr Jackson certainly seemed to believe that this was the case. In a letter to the Acting Secretary of the Commonwealth Citizens Consultative Committee, written on 1 January 1970, he claimed that Nottingham's provision for the teaching of immigrants was the best possible and that it would stand comparison with that existing anywhere in the country. As there are many who disagree with this claim it is important that some indication is given of the kind of provision which is made elsewhere. Despite the varied forms which it takes, some kind of intensive and separate teaching is almost invariably involved. Sometimes children are withdrawn from ordinary classes for extra tuition. In other places special language centres have been established. But, whatever the particular administrative arrangements, special provision of some kind is made during normal school hours.[43] The case for this was put very clearly in the publication *The Education of Immigrants* issued by the Department of Education and Science in 1971.

> Some authorities place all immigrant pupils without differentiation in classes appropriate to their age. (They) . . . then follow the accepted school timetable, joining in all activities and lessons with the English children. In such conditions . . . children for whom English is a second language acquire some spoken English and start to read and write. However, many children may learn only an unstructured form of English, a collection of vocabulary items – a language inadequacy which is a severe handicap in the later stages of education. . . . The belief that young immigrant children will pick up their language from their English friends and classmates is not now generally accepted by teachers experienced in this work. Some more positive and systematic approach is thought to be necessary.[44]

What then of the kind of provision made in Nottingham? Hawkes, in his survey of teaching methods, summed it up as follows:

> Nottingham is the champion of those who believe in meeting the special linguistic and other needs of immigrant children *without recourse to intensive separate teaching of any kind.*[45] (my italics)

In other words Nottingham's provision has lacked what, according to the Department of Education and Science, most experienced teachers consider essential. This is not to say that no extra help has been provided. New nurseries have been opened in areas of high immigrant concentration, nursery nurses have helped out in some ordinary infant classes and there has been an effort to keep classes at a below average size. At the secondary stage a few schools have had additional members of staff to help cope with newly arrived immigrants and some further classes have been held in the early evening after school. In addition, a general education course preparatory to normal further education classes has been arranged at a local college of further education for older immigrants.[46]

There is no simple way in which to determine the adequacy of these provisions. What is clear is that some of them were introduced very late in the development of the problem and can have made little impact on it. The general education course, for example, was not started until September 1969 and had only sixteen pupils in its first year. It is also clear that the small class policy has not always been successfully maintained. In the article by the Director of Education mentioned above he stated that a maximum of 30 children in a class would 'not be an unreasonable requirement' for the schools in which immigrants were concentrated. He added that 'the school premises are, however, quite inadequate for this purpose. Every effort is being made to keep the size of the classes *below 40,* but this is becoming increasingly difficult' (my italics).[47] Finally, it is clear that many people in Nottingham, including educational experts, consider that the provisions have been far from adequate. One body which has been concerned about them for several years is the Commonwealth Citizens Consultative Committee (now the Nottingham and District Community Relations Council).

In January 1967 the Secretary of the Consultative Committee was asked by his members to ask the Director of Education for permission to approach the Headmasters of appropriate schools in order to find out what difficulties they were experiencing with immigrant children.[48] Permission was refused.[49] Following this, a delegation from the Committee met the Director and discussed the general situation with him. He seems to have argued that the problem of recently arrived Asian children had been exaggerated and reminded the delegation of the existence of special evening classes in English which the children could begin at the age of fourteen. In reply, the delegation reiterated its opinion that not enough was done in the schools during normal hours and expressed concern over the consequences which might follow from a failure to make the necessary improvements.[50] In the meanwhile, groups of University students had initiated a scheme to teach immigrant children English in their own homes. By the end of 1968 it had come to involve as many as 110 volunteers. When the scale of this enterprise and the extent of the need which it indicated was drawn to the attention of the Consultative Committee, the Director of Education was asked to meet a second delegation.[51] This time, however, he declined to do so.[52] By 1970 the Committee was still convinced that more special provision was needed within the schools but was equally convinced that further efforts to persuade the Director of this were unlikely to be fruitful.

As a result they adopted a different tactic and set about organising their own Summer School Language Project. It was intended not only to provide additional language teaching for immigrant children with language difficulties, but also to demonstrate the need for special language tuition within the schools. A grant of £700 was obtained from the Community Relations Commission and a request made to the Director of Education for the use of a school during part of the summer holidays. He replied that it was during this part of the year that major maintenance and cleaning was carried out in the schools and that for this reason no school could be made available. He also suggested that in order to avoid a breach of the Race Relations Act it would be necessary for the Committee to provide for *all* children with language difficulties and that this could involve as many as 2,000 children.[53] The Committee was disappointed with this response – particularly the Director's invoking of the Race Relations Act as an argument against them providing additional help for children in need. They were also concerned by an additional comment in his letter which suggested that 'most' West Indians in Nottingham's schools could be said to have 'language difficulties'.

In the event, the Summer School eventually went ahead without the LEA's help and whilst the Committee felt it had several weaknesses it seemed, on the whole, to have been a successful exercise.[54] As a result, a similar school was planned for 1971. Again the LEA was invited to participate and again it declined to do so. And, in a letter to the Consultative Committee, the Director of Education claimed that he had not found headmasters or teachers enthusiastic about the project or much concerned to support it.[55] Yet, shortly afterwards, it seems that the city's branch of the NUT passed a motion supporting the School and urging more positive aid for immigrant children.[56] The Corporation also declined to make premises available and declared itself unable to endorse an application for Urban Aid which the Committee had hoped would supplement the grant of £550 given by the Community Relations Commission.[57] Despite this, and with considerable publicity, the project went ahead. In 1972 the LEA announced that it was to run its own Summer School.

This sequence of events has been described to indicate the way in which one group of people reacted to the LEA's provision for immigrant children. Not surprisingly, concern has also been expressed over the years by leaders of several of the city's immigrant organisations. But however adequate or inadequate the provision is, or has been, it seems to be generally agreed that a great many immigrant children have not achieved and are still not achieving educational levels commensurate with their real abilities. This is perhaps best illustrated by reference to Nottingham's West Indian school children. In an article published in 1972 Lancelot Christopher expressed concern at their poor educational achievements and argued that much more could be done for them at school.[58] Mr Jackson, in contrast, seemed to believe that all that could be done was being done. Nevertheless, there appears to be little or no disagreement between Mr Christopher and Mr Jackson about the actual performance of West Indian children, for in a letter to the Consultative Committee the latter expressed his anxiety that many West Indian children were passing through the educational system with such low levels of attainment that they were in danger of constituting a second-class community.[59]

Mr Jackson's fears seem to be well justified. Whereas about 21 per cent of the total secondary school population were in grammar schools in 1972 this was true for only about 3 per cent of those children born to West Indian parents. The corresponding figures for the Indians and Pakistanis were 15 per cent and 8 per cent – higher than the West Indian figure but both still markedly below the overall level. It must be emphasised that these figures are for children born to immigrant parents but who may not themselves be immigrants. In fact about one-half were born in this country. And, what is particularly striking, is that in the case of the West Indians and Indians those born in Britain were doing only very slightly better than those classified as immigrants by the Department of Education and Science. Only about 4 per cent of those born in Britain to West Indian parents were in grammar schools as compared to about 2 per cent of those classified as immigrants. The respective figures for the Indians were 16 per cent and 15 per cent. Only in the case of the Pakistanis, with figures of 22 per cent and 4 per cent, was there a marked difference. But, to the extent that both absolutely and proportionately far fewer children have been born to Pakistani parents in this country, they are not a typical group. Such figures deserve much more thorough investigation than is possible here. What is quite apparent is that, at least in the case of the two largest coloured groups, those children who were born in Britain and have had a full British education are still very much under-represented in Nottingham's grammar schools.[60]

As yet no complete picture of the jobs obtained by coloured school-leavers is available.[61] But, to a great extent, it is bound to reflect their distribution in the schools. So, whatever their real ability, it seems likely that most of the present generation of young coloured people will finish up in relatively menial jobs. Moreover the study of Jowell and Prescott-Clarke already referred to suggests that at least the better qualified amongst them may encounter discrimination. For this reason it is worth noting the comment made by Eric Irons (the Education Committee's Organiser for Commonwealth Immigrants, and someone often criticised for presenting an unduly optimistic and complacent portrayal of the situation) in his 1972 Report.[g]

[g]   For example: 'Every year one gets a glowing report from Mr Irons (Organiser for the Work with the Commonwealth Immigrant Community). One hears of the growing confidence of the younger section of the coloured community. This is certainly not true amongst West Indians. Question the youngsters on the street; ask them about their employment . . . and you will get a completely different picture!' See Lancelot Christopher, 'West Indian Education in Crisis', *Race Today*, vol. 4, no. 6 (June 1972).

... from personal observation and discussion with the Principal Careers Officer it would appear that immigrant school-leavers had to be submitted to potential employers several times more than normal before they were finally placed.[62]

All this suggests that the majority of coloured youngsters may become concentrated at the lower end of the occupational hierarchy like their parents before them. But, for the kind of reasons outlined in Chapter 2, they are much less likely to be willing to tolerate such a state of affairs – especially if the advantageous employment situation enjoyed by the area were to deteriorate.

In fact there are signs that such a deterioration may have already set in. As Table 18 shows, the level of unemployment in Nottingham was consistently below the national average during the period from the early 1950s to the mid 1960s. Since then the unemployment rate has usually been a little higher than the national average. Moreover as the Notts./Derbys. Sub-Regional Planning Unit made clear in its 1969 report, the prospect for the remainder of the 1970s and 1980s is not encouraging.

> In general there is no reason to suppose that male employment opportunities in the Sub-Region, which have recently been deteriorating, will get better during the next fifteen years or so unless measures are taken to stimulate growth. . . . In all parts of the Sub-Region the labour surplus is likely to occur mainly among the less skilled, as indeed for the nation as a whole. . . . Unfortunately it is not easy for unskilled people with consequent low income levels to move house or travel long distances to work in order to overcome a local shortage of jobs.[63]

It is not possible to predict just what effect such a deteriorating economic situation will have on race relations. Much will depend upon the precise character of the changes that occur. But there can be little doubt that racial distinctions will appear more salient than in a stable or improving situation. There is a greater possibility that members of the white indigenous population will feel resentful towards coloured people better placed than themselves. There is a greater possibility that preference will be given to white people when scarce jobs are allocated. There is less possibility that sufficiently strong action will be taken to ensure that coloured people do not face discrimination when seeking jobs. And there is a greater possibility that coloured people will refuse to acquiesce if they feel they are being kept at the lower end of the occupational hierarchy.

In this chapter it has been suggested that Nottingham's adult male coloured Commonwealth immigrants were attracted to the area because jobs were readily available. Most often they came without marketable skills and were prepared to do almost any kind of work. The minority who came looking for particular kinds of employment were usually successful and amongst the vast majority of those interviewed there was no evidence of anything other than the most realistic of job aspirations. When interviewed, all but a tiny handful were in regular employment and indeed the majority had suffered no unemployment since obtaining their first job in Britain. However, they were very much concentrated at the lower end of the occupational hierarchy and, compared to the work-force as a whole, very much more concentrated in particular industries. It has also been suggested that the immigrants do not constitute any significant threat to the economic security of the white indigenous workers. They tend to occupy the kind of jobs least attractive to white workers and the extent of their voluntary membership of trades unions seems to suggest that, at least in the work sphere, they are willing to identify their own interests with them. Nevertheless, most of the white respondents still see coloured immigrants as outsiders who do not really belong here, rather than as relative newcomers who are otherwise ordinary members of the work-force. Even so, unless there are substantial economic changes which find a particular form of expression at a local industrial level, it was suggested that this lack of acceptance is not of itself likely to manifest itself in overt hostility.

What seems more likely is that coloured workers will begin to protest, to a much greater extent than at present, about the way in which they are or believe themselves to be treated. For, although most immigrants had only modest ambitions and were very realistic about their skills, a significant minority did express dissatisfaction about some aspects of their work. There was almost universal dissatisfaction about the employment prospects for coloured workers as a whole. Almost all of those interviewed were convinced that there was widespread racial discrimination in employment and that this made it particularly difficult for those with the requisite ability and training to get clerical, supervisory and other such skilled jobs. Moreover, even though most of those interviewed had only looked for fairly menial jobs, over half were sure that they had on one or more occasions been victims of discrimination themselves. Though many English people (some of them very influential) prefer to attribute such allegations to misunderstandings and over-sensitivity, the available objective evidence comes down quite clearly on the side of the immigrants. It also indicates that racial discrimination cannot be satisfactorily handled by the machinery laid down in the 1968 Race Relations Act.

Towards the end of the chapter the prospect for the children of the immigrants was discussed. It was suggested that even in the unlikely event of discrimination disappearing their future seems to be far from bright. Whether born abroad or in Britain they are very much under-represented in the city's grammar schools. And, although such under-representation may not be peculiar to Nottingham or indeed to coloured immigrants, there is a great deal of evidence which suggests that Nottingham has done much less for its immigrants and coloured children than other LEAs. Thus amongst both immigrants and their children there will be a large and growing number who are employed in fairly menial jobs not commensurate with their abilities. This will no doubt help reinforce the already prevalent stereotypes about the capabilities of coloured people. Furthermore, especially since a job sets limits to so many other aspects of life, it will result in growing dissatisfaction amongst the immigrants and, even more so, their children. As things stand at present future confrontations along racial lines seem very likely.[h]

[h]   After this chapter was written a very serious dispute between Asian and English workers broke out in nearby Loughborough. The seriousness of the conflict was so pronounced that the Secretary of State for Trade and Industry ordered a public enquiry into the affair. A short account of it is included in Chapter 8.

6
Race relations and politics

Ever since the late 1950s matters relating to race relations have been of major political significance. Although immigration from the Commonwealth was not an important issue in the 1959 Election, the campaign for the introduction of control over it was by then already well-established. At the Conservative Party Conference in October 1961 as many as 40 of the 576 submitted resolutions featured the subject of immigration (as many as on the Common Market and twice as many as on Education) and the composite resolution put to the Conference demanding urgent action was passed by an overwhelming majority.[1] Less than a month later a Bill was introduced into the Commons and by June of the following year it had become law. The issue divided the major parties. Indeed so fiercely did the opposition parties fight the Bill that the Government was obliged to use the guillotine.

Despite the introduction of the Act, immigration continued to be a matter of great concern to the electorate. Yet, in the 1964 General Election, it figured as a prominent issue in only a small number of constituencies. By then the Labour Party had shifted its ground and was no longer opposed to the principle of control and there seems to have been a tacit agreement of central party headquarters to try to prevent it from becoming a major factor in the election.[2] It remained for individual candidates to exploit the potential political significance of the issue. This was done most dramatically in the Parliamentary Constituency of Smethwick. Alderman Peter Griffiths, the Conservative candidate, based his campaign 'on the twin planks of being a local man and an anti-immigration candidate'.[3] Patrick Gordon-Walker, the Labour choice and sitting member, tried to avoid the immigration issue but was constantly confronted with it. The extent to which it dominated the Smethwick election is reflected in the amount of attention devoted to it in the local weekly newspaper. In the three relevant editions, 55 per cent of the space devoted to the election was mainly about immigration and a further 16 per cent was partly concerned with the topic. The outcome of the election is well known. There was a swing to Griffiths of 7·2 per cent – the largest pro-Conservative swing in any constituency in the United Kingdom. Moreover, the swing was as much as 8·8 per cent against even the regional average for the West Midlands.[4] Yet it must be emphasised that it was the quite exceptional nature of the result which has made it such a prominent feature of the accounts of the 1964 Election Campaign. In the vast majority of constituencies immigration was not an important issue.

It proved to be even less prominent in the 1966 General Election. The new Conservative leader, Mr Heath, publicly declared his opposition to the kind of campaign which had been fought by Peter Griffiths in 1964. The latter, of course, lost his seat. But those who saw the decline in the attention paid to immigration in the election as evidence that it had lost its political significance were very mistaken. They seem to have assumed that politically significant issues are those which alter the relative standing of the major parties and that all politically significant issues will feature prominently in elections. Since the immigration issue did not figure prominently in the election or alter the party balance, it seemed to many to have lost its political import. It is true that for an issue to become important in an election it must, as Butler and Stokes put it, 'excite genuine and strong attitudes in significant parts of the electorate'.[5] But this is a necessary rather than a sufficient condition and two others must be met before an issue becomes prominent. The issue must be one on which opinion in the electorate is not evenly balanced and, more important in this instance, it must be one on which the parties are clearly divided. It has already been noted that by 1964 the parties had begun to come together on the issue. By 1966, the process of convergence had gone very much further. Indeed the new Labour Government had responded so much to the public clamour for more stringent control that it had introduced a ceiling of 8,500 on the number of vouchers which could be issued under the Commonwealth Immigration Act in any one year. Moreover, it will be shown later in the chapter that in Nottingham and elsewhere the electorate did not see any marked differences between the parties on the issue. In other words, the immigration issue had not lost its actual or potential political significance by 1966. It was rather that the convergence of the parties in the eyes of the electorate prevented it from being reflected in the campaign.

If there could ever have been any doubt about the potential electoral significance of race and immigration, it was shattered by the dramatic entry of Enoch Powell onto the scene in the late 1960s. His extraordinarily well-publicised speeches caused him to be sacked from the Conservative Shadow Cabinet and thousands of white workers demonstrated and even went on strike in support of his views. His role in the 1970 Election Campaign was no less startling and it has been suggested that it may have made a substantial contribution to the detachment of white working-class support from the Labour Party – one of the ingredients which seems to have helped bring the Conservatives their unexpected victory.[6]

In this chapter an attempt will be made to explore several political aspects of the race relations situation – some of which have been very much neglected to date. It will begin with an examination of the electoral behaviour of the coloured immigrant sample. This is especially worthwhile since until recently there has been a tendency to concentrate on the effect the race issue has had on the electoral behaviour of whites. Or, to be more precise, there has been a tendency to concentrate on the extent to which the election swing in constituencies with large coloured populations has differed from those elsewhere. So for example, when Deakin concludes that 'the issue of coloured immigration cannot be shown to have had any significant political impact on the British General Election in terms of voting behaviour' what he means is that 'in seats significantly affected by immigration the swing to Labour was 3·8 per cent compared to 2·6 per cent for the United Kingdom as a whole'.[7] Indeed, in his essay on *Colour and the 1966 General Election* hardly any mention is made of the effect the race issue may have had on the electoral behaviour of the immigrants.[a] This narrow approach and almost complete disregard of the direct rather than the indirect political influence of Britain's coloured minority is no doubt due in part to the fact that they constitute only a small part of the electorate. But, because in most constituencies they are not sufficiently numerous to swing an election result one way or another does not make their political attitudes and behaviour any less interesting or worthy of study. As Katznelson has noted, immigrants have usually lacked the resources of 'property, money, skills and in many cases even minimal literacy' when competing for such things as jobs and social status. This makes their use of what has been to hand especially interesting. And, as he observes, 'the only resource uniformly available to West Indian, Indian and Pakistani immigrants in Britain has been the vote'.[8]

Following this material there will be a discussion of the significance which the respondents themselves seem to attach to their political behaviour and what implications this may have for party politics in Britain. Then there will be an examination of the alternative forms of political action and expression which are, in principle, open to those members of the electorate (who figure prominently amongst those in the sample) who do not feel that the present party-political structure gives sufficient heed to their political demands.

The interviews were conducted between the 1966 and 1970 Elections and so it will be useful to begin with a description of the 1966 Election Campaign in the Nottingham Central Parliamentary Constituency to provide a background

[a]   Deakin's discussion of the 1970 Election does include material on the direct significance of the immigrant vote. N. Deakin, 'The Minorities and the General Election 1970', *Race Today*, vol. 2, no. 7 (July 1970).

against which to discuss the information collected. From 1955 until 1964 the
seat was held by the Conservatives. However in 1964, in a straight fight with
the sitting member Lt. Col. Cordeaux, a London solicitor Mr Jack Dunnett
won the seat for Labour. His majority of 2,128 represented a swing to the
Labour Party of 5 per cent compared to a national swing of 3·5 per cent. When
he came to defend the seat in 1966 it was as Parliamentary Private Secretary to
the Minister of Aviation – although some of his constituents were probably
more aware of the fact that he was Chairman of Brentford Football Club.[b]
He also seems to have gained the reputation of being a good constituency MP
and had held surgeries most weekends since winning the seat. His opponent,
Tony Mitton, Chairman of his family's engineering firm in Birmingham, was
fighting his first election.

Both candidates adopted a moderate position on immigration control.
Indeed Dunnett chose not to mention it in his electoral address. Mitton mentioned twelve items in all and immigration was one of the five to which he
devoted most attention. But his treatment of it was far from controversial and
in keeping with official party policy. Although a 'new boy', he adopted this
stance in the face of pressure from some members of the local party who
wanted him to take a much stronger line.

Although the subject of immigration was raised occasionally during the
campaign it did not become an important issue. Only half a dozen letters about
it appeared in the local press and, according to the Letters Editor of the paper,
this was an accurate reflection of the level of submissions. A fairly lengthy article which appeared one week before polling day and could conceivably have
triggered-off a series of letters seems to have gone almost unnoticed. Entitled,
The Immigrant Factor: How Will the Newcomers Affect Voting? the article
opened: 'When the talk in pubs and clubs comes round to elections – as it so
often does just now – and Central Nottingham is mentioned, it is not long
before someone says darkly, "Of course Dunnett got in on the coloured vote
last time". Did he? The answer may be yes.'[9] Following the article only one
further letter on immigration was published. Similarly, the candidates were not
faced with many questions about immigration during their canvassing or their
public meetings. In the course of visiting in the region of 300 households a day
Dunnett was confronted with the subject only about half a dozen times. In his
public meetings it arose no more than twice. Mitton did have one thinly
attended meeting at which the issue of immigration control was prominent, but
the discussion was very restrained and, overall, his experience was very similar
to Dunnett's.

With a majority of only just over 2,000 the Labour Party could not afford to

[b]   He has since become Chairman of one of Nottingham's two League sides –
      Notts. County.

ignore the immigrant vote. But those organising its campaign were confident that the only problem was the size of the immigrant turn-out – they did not believe that very many immigrants would even consider voting Conservative. A nucleus of a dozen regular immigrant supporters, who frequently enlisted other less committed helpers, were used to canvass areas with particularly high concentrations of coloured people. An election message was translated into Punjabi, Urdu and Hindi and widely distributed. The Conservatives, for their part, did not expect many immigrant votes and made little attempt to get them. Indeed in the early days of the campaign Mitton implied that he was not altogether happy about all of them having a vote. In the *Guardian Journal* of 16 March 1966 he was quoted as saying: 'I feel very strongly that if they don't understand English, they should learn it before they cast their votes because so much is at stake.' Despite this he did make some use of two coloured workers and late in his campaign agreed to the suggestion that his election address be translated for the benefit of those with poor English. A statement in Urdu alone was eventually printed but was probably not very widely distributed.

In addition to those immigrants who worked with the two parties there were others who made a more independent contribution to the campaign. For example, they organised a forum on the final Sunday evening before the poll at which Labour, Conservative, Liberal and Communist candidates from three Nottingham constituencies were able to explain their policies and answer questions. In spite of an alternative political attraction (George Brown, the then Deputy Prime Minister, was addressing a public meeting in the room immediately below) about 150 people were present and it was undoubtedly one of the liveliest meetings of the whole campaign. On another evening the local paper carried an offer of help from the Officers of the Indian Welfare Association to those Indians (or Pakistanis) who found it difficult to follow the party manifestos. In addition, a four language leaflet was issued in the names of three prominent Asians urging their compatriots to vote Labour. Though they signed the appeal as private citizens they were well known as officials of the Indian Workers Association and Pakistani Welfare Association.

The final result was a victory for the Labour Party. Jack Dunnett increased his majority from 2,128 to 6,426. As elsewhere the presence of coloured immigrants did not seem to check the swing to Labour. In the country as a whole it was 2·6 per cent. In seats with substantial immigrant populations it was 3·8 per cent. The swing to Labour in Central Nottingham was 6·1 per cent.

As Table 23 shows, the contribution which the constituency's male coloured immigrants made to this result was proportionately less than that made by white residents. During the construction of the sampling frame all those adult males who were contacted were asked if they had been registered to vote in the

1966 General Election. Those who had were also asked if they had voted.[c] It was found that the native whites were much more likely to have been on the Register. But amongst those registered it was the Indians and Pakistanis who were most likely to have voted. So, although overall participation was still highest amongst the whites, the level amongst the Indians and Pakistanis came close to it, and it was mainly the lower level of participation of the more numerous West Indians which depressed the participation figures for the immigrants as a whole.

Table 23 Participation in the 1966 General Election

	Native whites %	All coloured immigrants %	West Indians %	Indians and Pakistanis %
Registered	89·9	73·2	76·2	67·4
Not registered	10·1	26·8	23·8	32·6
No. respondents	2,145	291	193	98
Registered and voted	68·3	76·1	70·8	87·9
Registered but did not vote	31·7	23·9	29·2	12·1
No. respondents	1,928	213	147	66
Registered and voted	61·3	55·7	53·9	58·2
All who did not vote	38·7	44·3	46·1	41·8
No. respondents	2,145	291	193	98

The kind of answers given to account for their non-registration by those immigrants later interviewed were quite different from those given by the white respondents. Almost all of the former said that they did not know of, or understand, the registration procedure. The white respondents had all either moved recently or simply forgotten to fill in their registration form. The answers given by those in both groups who had been registered but had not voted were very similar. About half gave answers which had political significance: they either said that there was no point in voting (because, for example, there was no

[c] The answers were checked against the relevant ward registers for the Constituency. In the score or so cases (out of 2,436) where there was a discrepancy, the respondents' answers have been altered. They consisted mainly of non-voting immigrants who incorrectly believed they had been on the register.

difference between the two main parties) or they expressed a complete disinterest in politics. About half of the remainder in both groups gave more mundane reasons – for example illness or temporary absence from the constituency on the day of the poll. The incidence of registration and voting amongst the immigrants varied with their length of stay in Britain. Indeed those who had arrived before 1957 were as likely to be on the register as the English respondents.[d] The extent of registration and voting also varied with the educational level and social class position of the immigrants.[e] Thus it was the poorly educated, unskilled, recent arrivals who were more likely to have been unregistered, or, if registered, to have failed to vote.

Failure to register or to vote seems to have been indicative of a more general lack of enthusiasm for politics. For example, only 52 per cent of those who had not been interested in politics in their home countries had voted – compared with as many as 80 per cent of those who had been politically active. Furthermore, whilst only 9 per cent of the unregistered were able to recognise four or more of the names of seven British politicians, this was accomplished by 68 per cent of those who had voted. Yet even amongst the voters the level of interest and involvement in British politics was low. Only two immigrant respondents were members of political parties and, at least as measured by familiarity with the names of political figures, there was evidence of considerable political ignorance.

All immigrant respondents were given the following 7 names and asked if they could identify them: Harold Wilson, Edward Heath, Jeremy Thorpe, Roy Jenkins, Jack Dunnett, Tony Mitton and Peter Griffiths. Only 5 per cent could identify them all. Moreover, as Table 24 shows, 7 per cent could not identify any of them. The average score for the sample was only 2·9. Whilst a corresponding set of questions was not put to the English respondents it seems likely that they would have been able to identify more names than this.

Not surprisingly, almost all the respondents knew that Harold Wilson was

[d]   Ten per cent of those who arrived before 1957 were unregistered. This compares with 20 per cent for those who arrived in the period 1958–61 and 46 per cent of those who arrived in the post-1962 period. Similarly, 73 per cent of those who arrived before 1957 had voted and this compares with 53 per cent of those who had arrived since 1962.

[e]   Forty-six per cent of those who had received no formal education were unregistered. The corresponding figure for those with a minimal education was 19 per cent and that for those with more than a minimal education, 3 per cent. Twenty-six per cent of those in the Registrar General's social class 5 were unregistered, compared to 19 per cent for social class 4 and 3 per cent for social classes 1 to 3a. Similarly, whereas as many as 83 per cent of those with more than a basic education had voted, the corresponding figure for those without any formal education was 38 per cent. And, whilst 82 per cent of those in classes 1 to 3a had voted, this was true for no more than 61 per cent of those in social class 5.

Prime Minister. But, the then Leader of the Opposition, Edward Heath, was known to far fewer of the immigrants – and to only a small minority of the Pakistanis. The next most recognised name was that of Jack Dunnett, the Constituency's MP, and it is interesting to note that he was better known to the Pakistanis in his constituency than was the then leader of the Conservative Party. His opponent at the 1966 Election had obviously made virtually no impact on the immigrants. But perhaps the most surprising finding was how few immigrants were familiar with the much publicised name of Peter Griffiths.[f]

Table 24 Recognition of British political figures

	West Indians %	Indians %	Pakistanis %	All %
Harold Wilson	99	89	77	93
Edward Heath	74	52	18	59
Jeremy Thorpe	44	22	9	34
Jack Dunnett	53	41	32	47
Tony Mitton	10	7	—	8
Roy Jenkins	35	22	23	30
Peter Griffiths	31	7	—	20
No. respondents	72	27	22	121

This low level of interest in *British* politics does not necessarily reflect a similar level of interest in other political matters. Indeed, as many as 61 per cent of the respondents said that they had been interested in politics in their country of origin and, whereas less than 2 per cent were members of *British* political parties, the corresponding membership figure for parties at home had been 20 per cent. This would suggest that it is the feeling of being an outsider in this country, rather than a lack of political consciousness, which determines the low level of involvement in British politics for many immigrants.

As Table 25 shows, almost all of those immigrants who turned out at the 1966 Election voted Labour. That so few voted Conservative confirms the expectations of both Labour and Conservative party workers. Only amongst the Indian respondents was there any sign of a significant non-Labour vote and, with 27 per cent of them voting Conservative, they behaved in an almost identical fashion to the white voters.

[f]   At the time the questionnaire was constructed Enoch Powell had not yet hit the headlines on the subject of immigration and Peter Griffiths was the most controversial figure on the scene.

Table 25 Voting in the 1966 General Election

	Native whites %	West Indians %	Indians %	Pakistanis %
Voted Labour	70	96	73	100
Voted Conservative	28	4	27	—
No answer	2	—	—	—
No. respondents	89	53	15	14

All respondents were asked why they had voted for the party of their choice. As expected, the most often cited reason given by the whites who voted Labour was that at the time they believed that it represented the interests of the working class. The following quotations are illustrative of the 53 per cent of answers which were in this vein.

> I've always voted Labour. I've always been a working-class man and I've been led to believe that Labour are working-class.

> There's not much choice for the working man. I can't see any reason for voting for the Conservatives. We've got no capital – we're not in their class.

> I was a miner at the time so I had to vote Labour. It's the only party for a miner to vote for.

> The Conservatives have all the money. Labour's for the working class. I've always voted Labour.

> I think it's because I was born into it and I don't see why a working-class man should vote the opposite side of the fence.

Only 18 per cent of the immigrants who voted Labour gave similar replies. Rather more (38 per cent) saw their self-interest primarily as coloured immigrants rather than members of the working class.

> Well for a start I thought Labour would have a chance of doing more for foreigners. I can remember reading a paper saying that the other government wanted to send foreigners back. Wilson was talking on our behalf so I thought he might do something better for us.

> Well I hear – I don't know if it's true – that the Conservatives don't like the coloured people and don't want us here. But the Labour they do a lot for us so I give them my vote.

> Labour stands up for coloured people. If the Conservatives had their way we wouldn't be here.

> I heard Wilson say some things about coloured people and they wasn't bad – they was friendly.

Because I think this Government favours us a bit. They want us to get acquainted with their way of life so we can move towards integration. They don't like the colour bar. They set up an organisation to stop discrimination – though still many factories and works practise it. But the Government's tried to stop it. I thought Labour is good so I voted for it.

Tories were definitely against coloured people coming into the country so I've always voted Labour.

A further 16 per cent of the native whites claimed to have voted Labour for little other than force of habit. Not a single immigrant answered the question in this way. It is true that 12 per cent (all Jamaicans) said that they had voted Labour in Britain because they had always voted Labour at home and that this is tantamount to voting from force of habit. However, in this instance, the consequence was quite different for the Jamaican Labour Party is more 'conservative' than its main rival, the People's National Party. The only other significant way in which the answers of the Labour voters differed is that 14 per cent of the immigrants (but none of the indigenous voters) said that they had no particular reason for voting Labour. Very often this meant that they had blindly followed someone else's advice.

The most interesting aspect of these answers is undoubtedly the fact that, compared to the white voters, relatively few of the immigrants said that they had voted Labour because it represented their interests as members of the working class. But, in this particular instance, presenting the findings for the immigrants as a whole masks a marked difference between the West Indians on the one hand and the Indians and Pakistanis on the other. For whilst the Indians and Pakistanis gave reasons to do with their position as coloured immigrants as frequently as the West Indians, they also gave reasons to do with 'class' as frequently as the whites. It was the West Indians amongst the immigrants who scarcely ever expressed themselves in class terms.

The small number of white voters who supported the Conservatives gave a variety of reasons for their choice. Most often mentioned were the Conservatives' preference for private enterprise and their supposed efficiency.[g] Three of the four immigrants who voted Conservative said that they did so because as landlords they had been badly affected by the Labour Government's Rent Act. Not one of the more numerous white Conservatives gave such a reason.

[g] Conspicuously absent was the deferential type of answer so much discussed by other writers. See for example R. T. McKenzie and A. Silver, *Angels in Marble* (London, Heinemann, 1968) and E. A. Nordlinger, *The Working-Class Tories* (London, MacGibbon and Kee, 1967). For an excellent discussion and critique of the notion of deference by these and other writers see Dennis Kavanagh, 'The Deferential English: A Comparative Critique', *Government and Opposition*, vol. 6, no. 3 (1971).

Table 26 Voting in the 1964 General Election

	Native whites %	West Indians %	Indians %	Pakistanis %
Did not vote	21	35	41	45
Voted Labour	52	61	30	50
Voted Conservative	22	4	18	5
Other answers	5	—	11	—
No. respondents	124	72	27	22

Most of those respondents who had voted in 1966 had also voted in 1964. As Table 26 shows, in this instance too, the immigrants were less likely to have been registered and the proportion of them who had cast a vote was proportionately smaller than amongst the whites. Moreover, the way in which the votes were distributed between the parties was very similar to the pattern obtaining for 1966. In both samples clear majorities had voted Labour, but again there was greater minority support for the Conservatives amongst the indigenous voters. Amongst the immigrants it was again most noticeable amongst the Indians. Respondents were also asked about their behaviour in the previous Council election. Table 27 shows that the replies followed the same pattern as for the 1964 and 1966 General Elections. The only difference in this case was that a greater proportion in both samples had abstained.

Table 27 Voting in previous Council Election

	Native whites %	West Indians %	Indians %	Pakistanis %
Did not vote	48	68	67	68
Voted Labour	34	28	18	23
Voted Conservative	16	4	15	—
Other answers	2	—	—	9
No. respondents	124	72	27	22

To this extent then, the voting record of the two groups seems to have followed a fairly consistent pattern. However, when respondents were asked about their future voting intentions there were signs that the pattern might be beginning to break down. The most obvious indication amongst the white indigenous respondents was how many of them had become uncertain about voting Labour. For whilst the support for the Conservative Party had shown only a small increase, support for the Labour Party had slumped. Even so, it was amongst the immigrants that disenchantment with the Labour Party was most marked. The proportion of immigrant voters who had supported Labour in 1966 was as high as 93 per cent. The proportion of those interviewed who said that they would vote Labour 'if there was a General Election tomorrow' was as small as 23 per cent. Most striking, apart from this, was the large proportion who said that they did not know how they would vote – or that they would definitely not be voting. It is appreciated that questions about future voting intentions may be worth little as predictors of actual electoral behaviour except when they are put at a time when an election is imminent – but they are interesting as rough and ready indicators of the extent of really solid support that a party enjoys. Looking at these findings, it is clear that the Labour Party can no longer count on the continued support of almost all coloured immigrant voters.

Table 28 Future voting intentions

	Native whites %	West Indians %	Indians %	Pakistanis %
Would not vote	14	21	4	5
Would vote Labour	31	25	15	23
Would vote Conservative	35	22	37	4
Don't know	14	31	44	68
Other	7	1	—	—
No. respondents	124	72	27	22

So far attention has been concentrated on a straightforward description of the political actions of the respondents and almost nothing has been said about the significance which they themselves attach to such actions. For instance, whilst the proportion who did not vote in 1966 has been noted, there has been no discussion of what the abstentions meant to those concerned. Many people simply assume that all non-voters are apathetic about politics. Yet it was shown above that some of the answers of those who had abstained indicated an interest, rather than a lack of interest, in politics. Perhaps the clearest example of this is those respondents who said that there was, in their opinion, so little difference between the two major parties that there was nothing to be gained by voting. It is important to emphasise this kind of point for there has been an unfortunate tendency, on the part of many of those who have investigated electoral behaviour, simply to make assumptions about the significance which members of the electorate give to their votes. This is very apparent when one examines the literature on the class basis of British politics. As Butler and Stokes have pointed out:

> In contemporary interpretations of British voting behaviour class is accorded the leading role . . . But, in view of the large amount of attention focused on the correlation between class and party in Britain, the evidence about the nature of the link remains oddly limited . . . First, too little attention has been paid to the beliefs that link class to party in the voter's mind; the system of ideas, the attitudes, motives and beliefs which lie behind the observed differences have been largely neglected. Second, treatments of class alignment have tended to be static in their approach.[10]

No doubt encouraged by the apparent consistency in voting behaviour, as well as the fact that party support divides so clearly along class lines, there has been a strong propensity to assume that most voters see the choice between the parties as clear-cut, and that the significance of the votes cast for the two main parties by the majority of the electorate is self-evident.[11] Members of the working class obviously vote Labour because it is the party of the working class and members of the middle and upper classes vote Conservative because that party represents their class interests. What is not self-evident is the significance of a vote for those who deviate from the class pattern – for example working-class Conservatives. But, otherwise, it is very often assumed that the significance of Labour and Conservative voting can be easily discerned in the different class characteristics of those who vote Labour and Conservative.

In comparison with other countries, and in terms of the origins of, as well as financial and electoral support for, the two main parties British politics is not unreasonably characterised in class terms.[12] There is also some evidence that many electors, and especially working-class electors, do see politics in terms of class interests.[h] In other respects, the appropriateness of such a characterisation is open to question. The parties no longer mirror class interests in either

----

[h]   'Seven in eight of our working-class Labour supporters gave evidence of seeing politics as the representation of class interests, and almost half of these regarded such interests as opposed. Among middle-class Conservatives fewer than one in three gave evidence of seeing politics in terms of the representation of class interests.' D. Butler and D. Stokes, *Political Change in Britain* (London, Pelican, 1971), p. 121. However, they also note that in both the working class and middle class the proportion holding such views is conspicuously smaller in those who have entered the electorate since the War. See p. 151.

their composition,[i] or in terms of the policies which they pursue when in office.[j] It can be also argued that electors increasingly find the class image of the parties unconvincing. If any of these assertions is correct it is obviously risky to make assumptions about the significance of a vote cast for either of the parties from the class situation of the voter. Moreover, this has important implications for the politics of race relations. If, for example, many members of the working class no longer feel that they have a champion in the Labour Party then they may begin to turn elsewhere for political representation. Furthermore, should the long-established class pattern of British politics be breaking down, then it will be more difficult for coloured people to become an undifferentiated part of existing political groupings – especially since their very presence in this country may be one of the factors leading to the breakdown of the traditional pattern. Then they too may have to look elsewhere for political representation – or else remain the non-participants in British politics which effectively they are at present. Because of these possibilities a series of questions was put to respondents in an effort to establish what they felt about the choice offered to them at elections.

The first question was: 'What would you say are the main differences between the Labour and Conservative parties?' By implying in the wording of the question that significant differences did exist, respondents may have been discouraged from suggesting that this was not the case. On the other hand, it does render the fact that so many did make such an assertion all the more striking. As many as 23 per cent of the immigrants and 39 per cent of the native whites voiced opinions of this kind.

> When they want to get elected then they make promises and seem different – but when they get in then there's no difference at all.
>
> There's no difference. A dog is a dog whether white or black. A change in colour does not alter the fact that it is a dog. They just bark differently.
>
> To my foolish idea both are the same thing – both come under the same heading.
>
> If you permit me to tell you the truth they are both the same.

[i]   In the inter-war years 72 per cent of Labour MPs were rank and file workers and only 15 per cent were university educated. By 1966 the proportion of workers had fallen to 30 per cent and the proportion of university graduates had risen to 51 per cent. The change was even more dramatic at the top of the party. At the beginning of 1969 only one member of the Labour Cabinet had an occupational past that could be described as manual. Butler and Stokes (1971), pp. 153–4.

[j]   Perhaps the most notable example of this fact, as Butler and Stokes point out, 'was the adoption by Labour Chancellors in the middle 1960s of economic policies that would heighten unemployment and lower the real incomes of working people in order to defend the country's international balance of payments and defend the pound'. Butler and Stokes (1971), p. 155.

No difference at all – they're both rotten.

There isn't one – they both line their own pockets.

None – they're all after the working-man's money.

There's little difference now. They all make promises and don't keep them – just for vote catching it is.

There's no difference. They both spend all their time pulling each other to pieces.

As they are now there's not much difference between the parties. Once they're elected into power they forget all their promises. I've no faith in politicians at all.

A further 35 per cent of the immigrants and 8 per cent of the whites said that they were not familiar with the differences between the parties. Thus nearly 60 per cent of the immigrants and 47 per cent of the natives said that they could not distinguish between the parties or did not believe there was anything between them to distinguish.

Only two differences were mentioned by more than 10 per cent of the respondents in either of the two samples. Twenty per cent in both said that the Labour Party, unlike the Conservative, represented the interests of the working class.[k] For example:

I think that on the whole the Tory party is more for the 'society people'. There are 'society people' in the Labour Party, but it is still much more for the working-man.

Labour is in to provide work for the working-man. The Conservatives are for business people and only care for property owners. They've never done anything for the working-man.

A further 12 per cent of the white indigenous respondents, but only 4 per cent of the immigrants, made reference to the Labour Party's association with nationalisation.

Labour wants to nationalise everything and the Conservatives want free enterprise.

Without doubt, the most significant feature of the replies to this question was the large number of respondents, in both samples, who were convinced that no major differences existed and also, in the case of the immigrants, the large number who said that they did not know if there were any.

A second question put to all respondents was: 'Do you think it makes much

[k]   Again, as in the case of the answers given when immigrant respondents were asked why they had voted Labour in 1966, it was primarily the Indians and Pakistanis, rather than the West Indians, who offered this kind of view. Whereas a class perspective was expressed by 35 per cent of the Asians, it was mentioned by only 8 per cent of the West Indians.

difference *to the country* which of them wins an election?' As many as 46 per cent of the white indigenous respondents and 35 per cent of the immigrants said that they did not think it did.

> No, because no matter who's in they're going to pull each other to pieces and bash the working-man.

> No – the country runs itself!

> No. They only promise to do different things so that the public will vote them in. Once in power they do exactly the same as each other.

> How will it make a difference – you tell me – they're just the same.

> No – both parties make a mess of it. The only real difference is that the Conservatives kept quieter about it.

> It doesn't make any difference to the country. It only makes a difference to a party leader and his followers.

A further 21 per cent of the immigrants, and 4 per cent of the native whites said that they did not know whether or not it made any difference. In other words, half of the whites and well over half of the immigrants were not convinced that the election of one party rather than the other made any appreciable difference to the country. Most of the remainder were of the opinion that the country would be better off under the Conservatives.

> Yes – everybody wants the Tory Government again you see – because Labour has failed from its promises that it made. Most of the coloured people – you can meet them out in the street who voted Labour and you can hear them say – I'll never vote Labour again – it's true.

> I don't agree with the Labour Party's principles. Look at all this money they keep lending abroad. I don't agree with it at all. They're going to lend Egypt some money – they should be looking after this country first. Their lending's free of interest – that's bad business.

The third question in the sequence was: 'Do you think it makes much difference *to you personally* which of them wins an election? Once again, the most striking feature of the replies was how few of the respondents thought that it did. As many as 61 per cent of the whites and 42 per cent of the immigrants said that it made no difference. Moreover, a further 14 per cent of the immigrants said that they did not know whether or not it made any difference to them.

> No, quite honestly. They both hammer the working-man. If they can't tax him on drinks they will on cigarettes or something else. They'll get at him somehow.

> It should do – but it doesn't. If the Labour Party was what it's supposed to be it should help the working-man – but it's just the same as the other.

> No – I'm not sure really why I vote Labour. You have to accept things. I do my duty and vote.

> No. We should be better off under Labour but we aren't.

> It doesn't affect me brother. I just keep going.

Those who believed it made a difference usually added that they would be better off under the Conservatives. The reason most often cited for this view was that the Labour Party had brought about increased prices and put jobs in jeopardy. So it is possible that the continuing economic difficulties and even faster inflation since the election of a Conservative Government in 1970 will have now made even these respondents doubtful about the differences between the parties.

> Well it has done with my job – because they can't afford to buy the fat abroad to make the soap. I'll become redundant soon – don't know what I'll do next.

> We lived better and with less struggle than before Labour came in. If Mr Wilson came into this house tonight we'd be starving next week!

Some of this dissatisfaction with the Labour Party could be a reflection of the difficult economic situation which existed at the time, and the unpopular measures which were being taken by the Labour Government in its efforts to deal with it. On the other hand, the widespread belief in the essential similarity of the two parties is far less likely to be due to circumstances existing at a given period in time. Other evidence does exist to suggest that it is more deeply rooted. In 1963, in the first of three surveys, the following question was put to approximately 2,000 voters in Butler and Stokes' stratified random national sample: 'Considering everything the parties stand for, would you say that there is a good deal of difference between the parties some difference, or not much difference?' Since the phrase 'considering everything the parties stand for' is more inclusive than that in my own question (which asked respondents for 'the main differences between the parties') it is more likely to produce statements of difference. Nevertheless, 34 per cent said that there was not much difference – as many as said that there was a good deal of difference. Furthermore, as many as 48 per cent agreed with the proposition that 'there was once a time when there was more of a difference between the parties than there is now' – and no more than 27 per cent disagreed with it.[13] This is consistent with the findings of the Gallup Poll's repeated sampling of opinion on the question of whether 'there is any really important difference between the parties'. Despite short-term fluctuations, especially at the onset of election campaigns, the long-term trend in the proportion who consider there is an important difference is undoubtedly downwards.[14] Another question put to Butler and Stokes' respondents in their 1964 survey was: 'Do you think that the fact that Labour won the election will make any difference to how well off you are?' Only 37 per cent said 'yes' and 48 per cent said 'no'.[15] In their third and final survey, in 1966, their respondents were asked the following general question: 'Do you think that what the Government does makes any difference to how well off you are?' Twenty-six per cent thought it did not. Yet when those who said it did make a difference were asked the following two *specific* questions it became apparent that over 60 per cent of them actually felt it did not. The questions were: 'Has the Labour Government made you better or worse off or hasn't it made much difference?' and 'If a Conservative Government had come in, would it have made you better or worse off or wouldn't it have made much difference?' In reply to the first, 56 per cent said that the election of a Labour Government had not made much difference. In reply to the second, 53 per cent said that if the Conservatives had been elected it would not have made much difference.[16]

It is quite probable that many of the respondents in the Nottingham study who were very critical of the Labour Government when interviewed still voted for it when the 1970 Election came round. Whether or not they did so with enthusiasm and conviction is another matter. It may well be that they, and others like them, did so not because they had changed their views in any fundamental way, but because no other acceptable alternative had presented itself. Unfortunately, there is no way of showing how firmly held were the beliefs expressed in the interviews. All that can be said is that the impression gained in the course of the study was that, in very many cases, they were deeply held and had developed over many years. When the long-standing insecurity and relative poverty of most of those interviewed is taken into account it is certainly not difficult to imagine how such views could have developed. They are also consistent with other well-established facts such as the declining turn-out in successive elections in the post-war period. In 1950 the turn-out in the Nottingham Central Constituency was as high as 82·9 per cent. In the subsequent elections it fell fairly steadily and reached a new low of only 60·5 per cent in 1970.[*l*]

Finally, in this sequence of questions, all respondents were asked: 'Would you say there is any difference in the attitudes of the Labour and Conservative Parties towards coloured immigrants?' As many as 20 per cent of the native whites said that they did not know whether or not there was any difference.

[*l*] See F. S. W. Craig, *British Parliamentary Election Results 1950–1970* (London, Political Reference Publications, 1971). A similar decline is evident nationally. Butler and Stokes point out that there are also other signs of a weakening of class alignments – for example, the increasing volatility of the electorate in recent years.

However, over half of them (53 per cent) were convinced that there was none.[m]

> No – both sides import them and land the country with paying for them.

> I haven't noticed any. They must all look to coloured people otherwise they wouldn't keep bringing them in.

> Certain MPs on both sides favour them. It's just one of those things – some are for it, some aren't. It's the same on both sides.

> Only in theory. Both say they'll deal with the problems of immigration when they're in opposition but continue to let them into the country when they're in power.

> No I think they're both the same. One MP says one thing and another in the same party says another.

Only 25 per cent of the native whites suggested that there was a difference and, of these, all but a handful said that they thought the Labour Party more favourable to immigrants than the Conservative.

> Yes – Labour leans over backwards for them. They'd put in coloured candidates if they had them. They allow them to come in without any restrictions and let them live on National Assistance too easily.

> Labour are just out for votes and don't mind how they get them so they'll promise the coloureds anything to get their votes. The Conservatives realise you can't overflow the country with immigrants.

The fact that so few of the native whites did distinguish between the parties in this way should not be surprising. For, as was noted above, since the introduction of immigration controls in 1962, the parties have been moving closer together. But the fact that so many of the respondents seem to have been aware of the convergence, or at least aware of the absence of major disagreement, does help to explain why it was that, contrary to the predictions of several pundits, immigration did not become a significant issue in the 1966 Election. Not, it is quite clear, because the electorate were unconcerned about immigration but rather because the two alternative governments with which they were presented were seen not to differ on the issue. Moreover, these findings help to explain why Enoch Powell's outspoken speeches on race relations and immigration have been so well received in some sections of the population. He and only he, it must often seem, appreciates how ordinary people are feeling. His insistence that he is speaking on their behalf – and that it is his duty to do so

[m] Butler and Stokes asked their respondents the following question in 1966: 'Which party is more likely to keep immigrants out, the Conservatives or Labour, or don't you feel there is any difference between them on this?' Fifty-three per cent said that there was no difference. Butler and Stokes (1971), p. 599.

– must be especially gratifying. That many of those who support him may not always be familiar with the detailed content of his speeches is unimportant. To those who have grown cynical of politicians, and who believe that they are either unwilling or unable to appreciate the problems of ordinary people, Powell's identification with and apparent concern for them is sufficient.[n] The failure of both parties to win and keep the support of those native whites who, not unreasonably, often feel forgotten, renders the direct style of a politician like Powell so much more effective.

The replies from the immigrant respondents to the question were fairly similar to those given by the whites. A quarter said that they did not know if there was any difference between the parties. A further 34 per cent said that they were sure that there was none. For example:

> No difference at all. No one is concerned about us.

> No – they are more or less the same. We expected these things from the Tories – but not from the Labour Party. It was a big disappointment. The White Paper – it was very nice – but they have not done anything about integration. Only the negative things they have done.

> The watch and the clock keep the same time – only their faces are different.

> Before they got in power Labour was acting as if they favoured the coloured people but they've done nothing – I don't know if their hands are tied or what – but they're no different from the Conservatives.

> Both their attitudes is to forget everything and sweep it under the carpet. In their basic thinking they are both the same.

Only 39 per cent of the immigrants argued that there was a difference between the parties. Most, though not all, suggested that the Labour Party was more favourably disposed than the Conservative. But even some of these emphasised that the difference was not great.

> Yes – the Conservatives are not so keen on the coloured. They once say they want the coloureds to go right back.

> Labour is much better, Ted Heath's thinking of 'helping' us go back! They know they can't do it but they'll stir up the people that way.

> As I said earlier the Conservatives I don't think they much recognise colour – they are a most aristocratic people you know. They don't like the colour much at

[n]   Kavanagh has pointed out that members of the working class are more likely than members of the middle class to agree with such cynical views as: 'Politicians are all talk and no action' and 'Once they become MPs they forget about the people who elected them'. The evidence he quotes comes from National Opinion Polls (February 1968), and he calculated the following average agreement per class with such judgements: AB – 55 per cent, C1 – 62 per cent, C2 – 65 per cent, DE – 68 per cent.

all. If they get back again I don't know what they will do. They stopped the coloureds coming last time they was in. Labour is a bit more friendly – a bit more interested in the coloured people you know – but only a bit more. They say so but they don't do anything.

So here too is a group of disadvantaged people who, in the main, feel that neither of the two major parties represents their interests. Given the circumstances surrounding their relatively short stay in Britain this may not be surprising. But it must lead to speculation as to how they will behave in the future. One possibility is that ethnicity and colour will themselves become focal points for political organisation. For this reason a series of questions was put to immigrant respondents in an effort to establish what degree of enthusiasm existed for this kind of development. In each case the respondent was first asked for his view on members of his *own ethnic group* taking a particular kind of political initiative. Then he was asked for his view about the same initiative as a possible venture for *coloured immigrants as a whole*. In presenting the respondents' answers, however, we will first discuss all the views expressed on individual ethnic groups taking political action, and then those expressed on similar action by the whole of the coloured population.

It was pointed out above that some immigrant organisations in Nottingham had advocated that their members vote for the Labour Party in 1966 and that some immigrants had tried to organise a bloc vote for it. Consequently the first of the questions put to respondents was: 'Some people have suggested that it would help Indian immigrants (or Pakistani, etc., as appropriate) if they got together and decided to vote for the same party. What do you think of this view?' As Table 29 shows, in no case was a clear majority in favour of the suggestion. Indeed in the case of both the West Indians and Indians a clear majority was against it. The arguments put forward most often were that electors ought to vote as individuals or that such a move would make things even worse for immigrants.

This is absolutely wrong. We should not be tied to one party. We should look after our own interests as individuals. We are not sheep to be guided or pushed around by any one shepherd.

Everybody should vote as an individual. It is a 'free' country. Unlike our country no one individual can browbeat others or cajole them to vote for any particular party or candidate.

No, I don't agree. If the party you support is defeated then the other party will be opposed to you. It should be left up to the individual. The job of the leader is to tell their members what the parties stand for – not who they should vote for. I blame the Indian Workers Association for Gordon-Walker's defeat. You see they supported him publicly and so the local people turned against him.

I don't think that's right – I don't think we should vote together. If we did it would just make them discriminate more.

Some of the minority in favour of bloc voting mentioned that it had already been attempted.

Yes I think that is a good idea. Some people have said it was the immigrants who gave Labour their success in the last election. It's already happening.

We already do it – I fully approve of it.

Unity is strength. A stick may symbolise authority but it can easily be broken. Tie them together and they cannot be handled so lightly.

One vote polled individually will not be appreciated but ten polled together will command respect. This will benefit us.

In 1968, Mr Atwal, the General Secretary of the Indian Workers Association, fought the St AnnsWard Council election as a Labour candidate. In doing so he became the first coloured immigrant to contest an election in the city. Although neither he nor the other two Labour candidates were successful, and although he came last in the poll, he did manage to obtain 515 votes; no mean achievement for a coloured man in a local election in a safe Tory ward. In view of his relative success it was not a surprise when the analysis of the results showed a large number of immigrants to be in favour of the election of immigrant candidates. They were asked: 'Other people have suggested that Indian immigrants (or Pakistani, etc., as appropriate) should try to get other Indian immigrants (or Pakistani, etc., as appropriate) elected as councillors and MPs. What do you think about this view?' Majorities of Indians and Pakistanis voiced their approval as did almost half of the West Indians. Moreover, in all three cases, only a handful of respondents actually expressed disapproval of the idea.

If we are to have any future in this country at all that's what we need – even if it don't work now it may do later on.

Yes I think that is right. You would have more opportunity to make your point that way.

Well if an immigrant was to have some power it would definitely help the immigrants – yes. Someone has got to represent the immigrants in these places.

It would be good but I don't think this country would allow it. They wouldn't allow a coloured in the House.

A good idea but he probably would not be successful at the present – but perhaps in the future it would be different. But I'd support a Jamaican if he stood.

Well you have men here from Jamaica who would be quite capable of doing it but I don't know if they would get the opportunity. If they could get in it would be a good bit better.

However, some respondents did qualify their support for the proposal – either on the grounds that it would depend on the personal qualities of the candidate (16 per cent) or on condition that he was also prepared to represent his English constituents (8 per cent).

If he was a good man – yes.

It would be a good idea if we could get even one Indian elected – provided he hadn't a narrow view and represented the broad interests of the Indians.

Not unless he was very good and he was representing everyone.

That wouldn't be bad because we need somebody to speak for us – but he would have to speak for all of us – white and coloured.

Furthermore, whilst very few respondents were opposed to the suggestion, some 40 per cent of the West Indians and 20 per cent of the Indians and Pakistanis did doubt whether it would do any good.

They would only get elected if we all lived in a ghetto. But as we are now a candidate wouldn't have a chance. Anyway it's not his country – and even if he was elected what could he do against all the other MPs.

It's only a real possibility for a few seats. And only one MP wouldn't make much difference. He won't be able 'to lift our hay or give us a roof for our houses'.

I'm in favour – but only if he's very good and of course he may not be able to do anything. An Englishman with good views might be better.

Whilst most respondents favoured the election of immigrants as MPs or councillors, only a small minority favoured the idea of establishing separate political parties. The very notion of such minority parties may appear strange to those who tend to think of British politics only in terms of the two major parties. But it should be remembered that there are already many small political parties in this country and that elsewhere they are a great deal more common. Moreover, there have been newspaper reports that the Sikh community has already seriously considered establishing its own political party in this country. The question put to respondents was: 'I have also heard some people suggest that Indian immigrants (or Pakistani, etc., as appropriate) should form their own political party in this country. What do you think about this view?' The following quotations illustrate the kind of answers given by the 28 per cent in favour.

It is a good idea – provided we have honest leaders.

Do you think 'they' would allow that? It would be a struggle but in the future it might get started. If one did I'd definitely support it.

An Indian party would air our views. If not successful it would at least represent us honestly.

Our party is already in the making (i.e. a Sikh party) – someone told me about that.

This is not a bad idea. Our educated people could provide the leadership. They would look after our interests. Even if something substantial did not come out of it the Party would serve as a pressure group.

Two-thirds of the Indians and as many as half of the West Indians and Pakistanis were, however, positively opposed to such a proposal.

That's a bit funny – Jamaicans going to another country and doing that. It's best to stick to the parties we've got already.

I don't think that would be a good idea either – it would be like segregation. What you want is mixing – integration – you must learn to live together – you must!

It's nice to have your own culture. But to segregate yourself amongst the host community – that would be a wrong step.

No – if they do this it will cause race riots and that's what we don't want.

That would be like what Michael X is trying to do – it wouldn't be right – you must work through these parties we have.

It is clear that whilst most of the respondents did not feel that either of the two major parties either represented their views or were favourably disposed towards them, they were, nevertheless, very cautious about the particular political initiatives suggested to them. Only just over a quarter were in favour of bloc voting and the formation of separate parties, and some of the half who favoured the election of immigrant MPs and councillors felt it necessary to qualify their support for the idea. It is also clear from Table 29 that, on the whole, it was the West Indians who were least likely to favour the proposed tactics and the Pakistanis who were most likely to be in favour. The differences between the three ethnic groups in terms of their support for the proposals reflects, not only the greater cultural autonomy of the Indians and Pakistanis, but also the extent and character of the actual immigrant organisation which already exists in the city. All respondents were asked about their membership of immigrant organisations and whereas only 2 per cent of the West Indians were current members, the corresponding proportions for the Indians and Pakistanis were 47 per cent and 36 per cent respectively. Moreover, 90 per cent of the West Indians knew of no immigrant organisation to which they could belong. Only 37 per cent of the Indians and no more than 18 per cent of the Pakistanis were in this position. Of course there are several West Indian organisations in Nottingham. But they are much smaller and less influential

Black migrants: white natives

Table 29 Support for political initiatives

		Bloc vote by		Representative for		Political party for	
		Own ethnic group %	Coloured people %	Own ethnic group %	Coloured people %	Own ethnic group %	Coloured people %
West	For	18	19	48	50	28	26
Indians	Against	52	51	7	36	50	47
	Other	30	30	45	14	22	26
No. respondents				72			
Indians	For	37	26	59	48	26	22
	Against	59	56	11	22	67	67
	Other	4	18	29	30	7	11
No. respondents				27			
Pakistanis	For	45	36	68	68	32	36
	Against	41	41	5	5	50	41
	Other	14	23	27	27	18	23
No. respondents				22			

than their Indian and Pakistani equivalents. The fact that the Pakistanis tended to be more in favour of the suggested initiatives than the Indians may also be a reflection of the present state of immigrant organisation. For, although the Indian community is well organised, it is less unified than the Pakistani. It contains at least three major associations, each representing a different faction, whereas the Pakistanis have only one major group.

As was noted above, in addition to being asked for their views on the suggestions with respect to their own ethnic group, all respondents were also asked about them as regards possible initiatives for coloured people as a whole. In none of the three groups was there a consistently greater proportion in favour of this kind of combination. Indeed, as can be seen from Table 29, more often than not there was a fall in support for, or an increase in the proportion positively against, them. Given that combining in this way would undoubtedly increase the chance of success for such initiatives, this relative lack of enthusiasm may appear puzzling – especially to those who do not ordinarily distinguish between the constituent parts of Britain's coloured population – and it is worth mentioning at this stage that 16 per cent of the English respondents in the study seemed unaware of any differences between West Indians on the one hand and Indians and Pakistanis on the other. But, of course, whilst the Indians and Pakistanis in Nottingham do have much in common, the gulf between them and West Indian immigrants is still large. Whatever else might be said about their 'real interests' *vis-à-vis* the white British, there is no doubt that most coloured immigrants do not see themselves as belonging to a homogeneous group with genuinely common interests.

In the course of the interviews the Indian and Pakistani respondents were asked: 'What do you think of West Indians in general?'. The converse of the question was put to the West Indians. Perhaps the most striking feature of the answers was how many respondents were unable to offer any relevant comments because they had had no contact with members of the other group. This was the case for 33 per cent of the West Indians and 37 per cent of the Indians and Pakistanis.

The most frequent comment made by the West Indians, about the Asians, was the extent to which they were different and kept themselves to themselves. As many as 42 per cent made remarks of this sort.

> I don't think I like them very much. They speak their own language and I can't understand what they say. They are different – they don't try to mix so we don't try.

> They're clannish. Their way of thinking and behaving is entirely different from ours. I've known a few but it's hard to get through to them.

> Got no time for them – you can't speak to them at all – if you want them to do something at work you got to swear at them to get them to understand.

More explicitly critical comments were made by another 22 per cent.

> A people who 'grab' money!

> I don't think a lot of them. They don't look after themselves properly – their houses I mean.

> Well you see most of the Indians they, for some reason or another, they don't call themselves coloured – you know they think they're better than what we are.

No more than 11 per cent made what could be classified as friendly or not unfavourable remarks.

> They're very genuine people – they're nice.

> Well I don't have much to do with them – but they're OK I suppose.

Those Indians and Pakistanis who had experienced sufficient contact with West Indians to answer the question made more critical remarks than friendly. By far the most common complaint was that West Indians were rough, aggressive and generally uncultivated.

> He gets the money and spends – just like English people. Don't bother about the children or anything. I think he is crack-minded. He don't bother about anything. He says if I knock somebody and get trouble I don't care. He is very rough.

> Well they're not like us – take crime for instance – there isn't a day when one of them isn't in the paper for doing something. They are a bit more aggressive and crude – but that's just because they're ignorant. From the day we are born we are taught you must respect your elders – even if they are not any relation to you

> – and I think even among English people you don't find this sort of thing. But the West Indians don't seem to know how to behave – they're rude and rowdy you know – not like Indians or the English.

> This is a very serious question. Seventy-five per cent of Jamaicans do not work – all they do is go to the races and go out with prostitutes. They are tarnishing the name of the whole immigrant community. They do not use their brains – perhaps God willed it that way – I do not know. But they spoil things for all of us.

Only 30 per cent made favourable, or at least not unfavourable, comments.

> West Indians are good for us. If any Englishman fights us West Indians help us. Our own people run away.

> West Indians are good. If they were not here we would not have been able to live here.

> West Indians are OK – they are friendly when they speak to me.

Even more striking support for the contention that Indians, Pakistanis and West Indians do not see themselves as members of a single group with common interests came from the answers to another question. All West Indian respondents were asked: 'Do you think you have more in common with Indians and Pakistanis than you have with English people?' A corresponding question was put to the Indians and Pakistanis. As many as 83 per cent of the West Indians and 43 per cent of the Indians and Pakistanis said that they had most in common with the English. Moreover, a further 31 per cent of the Indians and Pakistanis said that as far as they were concerned they had nothing in common with either. No more than 8 per cent of the West Indians and 20 per cent of the Indians and Pakistanis felt that they had more in common with each other than with the English. This pattern of identification helps to explain not only the lack of enthusiasm for political action organised on the basis of colour but also why none of the organisations in Nottingham which represent all coloured people have more than a very small membership.

In principle, there are at least three ways in which coloured people can attempt to improve their disadvantaged position in British society by orthodox political means. The first approach is for them to become incorporated into the traditional class structure of British politics and, in the process, have their problems re-defined in class rather than racial or ethnic terms. The second is for them to organise along ethnic lines and, by means of pressure group tactics and/or the election of their own candidates where this is possible, seek to obtain improved conditions for their respective communities. The third is for all three major ethnic groups to organise around the common badge of colour and adopt similar tactics. However, for the reasons to be outlined, it seems most likely that things will continue as at present with coloured immigrants having virtually no direct influence in either local councils or Westminster.

The first possibility does not seem likely for several reasons. The native whites are not and do not seem willing to become colour-blind and if, as was suggested in Chapter 3, their prejudice is a 'normal' feature of British culture then there is little likelihood of any major change in this direction in the immediate future. Moreover, the West Indians, who are closest to the whites in terms of culture and sense of identity, are those least likely to adopt a class perspective in approaching politics. In any case if, as has been suggested, the traditional class structure of British politics is breaking down this will make it more difficult for coloured people to merge in an undifferentiated way into party politics. In suggesting a breakdown of the traditional class structure of British politics it is not being suggested that 'class' itself has become an outmoded category. But the evidence of the survey is that whilst many of the native whites (and some of the immigrants) do have a rudimentary if not necessarily well-developed class consciousness, they no longer see the party structure as reflecting it.

The second possibility seems more open to the Indians and Pakistanis than the more numerous West Indians. It has been shown that, in respect of culture and pattern of identification, the Asians have less in common with the British than have the West Indians and also that they are already much better organised and much more willing to think in communal terms. Moreover, the relative success of the Asians in commercial enterprise (in Nottingham and elsewhere) may help give more weight to any political activity they might organise. The West Indians, in spite of their disillusionment, often still cling to their links with British people, are less willing to consider separate political action and, despite having been in Nottingham appreciably longer than the Asians, are not at all well organised.

The third possibility – that all three ethnic groups combine under the common badge of colour – does not seem to be very likely on the basis of the available evidence. It has been shown that the vast majority of West Indians feel that they have more in common with the English than with Indians and Pakistanis and that, for their part, most Indians and Pakistanis feel either that they have more in common with the English than West Indians – or that they have nothing in common with either. Continuing prejudice and discrimination on the part of English people will almost certainly help to bring them together. Furthermore, it must be emphasised that organisations do not necessarily have to have massive grass-roots support before they can be influential.[o]

[o] It is not clear how much grass-roots support there is for the many 'black power' groups which have developed in the United States in recent years. But it seems possible that their influence is not commensurate with their actual membership or degree of committed support.

Nevertheless, in the short term, there does not seem to be much immediate prospect of a large and militant black power movement developing amongst Nottingham's coloured immigrants.[p]

This chapter, in addition to describing the political behaviour of the respondents, has also examined certain aspects of the political alternatives available to them. It seems clear that many of those who vote in General Elections do so not with any degree of enthusiasm or confidence but because there is no clear political alternative which appeals to them. They do not believe that the two main parties differ to any great extent, nor do they believe that it makes much difference to them personally which of them wins an election. The degree of deep-seated disillusionment with politics and politicians expressed in the course of the interviews was very striking.

The slump in the support for the Conservative Party shown in both by-elections and opinion polls since the 1970 General Election, and the failure of the Labour Party to benefit from this trend, has resulted in a great deal of discussion about the disenchantment of the electorate with the two major parties. However, it is clear from the findings reported in this study that the disillusionment was in evidence prior to the Election.[q] Of course some of the major political events of the last few years may well have reinforced it and made it more prevalent. The failure of the Conservative Government to obtain majority support for its decision to enter the Common Market (despite its election pledge that it would not do so before first obtaining the 'whole-hearted support of the British people') – and the apparent somersault of the Labour Party on the issue may well have had such effects. Equally important is the Government's complete reversal, with virtually no explanation, of its clearly stated view on the merits of a compulsory prices and incomes policy and the almost unparalleled inflation which has followed its promise 'to cut prices at a stroke'. However reasonable the explanations which politicians may be able to offer for such shifts in direction and apparent failures, there can be little doubt

[p]   It must be emphasised that this book is primarily concerned with Nottingham's coloured *immigrants*. The prospect for a 'black power' movement amongst coloured people born in Britain requires a separate discussion which cannot be attempted here.

[q]   It is usual to argue that the results of by-elections are not particularly important political indicators since they are rarely reflected in the outcome of a subsequent General Election. This may be an appropriate interpretation of their significance for psephologists who are primarily interest in *election results*. But it may be a quite inappropriate interpretation for those primarily interested in politics and political behaviour. Indeed the evidence and analysis presented in this chapter suggests that a by-election result may be a more sensitive and valid indicator of political feelings than a General Election.

that they will have brought about a further widening of the gap between politicians and those who elect them.

The particular decisions which have been taken by both parties on race relations and immigration over the years do not seem to have endeared them to either the immigrants or the native whites. Indeed the main effect of them has probably been to create further disenchantment all round. The first measure to control coloured Commonwealth immigration was introduced by a Conservative Government in 1962. It came only fourteen years after many Conservative politicians had expressed concern lest the implicit distinction in the category 'citizen of the United Kingdom and Colonies', which was contained in the Labour Government's 1948 British Nationality Act, might enable it to be used at some future date to introduce an 'artificial distinction' between British subjects. Within ten years there was instead a powerful lobby within the Conservative Party pressing for just such a distinction to be invoked to control the entry of coloured British subjects into the country. The shift in policy represented in the 1962 Immigration Act did not please the British subjects whose traditional freedom was now curtailed. Neither, however, did it do very much to satisfy those native whites who wanted control. By the time that the Act came into force there were already about one million coloured people in Britain and many felt that the legislation had come too late to be of very much value. The further restrictions brought into force in 1965, 1968 and 1971 may be seen as a recognition on the part of politicians that this was how many native whites were feeling. So, whilst these several restrictive measures may have been a response to native white opinion, they will often have been interpreted as a clear sign that too little was done too late rather than that the situation was always being closely controlled. The growing support for a policy of voluntary, or if necessary compulsory, repatriation is a further reflection of this kind of feeling amongst many white members of the electorate.

The same policies probably looked very different when seen through the eyes of the coloured immigrants. The increasingly tight controls and, with the 1968 and 1971 measures, openly racial character of the restrictions must have increased the disillusionment and cynicism amongst them. The more positive measures introduced by the Labour Government in 1965 and 1968 may even have exacerbated such feelings. I have already noted that many of those interviewed did not know that legislation prohibiting discrimination existed. Those who were aware of it were unlikely to be ignorant of the fact that the National Committee for Commonwealth Immigrants and the Race Relations Board had been set up in the same year that the Labour Government, far from repealing the Immigration Act which it had opposed when out of office, had introduced far tougher controls. The obvious weaknesses of the 1965 and 1968 Race Relations Acts certainly did not escape the notice of politically conscious immigrants and were seen as further evidence of the Labour Party's vacillations. Yet the same Acts were seen by many of the native whites as clear evidence that coloured immigrants were being put into a privileged position.

Those native whites who conceive of the various policies in the way suggested may increasingly turn towards politicians who favour repatriation policies. Disenchanted coloured immigrants may be attracted increasingly towards bodies which espouse notions of black power. Thus the policies and decisions of the parties may have served mainly to drive the natives and immigrants further apart.

In the final chapter I will argue that the various bodies which have been set up in an effort to improve race relations will prove unsuccessful and that this will be primarily because they are not well conceived rather than because they are short of manpower or resources. If the present, or another, Government does what many whites believe to be desirable, and what many others expect, and introduces a vigorous repatriation policy then it will be taking a further step along the same path. The main and perhaps only marked result of such a policy is likely to be a further deterioration in race relations and yet more disillusionment.

Clearly many of the natives and immigrants interviewed in this study and many other British people do not feel that the present party-political structure provides them with the means by which their interests can be met. That the immigrants should feel deprived of an effective voice when Westminster, Whitehall and virtually all local councils contain no Indians, Pakistanis or West Indians is not surprising – though the consequences are no less serious for all that. When so many of the native whites feel the same way it must surely concern those who assert the superiority of British democracy. It may be added that the more a political system loses its legitimacy the more the capacity of elected representatives to govern effectively is diminished. The possible implications of this for race relations must not be missed. History provides us with numerous examples of what can happen to ethnic minorities during periods when political orders become unstable.

7
Race relations organisations

There are many organisations in Nottingham which concern themselves with race relations. In 1970, in addition to individual members and representatives of statutory bodies, the Nottingham and District Community Relations Council contained representatives from over forty affiliated organisations. They ranged from the British Red Cross and the Diocesan Board of Moral Welfare to the Communist Party and the National Council for Civil Liberties and, as well as these, there were several other organisations – most notably the Indian Workers Association, the Black People's Freedom Movement and the Anti-Colour Bar Campaign – which had either left the Council or never been associated with it. To attempt to discuss the role played by such a large number of organisations is out of the question. But, as most of them exist primarily to perform other functions and have only an incidental interest in race relations, it is not unreasonable to concentrate on only a few.

The most obvious candidate for inclusion is the Community Relations Council for it is the only statutory or quasi-statutory body in Nottingham supported out of public funds which is charged with the improvement of race relations. It began its life in 1954 as a purely voluntary body. However, since the Labour Government established the National Committee for Commonwealth Immigrants (and then replaced it in 1968 with the Community Relations Commission) it has received direct and earmarked financial help to enable it to employ one or more full-time officers. In return for this financial aid the Council agreed, in 1970, to change its name from the Nottingham Commonwealth Citizens Consultative Committee to the Nottingham and District Community Relations Council and to adopt the Community Relations Commission's Model Constitution. In doing so it relinquished a degree of its autonomy. On the other hand, its affiliation to the Commission has made little fundamental difference to its structure or mode of operation. It is still composed of representatives from interested organisations plus a small number of individual members and carries out its activities via a full Council and Executive as well as through more specialised sub-committees. Since the Council is mainly composed of members from interested bodies it will be most convenient to discuss the role played by other organisations in terms of their relationship with the Council. Moreover, since the work of the Council has already been the subject of a detailed study by Katznelson, it will be profitable to begin the discussion by first summarising his conclusions.[1] Later in the chapter his account will be evaluated and criticised.

Katznelson begins his account by noting that the Council began its life in 1954 as the Nottingham Consultative Committee for the Welfare of Coloured People. It was established as a result of discussions between the Council of Social Service and the Council of Churches with the aim of helping 'the local coloured community settle down as happily and as easily as possible'.[2] No coloured people were present at the initial discussions although three members of the Colonial Social and Cricket Club were invited to a second planning meeting so that the Committee might 'hear from the coloured people themselves what they felt was needed'.[3] At the first official meeting of the new Committee, held in February 1955, the only coloured immigrants present were West Indians from the Colonial Club. These, according to Katznelson, were neither typical members of the coloured community nor leaders of it in any meaningful sense.[a] In any case they were outnumbered four to one by white representatives from voluntary agencies. Another obvious shortcoming of the Committee was that none of the city's political leaders interested themselves in its work. Moreover, during its formative years, even the representatives from the voluntary organisations were not regular attenders at its monthly meetings. The burden of the work that was carried out fell mainly on a small number of interested whites.

In its early years, he suggests that the Committee did do useful welfare work. However, its approach to such crucial matters as discrimination in housing and employment was characterised by extreme caution and it seems to have made little impression on the basic needs of the majority of immigrants. Although from 1957 the City Welfare Services Committee and the Education Committee did associate themselves with it (emphasising, argues Katznelson, its non-political welfare orientation) little was provided by the Council in the way of material or financial help. Furthermore, it turned down the Committee's specific requests for the appointment of a special welfare officer and the use of the city's information centre for weekly advice sessions.

It became impossible for the Council to remain completely inactive after the 1958 racial disturbances had put Nottingham's race relations problem on the

[a]   'Most of the Colonial Club's approximately 25 members were "old settlers" who had served with the RAF, married white wives, settled in Nottingham after the Second World War, and had middle class occupations . . . (They were) it is true, part of the visible immigrant élite, but they were leaders only in the sense of visibility. They failed to act successfully as a communications lynchpin linking West Indians to the existing social structure, and they failed to involve the people they claimed to represent.' Ira Katznelson, 'The Politics of Racial Buffering in Nottingham', *Race*, vol. 11, no. 4 (April 1970), p. 434.

front page of every national newspaper. But, 'in keeping with the city's tradition of amicable council politics, the parties responded to the politicisation of race by acting in concert to resolve their common problem by attempting to structure race relations and domesticate racial conflicts'.[4] In 1960 a West Indian from the Colonial Club who served on the Consultative Committee was appointed to a specially created post of 'Organiser for Educational Work Amongst the Coloured Communities'. Katznelson alleges that he was chosen at the recommendation of a leading member of the Consultative Committee who was well aware that the appointment was intended to be 'political primarily and educational only secondarily'. At the same time the Consultative Committee was given 'official recognition as a quasi-political institution' and awarded an annual grant of £500.

> Thus within a year of the disturbances, the political community had established officially sanctioned access points, both within and outside the local authority, for the coloured population. Neither access point provided for direct access to the political community; each acted instead, under the conceptual heading of liaison, as political buffers. Immigrant needs and demands were filtered through them: (the Organiser's) office dealt with individuals, the Consultative Committee with organised immigrant groups . . . (Moreover), by virtue of his institutionalised position (the Organiser) became the officially sanctioned leader of the city's coloured immigrants . . . and in interpreting the coloured immigrant community to his employers has identified intelligence, responsibility and stability with immigrant political docility.[5]

Katznelson contends that in an attempt to bring all the existing immigrant organisations within this structural machinery the Afro-Asian-West Indian Union and the Indian Workers Association were invited to join the Consultative Committee. However he adds that the affiliation of these two militant groups made things much more difficult for the established members. For, amongst other things, they insisted on debating fundamental questions about representation and the AAWIU members, in particular, made a conscious effort to politicise the Committee. They were not successful. So in 1963, as a result of a combination of pressure by the Committee's white leadership and their own belief that they could be more effective in their efforts to build a politically-conscious immigrant community if they disaffiliated from what they considered to be a tainted organisation, the AAWIU's representatives left the Committee.

From 1963 until 1966, he suggests that the Committee's non-controversial approach went virtually unchallenged by those who attended its meetings. Its Chairman was one of the city's Welfare Officers and its outlook was very similar to that which had existed in the pre-1958 period. In 1966 the Education Committee's Organiser of Work Amongst the Coloured Communities became the new Chairman. His approach to race relations was very similar to that of his predecessor and the dominant members of the Committee. He had welcomed the rejection of the AAWIU's proposals for the reform of the Committee and in his own Annual Reports had either ignored, or played down, the problem of discrimination and other controversial topics.

His election, however, coincided with the appointment of the Committee's first full-time officer and, according to Katznelson, it is evident that from this time on it began to adopt a more direct, although still far from aggressive, approach. For example, from 1967 onwards it made a series of requests to the Council for more special language provision for immigrant children. But, whatever their long term significance, such quiet efforts did not achieve very much and there is no doubt that the Council did not feel any need to be responsive to the suggestions of the Committee.

Katznelson concludes that 'Nottingham's quasi-political structural mechanisms to promote racial harmony clearly have been inefficient'. He suggests that 'this ineffectual record is directly related to the fact that the officially sanctioned race relations structures occupy an anomalous and essentially powerless position. They were created and supported by the political community and the local authority. As a result, their independence is compromised.' He also argues that 'by providing access to the immigrants' conspicuous, moderate, largely middle-class élite, the Committee not only has been unrepresentative, but also muffled immigrant protest and divided the coloured population. The politicisation of the black population is not only not encouraged, but has been actively discouraged; stability and harmony are stressed at the expense of political organisation'. Those who have gained from the arrangements are a 'small group of predominantly middle-class coloured leaders and the city's politicians. The former 'want recognition from the white community' and they 'have been granted a measure of paternal patronage'. The latter, however, have gained most of all for 'the city's integration structure – essentially a buffering one – has permitted them to manage the politics of race with a minimum of dissensus while simultaneously being able to assert that Nottingham has coped well with immigration'.[6]

Before making any attempt to evaluate Katznelson's thesis it is necessary to clarify what he means by the term 'buffering'. It is derived from Halpern's work on political modernisation and is one of six basic types of political relationship.[b] What distinguishes 'buffering' from the others is that it involves

[b]   'Buffering is that form of structured encounter between individuals or groups where the tension that accompanies changes in the balance of costs and benefits in encounters between self and other is managed by intermediaries. Such a position may be occupied by a mediator, arbitrator, broker, or by a concept . . . Buffering allows for change by permitting indirect and limited forms of conflict and collaboration.' Katznelson, 'The Politics of Racial Buffering', p. 436.

an indirect encounter between groups through a mediator. This not only has the effect of limiting the extent of communication between them, but also makes impossible direct, continuing and mutually agreeable mechanisms of tension-management. Furthermore, should the mediator be withdrawn, there is a possibility that the relationship might break down altogether. Thus there is little likelihood of 'buffering' developing into a 'modernised' relationship, i.e. 'one in which the linked participants each have the capacity to fashion change so that although the relationship is still a competitive one it has the capacity to transform unintended, uncontrolled change into justice'. Katznelson concedes that 'buffering' can sometimes promote constructive change. But to be really effective it would need to be representative, responsive and efficient and, in his opinion, the mediating structure in Nottingham is neither representative, responsive nor efficient.[7]

Katznelson's study contains many valuable insights and much of what he writes of the events in Nottingham is indisputable. However he presents an unjustifiably neat portrayal of them and this, coupled with a number of omissions and factual errors, causes him to draw a significantly distorted picture of the situation.

The Committee began in 1954 in much the way he suggests, although the idea for it was first suggested by a Liaison Officer for Jamaicans at the Colonial Office rather than by anyone in Nottingham. A growing awareness of such problems as poor housing amongst newly arrived Jamaicans had led the local Council of Social Service to contact their national body for advice. It was suggested to them that they discuss the situation with Ivor de Souza, a Liaison Officer for Jamaicans in Britain at the Colonial Office, and it was during his subsequent visit that he proposed the establishment of a Consultative Committee.

The immigrants who attended the first meeting were present at the suggestion of the West Indian who was later to become the Council's Organiser for Work Amongst Coloured People – but, in the main, they were already known to the members of the Council of Social Service in attendance. As Katznelson emphasises, they were not typical members of the growing West Indian population. He also contends that they were not leaders of it in any meaningful sense. This, he argues, proved to be a serious shortcoming for 'they failed to act successfully as a lynchpin linking West Indians to the existing social structure, and they failed to involve the people they claimed to represent'. Although it is almost certainly true that their links with the West Indian community were not as strong as the white members imagined, certain comments need to be made about the way in which Katznelson presents this point. For example, he does not make it clear whether or not he believes that any other means of recruitment were readily available to the white organisers of the Committee. He does not give any evidence to support his clear implication that the members of the Colonial Club considered themselves to be 'representatives' of their fellow West Indians. Finally, he does not give any evidence to support his assertion that 'the new Committee was meant to link West Indian and local community leaders'.[8] My own research suggests that the founders of it were, quite simply, interested in trying to ease what they took to be the transitional problems of newcomers and saw their work as little more than an extension of the kind of welfare activity ordinarily carried out by the Council of Social Service. Moreover, the immigrants played a considerable part in such work. With the benefit of hindsight the inadequacy of their approach may be obvious – but it is crucial to have in mind a clear conception of the way in which the organisers saw the task which they had set themselves.

According to Katznelson, during its first few years, 'the Committee's limited activity made little impact on the basic needs of the majority of immigrants'. All he concedes is that it 'did on occasion do useful peripheral welfare work'.

> ... relatives were put in touch; a depressed, lonely woman was directed to a neighbourhood Jamaican women's group; a student was helped to secure temporary work pending his National Service call-up. A Housing Association was formed, but as late as the summer of 1958 it had assisted only eleven families in any way. A 1957 course in basic English and the English way of life had twenty openings yet attracted an average of three pupils to each class session. Only twelve immigrants came to the first twenty-eight weekly advice sessions; the number of enquiries rose substantially during the 1957–8 recession to almost eighty a month, most concerning employment. The Committee, however, found itself 'unable to be constructive in most cases'.[9]

A. F. Laird and D. Wood, two of the founding members of the Committee, have complained that this list is 'hopelessly inadequate'. They suggest that:

> Some of the Committee's most useful achievements were in placing people in employment and carrying out experimental training schemes for local industry, and arranging in co-operation with the Local Education Authority and Technical College courses for female machine operators, and Leadership training with the LEA and Workers Education Association. One major breakthrough was achieved when, solely due to the Committee's efforts, the City Transport Department agreed to employ coloured bus-drivers – as opposed to conductors only, in 1956–7.[10]

Katznelson agrees that his list was not (and could not be expected to be) complete, but he suggests that the additional items cited by Laird and Wood simply confirm the observations he had made.

> The Committee's courses were ill-attended, despite promising starts. In spite of its attempts to help the city's West Indians secure work, the Employment Sub-Committee found itself 'unable to be constructive in most cases'. In short the

impact the Consultative Committee made on the lives of the West Indian immigrants was minimal.[11]

There can be no doubt that the pre-1958 Committee was preoccupied with individual welfare problems and that their attempts at educational work were not very successful. Whether or not it is appropriate to label their activities as 'useful peripheral welfare work' depends on the way in which the problem of race relations is conceptualised. Katznelson, presumably, describes it in this way because he does not believe that this kind of welfare work did, or can, make much impact on the fundamental problems involved. Yet it must be remembered that those concerned came into the Committee via orthodox voluntary social work and considered help to individuals to be their primary objective. So, for example, when one reviews their rejection of the Trades Council's idea for a public forum on discrimination because 'it might lend unhealthy significance to the problem which could best be solved by more quiet and constructive steps', it is not sufficient simply to assume that they did so because they wanted to 'play-down' the matter.[12] It must be appreciated that they really did believe that they were faced with a transitional problem which could best be handled on an individualistic basis. Moreover, there is evidence that when faced with a clear-cut case of discrimination they did make efforts to deal with it. Hence the significance of the example of the employment of coloured bus-drivers noted by Laird and Wood – about which Katznelson made no comment in his reply. Whether or not they can reasonably claim that the breakthrough was 'solely due to the Committee's efforts' is debatable, but the members of the Committee certainly did try to bring an end to this particular form of discrimination – and it is worth noting that their effort was made before the militant AAWIU became affiliated.[13] Furthermore, because Katznelson is so emphatic about the Committee's determination to avoid any political controversy, and its unwillingness to get to grips with fundamental issues, it is also worth mentioning that in 1957 very serious efforts were made to involve the trades unions, and that the Committee included a prominent advertisement for the openly political AAWIU in the handbook, 'Living in Nottingham', which it published for distribution to immigrants in the city.[14]

After the 1958 disturbances Katznelson argues that the 'issues of colour which, with the assistance of the Consultative Committee, had been kept off the local political agenda, now had to be dealt with politically, at least in the sense of trying to make them coherent and manageable'. The parties, he suggests, acted in concert in response to the situation by appointing the Leader of the Colonial Club to the specially created post of Organiser for Work Amongst the Coloured Communities. His 'appointment was complemented by official recognition of the Consultative Committee as a quasi-political institution. The Committee which had been financed by Pilgrim and Cadbury Trust grants was now awarded a £500 annual grant from the Council.' And he adds that 'in an effort to bring all the existing immigrant organisations within the structural machinery of the Committee, the IWA and the AAWIU were invited to affiliate after the 1958 disturbances.... Thus within a year of the disturbances, the political community had established officially sanctioned access points, both within and outside the local authority, for the immigrant population.'[15]

This account of the post-1958 arrangements contains several errors and omissions. The Committee had asked the Council for the appointment of a special welfare officer as early as 1955 and had been refused apparently on the grounds that it would not be proper to provide any additional service to that already available to the population as a whole.[c] The decision to appoint one after the disturbances (in 1959, not 1960 as Katznelson states) was, to this extent, an open admission that their earlier decision had been in error. But it was something which the Council knew would please the one body which had concerned itself with such matters before 1958, as well as the representatives of the West Indian Federation who had visited Nottingham after the disturbances and which, without any great effort on their part, would give the impression that prompt action was being taken to deal with the problem of race relations.[d]

[c]   Consultative Committee, 'Minutes', 13 April 1955. Katznelson seems very reluctant to accept that a formal request was made in 1955. In his answer to the criticism of A. F. Laird and D. Wood (*Race*, vol. 12, no. 2, October 1970, p. 238) he comments: 'The article did refer to the *formal* request made to the Council in 1958 to appoint a special Welfare Officer for coloured people, a request that was refused (his italics). Miss Wood and/or Mr Laird may have informally requested this appointment as early as 1955, but the Committee's Minutes record the request made in 1958.' However, the 'Minutes' of 13 April 1955 leave no room for doubt that a formal request was made and was formally refused in 1955.

[d]   The circumstances surrounding the particular appointment which was made has been the subject of disagreement. Katznelson suggests that it was made on the recommendation of Miss Wood, a leading member of the Consultative Committee. She denies that she was involved in the appointment. In an interview given to me before the publication of his article she attributed the choice made to the recommendation of Ivor de Souza, the Liaison Officer for Jamaicans in Britain, to whom reference has already been made. Certainly he was the person who first informed the Committee of the creation of the post (Consultative Committee, 'Minutes', 6 November 1958) and as the representatives of the West Indian Federation who had visited Nottingham had suggested such an appointment he was an obvious person to consult. Whilst Katznelson is correct in saying that it would have been odd if Miss Wood had not been consulted. I can see no reason why he should not be willing to accept her denial. There is, after all, no reason why she should deny any such involvement. She not only approved of the appointment which was made but would certainly have made the same recommendation as de Souza had she been consulted.

Katznelson's portrayal of the role played by the Organiser and his description of the latter's attitudes towards race relations seem to be accurate. It is true that 'despite his disavowal of political activities his structural role is a political one', and that up till 1972 not one of his twelve Annual Reports had contained any discussion of discrimination.[16] Neither, it may be added, had they ever contained any explicit discussion of the importance of the 'racial' element in community relations. What does emerge from the general tenor of the reports is the kind of view which was held by the members of the Consultative Committee in its early years – i.e. that the problems which arise are of a transitional kind which can best be tackled by quiet and constructive educational and community work.

Katznelson is also correct in pointing out that, by virtue of his institutionalised position, the Organiser became the officially sanctioned leader of the city's coloured immigrants and that many coloured people (and whites) defer to him for this reason. It is also the case that he has many critics amongst the coloured communities. Some object to the very existence of his Office and there was for a time a 'Campaign to Abolish Special Officers for Coloured People' in Nottingham. Its founders emphasised that 'the campaign was not designed as a personal attack on anyone holding such a post' and that 'it was the principle of dealing with coloured people as a separate group and the long term effects of this that was being objected to. . . .If ', they argued, 'the principle is established that we are a separate entity from the rest of the community then this is apartheid in its infancy.'[17] Other criticisms have been aimed at the way in which the Organiser portrays the race relations situation and, in particular, at the optimistic tone of his Annual Reports to the Council. They present, it is alleged, neither an accurate picture of the situation nor the real mood of the coloured communities. One militant West Indian dismissed the Organiser with these words: 'Well I think he is a downright Uncle Tom and that's my definition of him. He may be a decent fella in a way – but he's an Uncle Tom right enough.'

There is, unfortunately, no way of evaluating the work the Organiser has done for individuals – which is, after all, the main burden of his job. Neither is it easy to evaluate the extent of his influence. What is clear is that his views have not always held sway even on bodies like the Consultative Committee with which he has been so closely associated. For example, in 1961, the Committee declared itself opposed to immigration control and a letter to this effect was sent to the Home Office. This position was adopted despite the Organiser's expressed opinion that the Committee should concentrate on work in Nottingham and leave the matter of immigration control to politicians. He also argued against a meeting with local MPs.[18] And, shortly afterwards, when a sub-committee recommended precisely this course of action, he agreed with the Welfare Officer who was to precede him as Chairman that it would constitute unnecessary interference in an issue best left to the Government.[19] Despite this, a discussion was held with Central Nottingham's MP, Lt Col Cordeaux.[20] In December 1961 a further letter was sent to the Home Office and to local MPs outlining the Committee's opposition to immigration control. A suggestion in early 1962 that this opposition should be made public was also resisted by the Organiser. He maintained that whilst organisations represented on the Committee should be free to express their views if they wished, the Committee itself should not publicly express an opinion. His view was defeated by twenty votes to three.[21]

Katznelson suggests that the appointment of the Organiser 'was complemented by official recognition of the Consultative Committee as a quasi-political institution'. Precisely what is meant by this is not made clear. The only specific change which he refers to is the Council's decision to award the Committee a £500 annual grant.[22] Yet he must believe this to have been an extremely significant act for he subsequently claims that the officially sanctioned race relations structures were 'created' by the Council.[23] Clearly the acceptance of the grant made the Committee to some extent dependent upon the Council. However, his assertion that the post-1958 Consultative Committee was, like the position of the Organiser, a Council *creation* is extremely misleading. Moreover, his implication that both moves were part of a concerted and deliberate attempt by the Council to gain control of the City's race relations machinery is very questionable. If that was the Council's intention it is difficult to understand why resort was made only to the lever provided by a modest financial dependence. It seems much more plausible to interpret the grant as a reluctant concession without which the Council would have been obliged to explain why it had allowed the Consultative Committee to go out of business. Ever since its inception the Committee had lacked adequate finance. In 1956 it received a three year grant from the Pilgrim Trust. Towards the end of 1958, however, great concern was expressed because no further financial support was in sight.[24] A grant of £500 from the Cadbury Trust in early 1959 did enable the work to continue for another year but, by early 1960, the situation had again become critical and it was announced that funds would last only until May.[25] A little more time was bought when the Cadbury Trust was persuaded to make a further £250 available but, very obviously, without a more regular supply of funds the Committee was in real danger of collapsing. The Minutes of the meetings held during this period reflect the extent to which finance was a problem, and much of the Committee's time was spent in fund-raising activities. This then is the background against which the Committee requested the City Council for an annual grant and eventually received one of

£500.[e] Had the Council not made such a contribution it is probable that the Committee would have been unable to continue – something which could only have proved very embarrassing to the Council so short a time after the disturbances.

According to Katznelson, the third major development in the post-1958 period was 'the effort to bring all the existing immigrant organisations within the structural machinery of the Committee'. To this end, he asserts, 'the IWA and AAWIU were invited to affiliate'. In fact these two relatively militant organisations did not join in the way in which he suggests. In the case of the AAWIU his account is particularly misleading for it was not *invited* to join *after* the 1958 disturbances. On the contrary, it had *applied* for and been granted membership *as early as March 1956*.[26] The existence of the IWA, on the other hand, was drawn to the attention of the Committee in a letter from the Consular Department of the Indian High Commission in May 1959 and it was as a result of this that its President, Mr R. S. Sandhu, was invited to become a member.[27]

Katznelson's further contention that the Committee's activities after 1959 'passed through three discrete phases' as it 'sought to give content to the vague operational concept of liaison' is also open to criticism. Whilst the three periods did vary to an extent, they were marked by a much greater degree of continuity than he implies. The first period, from 1959 to mid-1963 was, he suggests, characterised by debates over 'fundamental questions of representativeness and responsiveness'.[28] There is no doubt that debates of this kind did take place and that the members of the AAWIU did try to politicise the Committee. However, the subjects most often discussed were housing, finance, immigration and employment. In short, Katznelson's labelling is a little arbitrary. Had the period 1959 to mid-1963 more or less corresponded with the period of the

[e]   Katznelson states that '*within a year of the disturbances* the political community had established official access points, both within and outside the local authority' (my italics), (*Race*, vol. 11, no. 4, April 1970, p. 436). The disturbances took place in *late August 1958* and yet he dates the appointment of the Education Committee's Organiser as *February 1960* (Ibid. p. 435). Nevertheless, this part of his conclusion seems to be correct for the Organiser's appointment actually ran from *1 March 1959* (Nottingham Council of Social Service, 'Fifteenth Annual Report 1958–9', p. 21). However, his assertion about the political community's access point outside of the local authority in the Consultative Committee does not seem to be correct. In the Nottingham Council of Social Service Annual Report for 1958–9 reference was made to the Organiser's appointment *and* 'the failure to obtain local authority aid'. In the 1959–60 Report it was noted: 'As stated in the last Annual Report . . . in the absence of any help from the Nottingham Corporation the Committee was obliged to make every effort possible to obtain finance from voluntary sources to carry on the work.' Not until the Report for the year 1960–1 is there a reference to a grant from the City Corporation.

AAWIU's affiliation with the Committee then his characterisation might be easier to sustain. But, as has already been noted, the AAWIU had been affiliated since early 1956, and its most prominent member continued to associate with the Committee for some time after 1963.[29]

The second period distinguished by Katznelson is mid-1963 to early 1966. With the departure of the AAWIU he alleges that there was a shift in the Committee's approach back to 'non-controversial liaison and integration work. . . . Appropriately, Nottingham's Welfare Officer served as the Committee's Chairman during this period of peripheral social activity, for in these years, from mid-1963 to early 1966, the Committee's outlook was very similar to its pre-1958 welfare, adjustment oriented approach'.[30] In fact the Welfare Officer in question did not become Chairman until December 1964.[31] More important is that, whilst this kind of work did predominate in the period mentioned, it is not the case that this constituted a significant shift in direction for the Committee. On the contrary, such work had always preoccupied the Committee – even during the period 1959–63.

The final period distinguished by Katznelson began in 1966 when the Council's Organiser became the new Chairman.

> More significant, though, was the appointment of William Taylor, who had previously worked at the national office of the NCCI, as the Committee's first full-time Secretary. Soon after his arrival, representatives of the local Labour, Conservative and Communist parties joined the Committee. Taylor attempted to have the Committee intervene discreetly but directly in political matters . . . for example, it requested that the Council pass a resolution, similar to one approved by the Camden Borough Council in May, indicating that the Council would require a non-discriminatory statement of intent from companies it contracted for goods and materials.[32]

This portrayal of the post-1966 period is also somewhat misleading. The Council's Organiser did not become Chairman in January 1966, but January 1967.[33] More significant is that the establishment of links with the political parties should not be seen as a novel departure to be associated with Taylor's arrival. Indeed the three main parties were represented on the Committee as early as 1960 and, although they did not continue their connection without break, it is obviously important not to ignore such a precedent.[34] In November 1964 the Finance Sub-Committee re-invited the Conservative and Liberal parties to send members to its meetings.[35] The Labour Party was already represented. After another break in its connection with the Committee the Labour Party asked if it could renew its affiliation in January 1966. As the policy of the Committee's parent body, the Council of Social Service, was to encourage all parties to be represented, letters of invitation were sent to the Conservative and Liberal Parties.[36] At this time Taylor had not yet joined the

Committee.[*f*] So, although the Conservative and Labour Parties did re-affiliate after his arrival, he was neither responsible for the introduction of the principle of political party affiliation nor the actual affiliations of 1966. Katznelson is also mistaken when he asserts that 'the admission of political representatives was approved only after heated debate on 17 October 1966'.[37] The Conservative and Labour Party affiliations were approved in April.[38] What was debated in October was a request for affiliation from the Communist Party. And, though some members were clearly uneasy about the possible implications of such a link, the debate was not heated and of the thirty-one people in attendance only one voted against the resolution to offer it membership.[39] Katznelson's observation that Taylor did encourage discreet, but direct, intervention in political matters is correct and important.[*g*] But he was given relatively little scope for such activity by his Committee and this lends reinforcement to the point that has been made about the very strong element of continuity which existed during the decade in question.

These errors and omissions in Katznelson's account are important because they seriously undermine his representation of the Consultative Committee's role in the development of the city's race relations. Perhaps because of the nature of his theoretical framework he exaggerates the significance of the political currents and events associated with its work. Moreover, his pre-occupation with the Committee's role as a buffer institution causes him to play down its other roles – for example as a welfare agency. So, however useful his perspective, it must be emphasised that it is only one of several which may be fruitfully employed. Therefore, in the remainder of the chapter, an attempt will be made to show how the Committee is seen by ordinary members of the immigrant communities and by immigrant leaders and how it has performed as a welfare agency, as a 'ginger-group' acting on behalf of the immigrants, and as an agency existing to promote 'better' race relations. Then I hope that it will be possible to evaluate Katznelson's as yet undiscussed claim that the Committee has muffled immigrant protest and divided the coloured population.

Most of the immigrants in the sample had not even heard of the Consultative Committee and the follow-up questions to those who claimed to have heard of it showed that only a small minority knew anything whatsoever about it. In other words, slightly over 90 per cent of the immigrant respondents held no

[*f*] At the Meeting of 17 January 1966 it was stated that he would be taking up his appointment on 1 February 1966.

[*g*] Miss Wood has pointed out to me that the first approach by the Committee to the Director of Education about the provision of special help for Asian children was also made some time before Taylor's appointment.

conception of the Consultative Committee at all. Those who did saw it primarily as a body which tried to help immigrants. Only two respondents described it as an organisation which tried to improve race relations. No more than two respondents judged the Committee to be successful at what they thought that it tried to do. The remainder either said that it was unsuccessful or felt unable to offer any evaluation of its work.

The twenty immigrant 'leaders' who were interviewed were all aware of the Committee's existence and most had at one stage or another been closely associated with its work.[h] Yet, only one of them considered that it was a highly successful organisation. Furthermore, there was an obvious relationship between the extent to which the leaders were critical of the way in which the Committee went about its business and the militancy of the group to which they belonged.

The sole enthusiast for the Committee summed up his appraisal of its work in the following words.

> They have done so much for the Commonwealth Citizens it is about time they realised what they have been given through this Committee. It is very successful – exceptionally.

He also added, in reply to a follow-up question, that there were no changes at all that he would like to see in the way in which the Committee was organised or in the things that it tried to do. The leader concerned belongs to the Indian Association which is the least militant of the Indian organisations in the city and which, the respondent himself emphasised, is concerned only with welfare work. Indeed, on controversial matters the Indian Association has even aligned itself on the opposite side to that of the other Indian groups. In Chapter 5 it was noted that the Indian Welfare Association and Indian Workers Association had made public protests about what they alleged to be the inadequate provision which Nottingham's Director of Education made for the teaching of English to Asian children. The Indian Association, in marked contrast, made a presentation to him on his retirement as a recognition of the efforts he had made on behalf of the same children. The spokesmen for the other Indian organisations also see the Indian Association as a non-militant group – although they tend to the view that its defining characteristic is not so much its non-controversial stance so much as the common economic interests of its members.

[h] By 'leaders' I mean nothing more than leading members of immigrant organisations. Obviously, there is no way in which to draw a random sample of such a mixed population. All that can be claimed is that the twenty 'leaders' who were formally interviewed were, so far as it has been possible to determine, fairly typical spokesmen for the organisations concerned.

> This is only a very small association. They have their business interests which draw them together – they have their houses you see. But they only have about twenty or thirty members. They haven't done anything to help the people you see – it is their business interests that unite them.

> It has ceased to exist as a public body. It exists only for the welfare of a limited number of people – its members. And most of them are landlords.

Whilst no attempt has been made to corroborate such statements the leader interviewed did own property and he was the only one to have consistently voted for the Conservative Party in both general and local elections. He stated that he voted Conservative primarily because the Labour Government's Rent Act had hit him hard. Moreover, the only Indian in the random sample who belonged to the Indian Association was a property owner on a very large scale.

Although those leading members of the Indian Welfare Association who were interviewed were not strongly critical of the Committee, they were certainly not completely satisfied with it. Whilst they considered that it served a useful purpose as an advisory and consultative body, they hoped for changes in both its composition and functions.

> More permanent staff are needed. It needs to be more ambitious and to widen its horizons.

> It is far too big a body. There are some members who only come and sit and then go home – and others who don't know what they are talking about. It's too full of sleeping partners – English and immigrant.

This moderately critical viewpoint is consistent with the Indian Welfare Association's position between the Indian Association on the one hand, and the more militant Indian Workers Association on the other. It was founded in 1966 as a result of a split within the Indian Workers Association. Whilst accounts of the circumstances leading up to the split differ considerably, there is agreement on the fact that the parent body is the more militant and openly political of the two. A leading member of the Welfare Association explained the difference as follows:

> The main difference is a political one. What we believe is that if we were a political association we could not render a good service to our members. Now in the Indian Workers Association there are those whose ideas are to the left. If they are feeling strong about this then that is alright – but the Association should not be political. They should only concern themselves with the welfare of the people. It was because of this that we had to split.

Unlike the Indian Association and Indian Welfare Association, the Indian Workers Association is no longer affiliated to the Consultative Committee and those of its leaders who were interviewed were much more critical of its role than their counterparts in the other two Indian groups. When asked: 'What do you think are the main things it tries to do?' one of them replied:

> It tries to pacify people who are frustrated as result of discrimination!

He continued:

> This Committee has not been able to do anything useful for the immigrants. Mr Taylor is a victim of the attitude of most educated Englishmen to state platitudes and ignore real issues.

When asked what changes he would like to see he emphasised:

> The Secretary must be an immigrant. Mr Taylor – nice though he is – just cannot communicate with the immigrants.

In the course of announcing his organisation's disaffiliation from the Consultative Committee the General Secretary of the Indian Workers Association complained that it had achieved nothing over the years. He dismissed its activities as 'a complete waste of time' and he informed those present that he had already conveyed this view to both local MPs and to the local political parties.[i]

None of the Pakistani leaders who were interviewed could be said to be enthusiastic about the Committee. The most favourable viewpoint came from a spokesman for the now defunct Pakistani Welfare Association. He saw the Committee as a co-ordinating body which existed primarily to focus attention on the most pressing problems of the immigrants and, in his judgement, it performed this role quite effectively. However, another leading member of the same organisation made far less complimentary comments. When asked: 'What do you think are the main things which it tries to do?' he replied: 'Well it doesn't try to do anything – it's totally unsuccessful.' So far as he was concerned the Committee was beyond reform and he suggested that most immigrant leaders of any standing were beginning to dissociate themselves from it. This marked disagreement does not seriously undermine the suggestion that the strength of the criticism expressed by the leaders reflects the character of the organisations to which they belong, for by the late 1960s the Pakistani Welfare Association had more or less ceased to exist as a formal organisation and certainly possessed no coherent membership or outlook.

The only large Pakistani organisation in Nottingham is the Pakistani Friends League. It was established, one of its leading members claimed,

[i]   Consultative Committee, 'Minutes', 3 March 1969. To write of the 'Indian Workers Association' without qualification is a little misleading, for there are two groups in Nottingham which use this name. Both, however, are more militant than the Indian Association and Indian Welfare Association and they differ, so far as the Consultative Committee is concerned, only in terms of the extent of their criticism of it. The quotations which have been used come from spokesmen of the less militant of the two groups.

because the officials of the Pakistani Welfare Association refused to submit themselves to an election. The same spokesman summed up its main functions as follows:

> We provide facilities for our members – we look after their welfare. We try to help integration and create a better understanding with local people and to be a link with the city officials. We also provide social and cultural facilities for our members.

He saw the Consultative Committee primarily as a link between the immigrant and indigenous communities. Whilst he considered that it was useful to have such a body, he emphasised that it was 'a paper tiger – it has no power'. He was also unhappy with the nature of representation on the Committee and the way in which power was distributed.

> I do not like the way people are represented on it. It has never been defined who represents who and why. Anyone can become a member and this affects the power of the groups. Sometimes committees (i.e. standing and sub-committees) are dominated by one particular group. People should only be on as representatives of groups and be responsible to them.

In short, the Pakistani Friends League is another moderate immigrant organisation whose leaders accept that the Consultative Committee could play a useful role but who are, nevertheless, far from satisfied with either the limited extent of its influence or the composition of its membership.

Although there are several West Indian organisations in the city, none of them appear to enjoy the same degree of grass-roots support as the Indian Welfare and Workers Associations and the Pakistani Friends League. The most important of them are the West Indian Nationals Association and the Black Peoples Freedom Movement. The former is a moderate organisation descended from the old Colonial and Sports Club. The latter, perhaps the most militant of Nottingham's immigrant organisations, is partly descended from the Afro-Asian-West Indian Union.

One of the leading members of the West Indian Nationals Association who was interviewed had been connected with the Consultative Committee for over four years. Yet he found it very difficult to specify the main things it tried to do.

> I'm not sure. It's a focal point for those interested and it is useful in disseminating information. Beyond that I've no clear idea what its role is intended to be. It does not seem to have any clearly defined objectives. There's far too much talk and far too little action. And it talks about too many things. As a result very little is done in any area.

The members of the Black Peoples Freedom Movement and the AAWIU who were interviewed were much more critical of the Committee. The most generous comments came from those who saw it primarily as a paternalistic body. Others clearly saw it in a much more sinister light.

I think the white people on the Consultative Committee are that backward in their thinking that they cannot communicate properly with a black man. They still believe that you need help – in a patronising way. Everybody needs help – I need help – but not the way that these people think about it you see. They are looking for somebody to wet-nurse and they have found themselves some black people. They are the sort of people who would go round with a tag – 'I help black men' – you see these are the people you can term 'nigger-lovers' – they're cranks. If they didn't have us to wet-nurse it would be somebody else. I've been to their meetings but I cannot get along with them. They still treat black men like children. It can't work – you see the basic foundation is wrong. I don't think that this sort of organisation can ever meet the needs of black people in this day and age.

The Nottingham organisation has been much concerned with the activities of the Consultative Committee. Since the racial disturbances the people in charge have tried to replace some of the Europeans with colonial stooges. This does not change the character of the Committee, whose purpose is to confuse the coloured people and the British Labour Movement, and to spread the illusion that something is really being done to solve the problem of immigrants from the West Indies and other colonial territories.[40]

At one time we thought we would be able to influence this body. But that has never happened. We have ended up at all times with constant rows and arguments. At first there were very few West Indians who were articulate, who were able to see through what people were suggesting or what they could do with the information they were collecting. Some of them on the Committee were – I don't suppose you should call them Uncle Toms here – but that's what they were. We collected information by interviewing people – I myself have taken part in this . . . and a Nigerian chap exposed this as a police spy bureau – because all the information we collected was being passed on to the police.

Whilst the views quoted immediately above may not be typical, it is quite clear that most immigrant leaders do not rate the work of the Committee particularly highly. As has been shown, even representatives of the more moderate organisations make fundamental criticisms of it. Moreover, there has been a marked decline in even the amount of formal support for the Committee in recent years. It has already been noted that both Indian Workers Associations have dissociated themselves from the Committee. The Black Peoples Freedom Movement, which was born out of a merger between the AAWIU and another much younger militant West Indian group, has never been affiliated. The more moderate West Indian Nationals Association withdrew its support in late 1972. Whilst its actual withdrawal was precipitated by the controversial decision to appoint Terence McCann to the post of Community Relations Officer (rather than the more experienced Vernon Clements, a West Indian JP, who already held the post of Assistant Community Relations Officer) dissatisfaction had been growing ever since its representatives had begun to clash with the Committee's new Chairman earlier in the year. A little later, for related although not identical reasons, the moderate Pakistani Friends League considered withdrawing from the Committee. This situation was precipitated by the resignation of the Committee's Treasurer, Mohammed Aslam, a local accountant and JP, from the Committee. He believed that the Officers of the Executive had improperly discouraged him from raising several potentially embarrassing financial matters with the full Committee which elected him and, as a result, had made it impossible for him to perform his duty as Treasurer. At the time of writing the League had not yet announced its decision. Nevertheless, it is clear that by the end of 1972 the Committee seemed to have lost the formal support of all but two of the important immigrant organisations in the city. Those that remained were the small and not very active Indian Association and the Indian Welfare Association whose leaders, it has already been pointed out, were themselves critical of certain aspects of the Committee's work.

It has already been mentioned that the original members of the Committee were primarily concerned with what they took to be the transitional problems of newcomers and that they saw their work as little more than an extension of the kind of welfare activity ordinarily carried out by the Council of Social Service. But, according to Katznelson, in 1960 welfare and individual liaison was taken over by the Education Committee's Organiser and the Committee turned its attention towards 'organisational group liaison'.[41] Its change of name, in the same year, from the Consultative Committee for the Welfare of Coloured People to the Commonwealth Citizens Consultative Committee was, he suggests, a recognition of the new division of labour. Laird and Wood, however, two of the leading members of the Committee for many years, deny that there ever was such a division of labour. On the contrary they note that 'the Committee, through the Council of Social Service Casework Section, continued to deal with welfare problems'.[42] The records show quite clearly that this was the case and Katznelson's unwillingness to concede the point is surprising. Moreover, his charge that Laird and Wood's claim is 'patently misleading since the Consultative Committee, now the Community Relations Council, has recently disaffiliated from the Council of Social Service, after many meetings and much anguish' is also puzzling.[43] Whatever changes occurred in the Committee's relationship with the Council of Social Service in 1970 are irrelevant to what it did between 1960 and 1968 – the period in question. Even so, as will be shown below, individual welfare work has still continued on a substantial scale since 1970.

What does lend apparent support to Katznelson's position is one of the recommendations which was accepted by the Committee when the Council of Social Service adopted its new constitution in 1965. It was resolved that 'the

Committee should act more as a central advisory body than it had hitherto done, and deal less with individual difficulties'.[44] Yet, despite the formal adoption of this shift in direction, individual welfare work undoubtedly continued on a significant scale. In the Annual Report for 1967–8, whilst it was stressed that the Committee did not undertake casework, it was also emphasised that 'many people consult us on their individual problems'.[45] Similarly, in the Annual Report for the year 1969–70, after the usual disclaimer that the Committee was not a case-work agency, it was added that 'invariably a number of individuals are referred to the Community Relation Officer for help and advice' and that such cases 'do take up a large part of the Officer's time'.[46] In the Report for 1971–2, it was reported that such work was becoming increasingly important.

> There has been a substantial rise in the numbers of individuals seeking advice. Over 550 people have called at the Office to seek help with problems relating to immigration, education, legal queries, employment and cultural difficulties. This work is time consuming and often emotionally charged, particularly in cases where the parents are trying to bring children to join them in this country but are having difficulties.[j]

In other words, whatever the official position in recent years, there can be no doubt that individual welfare has always figured prominently in the Committee's work. It has not, of course, figured in the deliberations of the Committee to the same extent but this is because such work tends to be carried out on a day to day basis by full-time officers without any reference to the Committee's lay members. Without a detailed scrutiny of case histories it is not possible to evaluate such efforts fully. But help has been given to thousands of individuals over the years and it may well be that this is the role which the Committee has performed most adequately.

Whilst the Committee has never publicly declared itself to be an interest group for the coloured immigrant communities it has, on several occasions, acted in such a capacity. However its efforts in this direction have often appeared half-hearted and it has been very reluctant to make use of even the limited means of influence at its disposal.

One of the earliest victories claimed by the Committee is in the field of employment.

> One major break-through was achieved when, solely due to the Committee's efforts, the City Transport Department agreed to employ coloured bus-drivers – as opposed to conductors only, in 1956–7.[47]

[j]   Nottingham and District Community Relations Council, 'Annual Report 1971–2', p. 2. This figure does not include the 437 cases dealt with in the same year by the affiliated Fair Housing Group Worker.

The problem was first raised with the Committee in September 1955 when it was decided that the Chairman should take up the matter with the Manager of the City Transport Department.[48] In reply to a letter from him the Manager explained that the training of coloured workers as drivers was still the subject of negotiations between the TGWU and the Department and, as a result, it was impossible to give the Committee any assurances about future recruitment policy. It was resolved to pursue the matter and further letters were sent to the TGWU and the leaders of the two main political parties in the city.[49] In December, after a reply from the TGWU stating that the matter was still under discussion, it was decided to try to arrange a meeting with the parties concerned.[50] So far as can be ascertained from the Committee's Minutes no meeting took place. Nevertheless, in January a further letter was received from the City Transport Department saying that in future there would be no discrimination and that coloured applicants would be treated as anyone else.[51] So, whilst the intervention of the Committee could have been significant, it certainly does not seem reasonable to claim that the Department's decision was taken 'solely due to the Committee's efforts' – especially since the matter was already under active discussion when the Committee made its first approach. Although the incident does demonstrate that the Committee was willing to make demands of the City Council on behalf of coloured people from an early date, note must be made of the methods employed and care must be taken not to exaggerate the influence of the Committee in the matter.

Throughout much of 1961 the Committee was concerned with the possible introduction of immigration control and in March it issued a press statement to make it clear that it was opposed to such a move. At the same time a sub-committee was appointed to consider what further action ought to be taken.[52] It recommended that a report on the local situation be prepared and that local MPs be invited to have a 'friendly' talk about the matter with a few of the Consultative Committee's members.[53] This was agreed but, after the report was prepared, a few of the members argued against the proposed discussions with MPs. According to one it would constitute unnecessary interference in Government matters. As a compromise it was decided to seek a meeting with a representative of the City Council's Housing Committee as well as local MPs in which it would be made clear that the discussions would be treated confidentially and that no press reports would be issued.[54] The militant AAWIU refused to take part in any discussions on such terms and at a subsequent meeting one of its spokesmen specifically asked for clarification on whether or not they were designed to bring about a change in the views of those who, like Lt Col Cordeaux MP, were in favour of control. In what seems to have been a carefully worded reply the Committee's Chairman explained that the object was to provide him with information on the current position of coloured immigrants in

Nottingham.[55] When the Commonwealth Immigration Bill was eventually published the Committee did send a letter of protest to the Home Secretary. Moreover, by way of a summarised account which appeared in the *Economist*, it seems that the Committee's unpublished report was used by Hugh Gaitskell in a speech opposing the Bill in the House of Commons.[56] However, what is most telling so far as the Committee is concerned is the extremely cautious way in which it expressed its view on what was a very heated and controversial issue. Although it is most unlikely that it could have done anything to prevent the introduction of the Immigration Act, there can be no doubt that it could have done a great deal more to make its views more widely known.

Such caution has been evident on many other occasions. In October 1963 the Secretary noted that at two recent national conferences concern had been expressed at the growing evidence of racial discrimination against coloured youngsters. She asked the members whether or not they considered that there was a similar problem in Nottingham which ought to be investigated. None of those present did consider it to be a particular problem and the Minutes do not suggest that any more extensive an enquiry was even contemplated. Some considered it would not be wise to raise the matter at all and one member expressed the view that if any problem did exist it was something which should be left to 'experts'.[57] In December 1965, a Pakistani member asked the Committee to consider the case of some local hosiery firms who, he alleged, did not pay full union rates to their Pakistani workers for overtime and night-shift work. The Committee seems to have been most reluctant to become involved and it was argued that, since the state of affairs described to them was not necessarily based on colour prejudice or exploitation, it could do more harm than good if the Committee were to concern itself with the matter. It was recommended that the Pakistani members at the meeting encourage their colleagues to join the relevant trades unions, if they had not already done so, and pursue the matter through them.[58] Seven years later serious industrial disputes involving Asian workers hit the local hosiery industry. They not only included cases in which Pakistani workers alleged that they were underpaid for overtime and night-shift work, but also cases in which it was claimed that they were discriminated against by both management and trades unions. There is no point in speculating on what might have happened had the Consultative Committee taken up the case of Pakistani workers in 1965 as Mr B. requested. By choosing not to intervene the Committee did relinquish yet another claim on the support of the immigrant population.

Although the Committee's characteristic caution has been especially evident in its dealings with the City Council this cannot be attributed solely to the fact that it is financially dependent on the Council. Indeed since 1966 the Committee has received the bulk of its finance from the National Committee for

Commonwealth Immigrants and its successor the Community Relations Commission. Furthermore, the Committee has on several occasions publicly declared its dissatisfaction with the grant from the Council which it contends is one of the smallest in the country.[59] Its caution is probably better explained by the fact that most influential members of the Committee either believe that public controversy is likely to be counter-productive or find such controversy distasteful.

One clear instance of the Committee's unwillingness to adopt an aggressive stance, and its readiness to concede defeat, can be seen in its attempt in 1967 to persuade the City Council to insert a non-discrimination clause in its contracts with firms supplying goods and services. The matter was first raised at a meeting of the Committee's Finance and General Purposes Sub-Committee when the Secretary informed those present that the Camden Borough Council had recently adopted such a proposal at the suggestion of the Camden Council for Community Relations. However, since some members suggested that such a request would constitute an attempt to dictate to the Council, it was decided to refer the matter to the next meeting of the full Committee.[60] There it was agreed that the Council ought to insert such a clause in its contracts and there seems to have been a fair amount of enthusiasm for the idea. The representative of the Labour Party (which at that time was in control of the Council) said that he had already discussed the matter with an Alderman on the Camden Council and that it was obviously an important step forward even though the clause might not be legally enforceable. Moreover, he was confident that the Council would respond favourably to the suggestion.[61] In the event, the clause was not adopted by the City Council, precisely on the grounds that it would be unenforceable. And, even though the proposal was strongly supported by the representatives of both the Labour and Conservative Parties on the Committee, the only further action taken was to pass on the relevant correspondence to the Race Relations Board.[*k*] No further efforts were made to pressure the Council into changing its mind, and the matter was quietly dropped.[62]

Although the Committee did not concede defeat so readily when it tried to persuade the City Council to make special in-school provision for immigrant children, its efforts were certainly characterised by the same kind of timidity.[*l*] After some preliminary discussions the Integration Sub-Committee decided to approach local Headmasters to discover the size and nature of the problem with which they were faced. To the surprise of the Committee's members, a

[*k*] At this time racial discrimination in the field of employment was not covered by legislation. However, the Race Relations Board was collecting information on relevant issues even if outside of its official scope.

[*l*] The main aspects of this issue have already been described in Chapter 5.

letter was received from the Director of Education in which he asked the Committee not to make an approach to Headmasters. Although this was felt to be an unsatisfactory state of affairs his request was accepted and a letter was sent to the Director inviting both him and the Chairman and Vice-Chairman of the Education Committee to the next meeting.[63] No reply was received. However, the Education Committee's Organiser for Work with Coloured People, who was a member of the full Consultative Committee, did suggest that it was confusing the political and administrative aspects of the problem by inviting the Chairman and Vice-Chairman of the Education Committee, as well as the Director of Education, to a meeting. He recommended that a delegation ought to visit the Director instead. This too was accepted and a delegation appointed.[64] When it reported at the next meeting it was made clear that the Director had been unwilling to make any concessions. Yet, short of agreeing that contact ought to be maintained with him and inviting immigrant groups to submit case histories of children with language difficulties, no further action was even discussed.[m] No less revealing about the Committee's attitude towards the Council is that although nothing whatsoever had been gained for the children, the Chairman expressed his satisfaction that there had been a good relationship between the Director and the delegation throughout the meeting.[65]

In a later meeting of the Committee a few members urged not only that the matter be taken up again but that, in view of the earlier failure, an approach should be made through political parties and councillors rather than the Council's officers. Whilst this proposal was accepted, the majority succeeded in deferring the date of the approach until after the Council elections in several months time.[66] Indeed, so far as can be determined, no such approach was made either before or after the elections. Thus, when at a later date the Chairman of the Sub-Committee in reporting to the full Committee gave an assurance that the issue would not be forgotten, but claimed that for the present all possible avenues had been pursued, she could only have had in mind what she and others considered to be *appropriate* avenues – for no serious attempt had been made to involve local politicians or make use of the mass media let alone any form of public demonstration or protest.[67]

In 1970, the Committee decided to hold a Summer School to provide at least a small measure of extra help for some of the immigrant children it believed to be in need. Despite some problems the project was an obvious success and it was decided to repeat the experiment on a larger scale in 1971. In 1972, the Education Committee decided to mount its own Summer School. This was

[m]   The names of over 100 children were obtained. They were not sent to the Director of Education because many of the parents concerned expressed fear that it might lead to discrimination against the children.

seen by the Committee as an acknowledgement of the educational value of such programmes.

> The local authority has acknowledged the contribution of such programmes and has decided to organise a summer project for the summer of 1972. We are naturally delighted to see the skills and resources of the local authority Education Department being utilised in the development of this project ... One of the roles of the Community Relations Council is to develop projects and to prove the need or the usefulness to the appropriate Department. In this case we surely fulfilled our role.[68]

If evaluated in isolation from the earlier efforts of the Consultative Committee the Summer School can be judged a success. When evaluated along with them, it represents a failure. The aim of the Committee had always been to persuade the Education Committee to provide substantial in-school help for immigrant children with language difficulties and in this respect it clearly failed. Indeed by 1972, when the Education Committee took over the Summer School, the original problem had virtually disappeared for by then there were very few immigrant children entering Nottingham's schools.

The promotion of 'harmonious race relations', or 'community relations' as they are now termed, has always been one of the primary concerns of the Committee. However, as Hill and Issacharoff point out in their study of the community relations movement, the notion of 'harmony' is somewhat ambiguous when applied to race relations.

> There is and always has been some confusion as to what objectives the movement should pursue, and as to whether the programmes recommended are relevant to the achievement of the over-all declared aims. ... If one ... does really want to see the rights of Commonwealth citizens protected and community 'harmony' maintained, one cannot escape from the fact that these two goals may be incompatible and that one may need to be subordinated to the requirements of the other. The particularly important point to be made about 'harmony' is that this may appear to exist ... even in a racialist society. Harmony itself does not indicate the existence of equality.[69]

The Consultative Committee, like similar bodies elsewhere, has never faced up to this problem. Indeed most of its members are probably unaware of it. This is partly because no effort has been made to develop an analysis of the phenomenon of British race relations on which to base practical policies – and some members would judge any attempt to do so to be a sterile academic exercise. As a result, the projects which have been undertaken to help bring about an improvement in race relations have only rarely been related to any general strategy, and the ways in which they are supposed to bring about an improvement have gone unexamined. In other words, they have been devised on an *ad hoc* basis and founded upon implicit assumptions of doubtful validity. In this, Nottingham's Consultative Committee seems fairly typical for Hill and Issacharoff in their study of eight similar bodies came to the conclusion that 'community relations practical work is confounded by its lack of theoretical founding'.[70] This is not to say that the Committee's ventures would have been much more successful had they been evolved from a clearer conception of the nature of race relations. Indeed it seems doubtful if any body like the Consultative Committee can reasonably aspire to make a significant impact on the fundamental features of race relations in Britain at this time. Nevertheless, it is telling that in over seventeen years the Committee has failed to produce a clear conception of the role it has to play.

The Committee's failure to develop activities based upon a clear and sound overall strategy can be illustrated in many ways. For example, in 1962, its Integration Sub-Committee put forward ten recommendations, most of which were obviously intended to facilitate 'integration'.[n] Yet the notion of 'integration' itself does not seem to have been examined, and certainly no definition of it was included in the paper presented to the full Committee when it was asked to consider the recommendations. In other words, precisely what the suggestions were meant to achieve could not have been obvious to those who discussed them. The first recommendation was that measures should be taken to increase the opportunities for Commonwealth citizens 'to meet English people in social and cultural activities in order to develop integration more rapidly'. However, the two specific measures mentioned seem to be contradictory. The first was that 'all help should be given to the Commonwealth Citizens Association to obtain a clubroom for their own activities', and the second that 'Commonwealth citizens should be encouraged to join existing clubs'. The next recommendation was that 'individual friendships should be stimulated through the giving of hospitality'. Yet this overlooked the obvious point that the giving of hospitality pre-supposes the existence of a fair measure of tolerance on the part of those concerned. Amongst the other suggestions were that 'at a future date a TV programme be arranged stressing the positive side of integration', that 'a Commonwealth Week in schools might be helpful', that 'the formation of a Commonwealth Citizens Drama Group might be considered in one of the local schools' and that 'the Libraries Committee produce a reading list on Race Relations and Social Anthropology'.

Behind each of these suggestions can be discerned one or both of two basic assumptions. The first is that contact between the members of different racial or ethnic groups will lead to greater tolerance, and the second is that by means of public education it is possible to reduce prejudice and discrimination.

[n]   They were discussed by the full Consultative Committee on 4 February 1963.

Moreover, the same assumptions lie behind most of the actual activities which have been organised or sponsored by the Committee in the last decade in its attempt to improve race relations. This becomes readily apparent if one examines the Committee's Annual Reports.

In the Report for 1964–5, the Committee began by stating that:

> During the past year the underlying chief motive for the Committee's work has been to provide opportunities to get to know and to understand the newcomers from India, Pakistan and the West Indies.[71]

To this end it organised a conference with the theme 'Pakistanis at Home in Britain' and was instrumental in the decision of the Junior Chamber of Commerce to invite representatives from the main immigrant groups to give talks on their experiences of life in Britain. Similar help to other organisations was listed amongst 'practical examples of integration'. Also included in the list was an appearance by 'Millie' the West Indian teenage pop-star at a dance organised jointly by the Commonwealth Citizens Association and The Cripples Guild. The dance, which raised £550 for the Guild, was described as 'an outstandingly successful event' – but whether from a financial viewpoint, or that of 'integration' was not made clear. In its 1967–8 Report the Committee claimed 'public education about immigration and race relations' as 'one of its principal tasks' and noted that over forty talks had been given in the previous year. It also recorded that:

> One of the most pleasing developments during the year was the extent to which organisations affiliated to the Committee have promoted functions which have encouraged better race relations in the City. For instance, the International Social Club have held a number of well-attended dances. The Commonwealth Citizens Association and the West Indian Students Association have also held some highly successful dances which, as well as being extremely enjoyable, have spread appreciation of West Indian culture.[72]

The 1969–70 Report drew particular attention to the lectures given to the police by the Committee's Officer.

> The Community Relations Officer has continued the programme of lectures to courses at the Police Training College, Epperstone, and there seems little doubt that these are having the desired effect. I would not claim that all is as we would like to have it, or that the pace of acceptance is as swift as we would like, but I am quite sure that we are progressing surely and irrevocably towards our goal.[73]

Reference was also made to the talks which had been given to other organisations and the report concluded:

> We must now move from the defensive to the offensive, attacking prejudice where it is to be found in the community and helping to educate the citizens of our country into the acceptance of a multi-racial society.[74]

The 1971–2 Report also drew attention to the conferences and talks which had been given in the past year and the new initiative of the Employment Sub-Committee which had published occasional papers for circulation to industry. Considerable satisfaction was also expressed with the second of the Carnivals which the Committee had organised.

> The greatest compliment paid to the Carnival was contained in a letter to the Evening Post from a self-confessed elderly person who expressed her joy at the colour and exuberance of the occasion. We accept that social events must not become the major point of our programme. We would wholeheartedly accept that people now require results in housing, employment and education but we would argue that cultural events such as the Carnival are necessary and helpful.[75]

This selection of activities constitutes only a small proportion of those which have been carried out by the Committee, but they are fairly typical and serve to illustrate the kind of measures which it employs in its efforts to promote more harmonious race relations. It is difficult to avoid the conclusion that they probably make very little impact on the situation and that the optimism about their effect shown by the Committee is unjustified. Whilst it is true that there is evidence that some kinds of inter-racial contact can lead to a reduction in prejudice, the necessary conditions are not present in the contact situations devised by the Committee. When those concerned possess equal status, are seeking common goals, are co-operatively dependent on each other and interact with the positive support of authorities, laws or customs then prejudice may decrease.[76] However, these requirements are not found in carnivals, dances or similar activities. As Hill and Issacharoff point out:

> At best social activities can provide the foundations upon which other things can be built . . . at worst they can become the most condescending kinds of events at which well-meaning 'liberal' people try to be nice to the 'foreigners'. Committees find it fairly easy to put on social events that will be popular with members of both white and black communities, but these may merely parallel activities organised communally elsewhere. A good modern dance will attract a large number of people from both West Indian and native communities, but similar events are likely to go on regularly anyway. There is nothing forced about these occasions, but do people interact on an inter-racial basis at them? Perhaps the best argument for community relations committees continuing to sponsor such events is that they may make money and publicise the committees in a favourable way.[77]

It should also be added that in any case those brought into contact by the Committee are very often those least in need of 'conversion'.

Similar doubt exists about the value of public education as a means of reducing prejudice and changing patterns of behaviour. This is particularly significant since the Community Relations Commission has increasingly emphasised 'community education' as the appropriate objective for their local committees.[78]

> Social psychologists can give us little guidance on the gains to be made by these forms of education. Such evidence as we have suggests that much that is designed to educate bounces off those who are ill-disposed to immigrants, or may, worse still, simply entrench their attitudes by antagonising them or forcing them to argue back . . . Furthermore, a great deal of the arguments and information put out by community relations committees only reach the 'converted' . . . For these reasons, there are good grounds for doubt about the effectiveness of many of the educational activities of community relations committees.[79]

The faith of the Commission in the efficacy of conferences, for instance, does seem naive. For, whilst they may be superficially impressive events, it is questionable whether many people other than the already committed attend. The same problem, about the composition of the audience, applies to lectures and talks. In any case, even in cases where attendance is involuntary, as in the lectures to the police, it is very doubtful if a series of brief talks can bring about any fundamental change in deeply held cultural preconceptions. One is bound to agree with Hill and Issacharoff that:

> The CRC seems to place great faith in conferences, lectures, news-letters, and pamphlets with little evidence that these overt media reach the right people and with no idea whether they will have any real impact.[80]

In short, the Committee has never addressed itself in any systematic way to the question of how best to promote harmonious race relations and its efforts cannot have had any lasting effect on more than a tiny proportion of those whom it would like to influence. But, even given a more systematic approach and greatly increased resources, it is most unlikely that the Committee could hope to make any headway given the size of the task which confronts it. And, since it has been reticent about acting as a pressure group for the immigrant population and has used only the most moderate of techniques when it has intervened, it would seem that the role which the Committee has been most successful in fulfilling is the very role which it has formally abandoned – namely that of the provision of individual welfare.

According to Katznelson, 'by providing access to the immigrants' conspicuous, moderate, largely middle-class élite, the Committee not only has been unrepresentative, but has muffled immigrant protest and divided the coloured population'.[81] Whilst it can be agreed that immigrant protest is relatively muffled and that the coloured population is divided, it is less certain that the Consultative Committee has been a crucial factor in bringing about this state of affairs. There are many other, more obvious, determinants and reference has been made to them in earlier chapters. In any case there is ample evidence that the existence of the Committee has not prevented the development of militant groups, whether inter-racial or coloured, or prevented the open expression of protest by even moderate organisations affiliated to it. So, even if it could be shown that there would have been more protest and less division had there been no Consultative Committee, it must surely be admitted that the Committee has not had much of a muffling or dividing effect.

Most of Nottingham's major immigrant organisations have, over one issue or another, publicly expressed their dissatisfaction with aspects of life in this country. In the late 1950s and early 1960s the most outspoken group was the Afro-Asian-West Indian Union. During the period of its affiliation to the Consultative Committee its political work continued and its newspaper 'Clarion', which for a time was published in Nottingham, carried the following statement in each edition.

> As a result of the imperialist oppression undermining the whole political and economic well-being of the colonial people, immigration to Britain in search of a livelihood has taken place.

> Even in Britain, colonial peoples find it tremendously difficult to overcome problems of housing, employment and racial discrimination. Only by organising can we overcome the imperialist oppression in the colonies, and our many difficulties here in Britain.

Its Secretary, George Powe, elaborated on this theme in his pamphlet 'Don't Blame the Blacks' in which he emphasised his view that 'the threat to the white worker is not the coloured worker, but the reactionary policy of the British ruling class'.

> We must remember that colour prejudice, like antisemitism, is a weapon of class rule, and as such must find no support in the ranks of those whose task is to establish a world that is free from want. It should be clear that to end race prejudice and the colour bar, which the ruling class use as their main weapon to divide the working class, the coloured and white workers must join in the common struggle against capitalism.[82]

Members of the AAWIU were largely responsible for the establishment, in 1964, of the Campaign to Abolish Special Officers for Coloured People, and were also openly critical of the Consultative Committee which they considered to be an example of those 'reactionary bodies which pose as organisations looking after the welfare of coloured people, which use flowery language about integration to try to impress us, and steer us away from the popular organisations which exist to help with any citizen's problems'.[83] Clearly the AAWIU was not significantly muffled as a result of its association with the Consultative Committee.

Public criticism has not, however, been limited to openly militant, left-wing organisations. At the Indian Welfare Association's Celebration of the seventeenth anniversary of the Indian Republic in 1967, its President Mr H. S. Kandola accused the Nottingham City Transport Department and a local bus company of practising discrimination and also noted that there were no coloured milkmen, postmen, traffic-wardens or policemen in the city. His audience included not only the Chairman and Secretary of the Consultative Committee, but also the Lord Mayor and the Chairman of Nottingham's City Transport Committee.[84]

In 1968, the General Secretary of the Indian Workers Association, Mr A. S. Atwal, alleged that Nottingham's Education Department was discriminating against trained Asian teachers.[85] In the following month, following an incident involving police and immigrant leaders, the Nottingham Indian Workers Association issued a press statement which read:

> We strongly condemn the alleged brutal police attack on our General Secretary, Mr Joshi, and other leading figures of the Indian Workers Association while on their way home from a peaceful demonstration in Birmingham.[86]

The statement claimed that the leaders were dragged away and beaten by the police and concluded that:

> This police attack on immigrant leaders, who fight against racialism, is a direct encouragement to the Fascist elements in this country.

Later in the year, the Indian Welfare Association renewed its allegations against the City Transport Department and challenged them to set up an independent enquiry. It also accused Insurance Companies of discriminating against coloured taxi-drivers and stated that:

> None of them are prepared to entertain their applications for full insurance cover, in spite of the fact that most of these drivers have good driving records and are experienced with driving conditions in the United Kingdom.[87]

Whilst the Pakistani Friends League seems less inclined to issue press statements and make specific allegations than the two Indian Associations, it too has made public criticisms of a more general kind on occasions. For example, at the Celebration of Pakistan's twenty-first anniversary, the Honorary Secretary of the Friends League included the following remarks in his address to an audience which included the usual selection of civic dignitaries.

> Many times we have asked ourselves what is the basis of the 'Immigrant Problem'. At last we have come to some understanding of its real meaning. We believe that recent events ... have shown quite clearly that it is the ideas and attitudes of British people with regard to 'race' and 'colour' which constitute the

real problem ... Immigration was not always a problem ... It only became a
problem when the sons of the Mother Country; West Indians, Indians,
Pakistanis, Asians and others began to immigrate to Britain after the Second
World War. They came for some of the same reasons which had led English
immigrants to go to their countries; some were looking for employment, others
for adventure, others again for political or religious freedom. But none came for
gold, slaves, land or conquest. Was it a backward looking historical viewpoint
which led the people of Britain to assume that they had come for those
reasons?[88]

Whilst this may not seem to have been a particularly hard-hitting speech, it
must be remembered that it was given by the leading member of a moderate
organisation on the kind of occasion when it was usual to make only the most
polite and inoffensive of remarks. Certainly the relative frankness of the comments surprised the dignitaries in attendance.

Protests were no less common in 1969. The most controversial issue was the
reluctance of the City Transport Department to allow Sikh employees to wear
turbans on duty. Other than the Sikhs themselves, the move to end the ban on
turbans was led by the militant and inter-racial Anti-Colour Bar Campaign.
The Consultative Committee supported the Sikhs but played a more quiet and
conciliatory role. The issue, which lasted for several months, became very
heated and a former city councillor even lodged a complaint with the Race
Relations Board in which he charged the Anti-Colour Bar Campaign with
stirring up racial hatred.[89] Later in the year the Indian Welfare Association
renewed its attack on the Education Department which it accused of showing
'complete indifference' to the problems of teaching English to Asian children
and, amongst other points, claimed that fear of victimisation was making immigrants reluctant to complain about discrimination in promotion opportunities to the Race Relations Board.[90]

The most significant issue in 1970 was the campaign to stop the tour of the
South African Cricket Team. The Anti-Colour Bar Campaign again played a
prominent part and was strongly supported by the Indian Workers Association and the Society for Protection against Discrimination and Exploitation
(SPADE) which had replaced the old AAWIU. In 1971, the main source of
concern amongst immigrant groups was the Conservative Government's Immigration Bill and seven organisations came together to organise protests
against it. In addition to the militant Black Peoples Freedom Movement, which
had replaced the short-lived SPADE, and the Indian Workers Association,
were the more moderate Pakistani Friends League, the Indian Welfare
Association, the West Indian Nationals Association, the West Indian Students
Association and Supreme Soromani Akalidal.[91]

Although this list of protests is not exhaustive, it shows that even the
organisations affiliated to the Consultative Committee are capable of public

protest and when doing so have not felt obliged to follow its example. The developments which took place in 1971 over the Immigration Bill are particularly significant for they brought together seven immigrant groups not all of which were affiliated to the Committee, and which had widely differing outlooks. Moreover, it is interesting to note that the Chairman of the steering-committee was Mohammed Aslam JP, the Honorary Secretary of the moderate Friends League and Treasurer of the Consultative Committee. So, whilst the amount of discontent revealed in the course of the interviews may not be reflected in the amount of public protest, it is very doubtful if the Consultative Committee has been a serious obstacle to its emergence. Perhaps the main weakness of Katznelson's analysis is that he exaggerates the significance of the Consultative Committee's role. It can be agreed that it has not pressed the claims of the immigrant population with particular vigour. But neither has it had much of an impeding effect on the development of immigrant protest.

So far only passing reference has been made to the inter-racial and militant Anti-Colour Bar Campaign. Although founded in June 1967 it is not mentioned by Katznelson and this is especially significant since it is undoubtedly the most vigorous protest group in the city. It was established following an allegation of discrimination against a Nottingham licensee which precipitated sit-ins and demonstrations.[92] Its Annual Report for 1968 made particular mention of the demonstration it organised against the Kenyan-Asian Bill, of its success in breaking up the Labour Party's May Day Rally (in protest 'against the Labour Party's racialist policies'), of its demonstration against Enoch Powell when he visited nearby Gedling ('this was most effective, Powell leaving at the end of the meeting across playing fields'), and of its protest at the appointment of a Fair Housing Group Worker (described as 'the apartheid measure of establishing a separate coloured person to handle immigrant housing problems'). In addition, it 'sponsored a meeting at which Paul Boutelle, an Afro-American, running as the Socialist Workers Party candidate for Vice-President of the USA, was the speaker'. In 1969 it organised a further meeting addressed by a number of nationally prominent black-power spokesmen. Later in the year its members were involved in demonstrations against the South African Ambassador in which a number of arrests were made and they were subsequently involved in a further demonstration against Powell in which coffee was thrown over him. And, as has already been mentioned, its members were very prominent in the protests over the Transport Department's policy on turbans, in the 'Stop the '70s Tour' campaign and in those against the 1971 Immigration Bill.

The aim of the ACBC is 'to oppose racial discrimination in all its forms, wherever it may be found'. Unlike the Consultative Committee it makes regular use of demonstrations and similar forms of protest and is as aggressive as the Committee is conciliatory. Indeed resignations from the local 'Stop the '70s Tour' Committee resulted from its unwillingness to commit itself on a policy of non-violent protest. At a public meeting one of its leading members declared:

> I am convinced there is a likelihood of violence at Trent Bridge. We must take it as a fact of political life that the form of such demonstrations cannot be guaranteed by any Committee. Our job is mobilising the maximum possible numerical support for a demonstration we intend to be peaceful. But we cannot police such a demonstration and we must not take up a position of condemning those who feel they must protest in another way.[93]

Whereas the Consultative Committee shrinks from political involvement, the ACBC wears its left-wing allegiances openly. Probably for this, more than any other reason, no links have been established between the two organisations – indeed the Consultative Committee has on occasions been the subject of the Campaign's criticisms.

This chapter, on organisations concerned with race relations, has concentrated on the work and role of the Commonwealth Citizens Consultative Committee and has been concerned with other bodies only in terms of their relationship with it. This approach has been adopted for three main reasons. The first is that the Committee is the only body of official standing in Nottingham, supported by public funds, which has a direct responsibility for the improvement of race relations.[o] For this reason alone it obviously merits close attention. The second reason is that several writers and observers have claimed that the Committee has done a great deal to improve race relations in Nottingham. For example, in 1967, Mary Grigg concluded that:

> There are no committees in the North as impressive as the Commonwealth Citizens Consultative Committee in Nottingham, which is a good example of how a committee can work effectively without being a political bulldozer or shirking the implications of power.[94]

Similarly, in the same year, in its Annual Report the NCCI claimed that:

> Because of its early start (the Consultative Committee) was able to anticipate and minimise many of the difficulties such as housing shortage, discrimination in employment, problems of immigrant relations, and youth problems. After so many years of solid work and pioneering activity, the Nottingham Committee ... may well set an example in the field from which many of the newer committees will benefit.[95]

---

[o]   The East Midlands Conciliation Committee of the Race Relations Board is based in Nottingham but its task is the prevention of discrimination rather than the improvement of race relations.

The third reason is that Katznelson, although reaching very different conclusions about the achievements of the Committee, also claims that it has played a crucial role in the development of the city's race relations. Had these several writers not made such considerable, and conflicting, claims about the Committee, it would probably not have figured so prominently in this chapter. Indeed, if the arguments which I have offered are correct, it would appear that they have seriously exaggerated the importance of the Committee. The evidence presented here suggests that it has made relatively little impact on race relations in the city and that the attention it has attracted far outweighs its real significance. This is not to say that it has not done very useful work. In particular, it may deserve more credit for its individual welfare work than it has received. But the lot of the vast majority of coloured people and the general pattern of race relations have probably been scarcely touched by its efforts.

8
Conclusions

At several stages in the course of the book I have drawn attention to the disillusionment and discontent to be found amongst Nottingham's coloured immigrants. In Chapter 2 I pointed out that many of those interviewed had been profoundly shaken by their initial experience of life in this country. Instead of a society in which hard work and ambition brought high incomes and security they found that discrimination often made it difficult for them to obtain jobs. Instead of an open and friendly welcome they found prejudice and sometimes open hostility. Experiences of rejection have been felt most strongly by the Jamaicans. Their strong sense of identity with Britain produced higher expectations and probably greater exposure to circumstances in which prejudice and discrimination were encountered. In other chapters I noted that most coloured immigrants are convinced that they do not have equal opportunities in either the employment or housing markets and that many of those interviewed are able to cite specific instances of discrimination in which they have been involved. Such experiences and feelings of rejection have inevitably affected the way in which the immigrants see their place within British society. Though the Indians and Pakistanis appear to have been less upset than the Jamaicans, it has not encouraged them to conform to British behaviour patterns and engage in inter-personal relationships with British people any more than is necessary. In the case of the Jamaicans, the feelings of rejection have been much more significant and have very often been more than sufficient to overcome the initially strong sense of identity which they felt for Britain.

The members of any immigrant group are likely to feel 'outsiders' to some extent – whatever the response of the indigenous population to their arrival. But in this instance the tendency does seem to be particularly pronounced. It has been fostered by several factors other than the nature of the welcome extended to the immigrants and the relatively marked cultural differences which exist between the Indians and Pakistanis and the British. Most of those interviewed came to this country for negative rather than positive reasons. Not only would most not have left home had conditions not been so difficult for them, but many would have gone to other countries had that been possible.

Moreover, most came not to settle but to work for a time and then return. No doubt influenced by the nature of their reception, and the relatively poor prospects before them in Britain, many remain reluctant to sever their ties with their country of origin and still express the intention to return home at a future, if unspecified, date. There can be little doubt that such factors serve to strengthen the tendency to withdrawal found amongst the coloured immigrant population.

If the feelings of rejection can be as great as has been implied then it would not be unreasonable to expect them to become manifest in clinical signs and symptoms in some cases. There is growing evidence that schizophrenia, for example, can be precipitated, or perhaps even caused, by difficult social circumstances. Thus it could be expected that rates of schizophrenia would be higher amongst immigrant groups, and coloured immigrant groups in particular, than in the indigenous population as a whole.[a]

Table 30 Schizophrenia (1963–9) and birthplace

Birthplace	Schizoid males %	Schizoid females %	Schizoid males and females %	Total population %
Great Britain	66·4	75·4	70·8	93·2
'New' Commonwealth	16·2	12·0	14·1	2·8
Elsewhere	17·4	12·6	15·1	4·0
No. schizophrenics	247	231	478	

A recent study has in fact shown this to be the case in Nottingham. Giggs obtained information on all persons classified as schizophrenics who were hospitalised for the first time from an address within the city boundary during the seven years 1963–9.[1] The relevant parts of his findings are summarised in Table 30. They show that the incidence of schizophrenia was significantly greater amongst the foreign-born population. Whereas they comprised less than 7 per cent of Nottingham's population in 1966, they constituted 29 per

[a] Schizophrenia has been defined by Mayer-Gross, Slater and Roth as: '. . . a group of mental illnesses characterised by specific psychological symptoms and leading, in the majority of cases, to the disorganisation of the personality of the patient. The symptoms interfere with the patients' thinking, emotions, conation and motor behaviour.' See *Clinical Psychiatry* (1970), p. 237. Bagley has also suggested that it so impairs the individual's capacity to adapt to his environment that 'it is virtually impossible for a schizophrenic to exist in an urban community without coming to the notice of the authorities'. See *Race Today* vol. 1, no. 6 (October 1969), p. 172.

cent of the schizophrenics. In other words, there were more than four times the number of foreign-born schizophrenics than would have been expected had they been evenly distributed amongst the total population. Moreover, the incidence amongst coloured immigrants (i.e. the 'new' Commonwealth born population) was greater than that amongst other foreign-born groups. Whereas the former comprised less than 3 per cent of the population, they constituted over 14 per cent of schizophenics. Those others born abroad comprised 4 per cent of the population but over 15 per cent of schizophrenics. Thus, whereas there were five times as many coloured immigrants as would be expected on the basis of a uniform distribution of schizophrenia, the corresponding rate for other foreign-born residents was less than four times. It cannot be assumed that the disproportionately greater extent of recorded schizophrenia amongst coloured immigrants is a result of the particular problems faced by them which have been discussed. Such problems do, however, constitute a possible explanation. The findings do not show that schizophrenia is *rife* amongst coloured immigrants. The figures represent differential rates and the actual number of schizophrenics which emerged in the coloured immigrant population in the period 1963–9 was only 68. However, as Bagley has indicated, 'the fact that schizophrenia is a relatively frequent diagnosis . . . suggests that there may be a similar excess of milder psychiatric states (depression, anxiety etc.) which do not come to the notice of the psychiatric services'.[2] If this is so it is even more likely that some of the responsible factors will be those unfavourable circumstances which have been described.

Evidence has also been presented at several stages in the book which suggests that such conditions will continue and perhaps even become intensified in the future. In Chapter 3 I suggested that most unfavourable attitudes towards coloured people have probably been culturally transmitted. Although this is not to say that some have not arisen or been reinforced by contact and competition or personality factors, the prevalence of unfavourable stereotypes amongst perfectly ordinary men and women, many of whom have had no close contact with coloured people, provides fairly strong circumstantial evidence that racial distinctions are built into our cultural definitions. It also implies that those who hold unfavourable views about coloured people are normal rather than exceptional. There is also little reason to suppose that either racial stereotypes or the commonly felt sense of superiority towards coloured people will disappear in the immediate future – indeed they are still being reinforced. In short, it must be anticipated that most British people will continue to show some antipathy towards coloured people for many years to come.

Whether or not such feelings result in positive hostility or open conflict will depend upon the kind of circumstances in which individuals and groups find themselves. Possible changes in those relating to housing and employment will be summarised below. But, before doing so, it is worth noting something of the organisational expression which has been and is being given to feelings of antipathy towards coloured people. Until very recently there was little or no organised opposition to them in Nottingham. For example, there was no equivalent of the Birmingham Immigration Control Association or any one of the many similar bodies found elsewhere. However, 1971 saw the development of the National Front in the city and its membership seems to have increased by as much as ten-fold during the Ugandan-Asian crisis in the second half of 1972. By the end of that year its strength was such that it planned to field several candidates in the next local government elections.[3] Whilst the Front has not made the same impact as in nearby Leicester, its establishment and rapid growth, after over twenty years without any organised opposition to coloured immigrants, may still prove to be very significant. At the very least the Front will probably keep matters relating to race relations and immigration in the public eye. It could become an organised focal point for much of the resentment revealed in the course of the interviews. Moreover, the general disillusionment with the two main political parties which became apparent in the course of the interviews must surely enhance its potential for further growth.

In Chapter 4 I suggested that the characteristics of Nottingham's housing market had, until recently, probably had the effect of reducing the likelihood of racial antipathy developing into open racial conflict. Given the existence of prejudice and the prevalence of the view that coloured immigrants are newcomers who should not automatically be treated in the same way as the indigenous population, this may not seem to be a very obvious conclusion. However, many of those who live in poor housing conditions appear to have become reconciled to them – and many even say that they are satisfied with what others would judge to be thoroughly inadequate accommodation. Moreover, many of those who express dissatisfaction complain about different kinds of factors. For example, some complain most, or only, about the kind of people who live around them. Others complain about one or more of the physical features of the area in which they live. Still others complain less about the area and more about specific housing conditions. In so far as this means that those concerned may be looking for different kinds of accommodation to remove the cause or causes of their dissatisfaction, it may have the effect of reducing the amount of direct competition between native whites and coloured immigrants for scarce housing resources. The amount of direct competition has also been influenced by the large quantity of cheap housing which has been available until recently. It was found that most of the immigrants interviewed had been able to buy their own houses. In doing so they had not affected the housing situation of most of their white neighbours. These were living, in most cases, in similarly substandard accommodation but were in no obvious danger of either finding themselves homeless or in worse housing conditions as a result of the immigrant influx. In any case, evidence was found that most of the native whites did not see any reason why coloured immigrants should not buy their own houses if in a position to do so.

However, the prospect of open conflict over housing seems to be increasing rather than decreasing. Slum clearance programmes have rapidly accelerated the decline in the availability of cheap rented accommodation. As a result, the residents of the inner zone are becoming more and more dependent upon council housing. For those whose houses are demolished, and who can afford and wish to live in council properties, this change may be inconsequential. But for those who, for whatever reason, begin to look for alternative cheap accommodation elsewhere it may be extremely significant. As the supply diminishes so conflict between racial groups becomes more possible. Relationships may also be affected by the growing discontent which is likely to arise as conditions of scarcity push up prices, and as the improvements elsewhere in the city make the poorly housed feel an increasingly conspicuous minority. Similarly, younger people, whatever their ethnic origin, are less likely to tolerate the conditions which many of their parents have tended to take for granted. In short, within the inner zone, in which competition for cheap accommodation between black and white takes place, the general atmosphere may become increasingly vexed and even potentially explosive.

At the same time, it is important to consider whether or not those coloured people who are in a position to buy themselves out of the inner zone into suburban privacy will be able to do so. As yet there is no firm evidence available on which to base a prediction, although it is certainly possible that many of them will encounter discrimination. What is more clear is that if they do meet it then, for reasons to be outlined below, the existing machinery laid down under the 1968 Race Relations Act may not be of very much help to them.

There is one further development in the field of housing which requires comment. It was announced in late 1972 that Nottingham's Fair Housing Group, which is attached to the Community Relations Council, had received support from the City Corporation to found a new Housing Association. This is not an entirely novel development. Indeed as long ago as 1956 the Commonwealth Citizens Consultative Committee established a Coloured People's Housing Association in the hope that it would bring about an improvement in the housing conditions of the immigrants. However, whereas this earlier venture was limited by its dependence on individual investment and, as a result, only raised sufficient capital to buy about 30 houses, the new scheme is backed by a Corporation loan of £500,000 in addition to an annual grant of £4,000 for a period of three years and other assistance. By any standard it is a substantial project and certainly the largest ever initiated by the Community Relations Council. Its aim is to buy, alter and modernise old properties within the inner zone and then rent them at the minimum cost to those in need of improved housing – irrespective of their racial or ethnic origin.[b] There can be little doubt that this initiative will do a great deal for a large number of families. But it is not likely to make any marked impact on the general trends which have been outlined. This is because it will be concerned primarily with providing *better* rather than *more* dwelling units. Consequently, the fundamental problem of the scarcity of cheap housing will be relatively untouched.[c] The establishment of such an association, on so large a scale, is a notable achievement for a voluntary group. But only a local authority programme backed by huge national resources can halt or reverse the housing trends which threaten to further exacerbate existing patterns of race relations.

In Chapter 5 I suggested that just as the arrival of the immigrants did not make much impression on the housing situation of the native whites, so it did not constitute much of an economic threat to white workers. The immigrants came to Nottingham at a time when jobs were readily available and most were prepared to do almost any kind of work. Those interviewed were found to be very much concentrated at the lower end of the occupational hierarchy and occupying the kind of jobs least attractive to white workers. Moreover, the extent of their voluntary membership of trades unions seems to suggest that, at least in the work sphere, the immigrants are willing to identify their own interests with those of white workers.

I also suggested that the most likely source of contention between white and coloured workers is the apparent unwillingness of many of the former to support equal opportunities for the latter. So long as the immigrants remain concentrated in the most menial of jobs and are willing to tolerate poor working conditions and little opportunity for advancement, and provided that jobs in general are not in too short a supply, then working relationships may remain fairly amicable. Given a more ambitious set of coloured workers who

[b]   It was hoped that particular consideration might be given initially to Asian refugees from Uganda.

[c]   Especially since it seems that Trent Polytechnic is to increase its student intake very considerably over the next few years and so create even more pressure for cheap flats and houses.

are less willing to settle for second best I suggested that industrial unrest might develop.

Since Chapter 5 was written two disputes have arisen in the Nottingham area which lend support to this appraisal of the situation. The first began in the middle of 1972 when 39 Pakistani workers at a factory in the Lenton district went on strike in protest against the redundancy of five of their fellow-countrymen. With the backing of the TGWU they asked the management to spread the available work in such a way that their colleagues could be reinstated. The strike began because the company turned down their request. When the strikers refused to return to work they were dismissed and an advertisement for replacements appeared in the local press.[4] This particularly infuriated the strikers since the advertisement simply offered 'wages up to £40 per week' without any qualification. As the district organiser for the TGWU pointed out, such wages could be earned only by working as many as 84 hours a week. The basic weekly wage was only £15 a week.[5] And, as he had emphasised at the very outset of the dispute, it was precisely because most of the Pakistani strikers were working an 84 hour week of seven 12-hour shifts that they had felt that it would be an extremely easy matter for the management to spread the load and avoid any redundancies. Eventually the five workers were reinstated and significant concessions obtained from the firm. In particular, it agreed to a reduction in working hours from 84 to 56 per week.

The vast majority of production workers at the firm were Pakistanis and neither they, nor the handful of white employees, were union members until the dispute began to develop. It seems that it was only when the possible advantages of union membership became apparent to the Pakistanis (and the white workers did not respond to their request for solidarity) that the TGWU became involved. But the way in which local immigrant organisations rallied to the support of the strikers was perhaps the most notable feature of the dispute. For example, when the firm advertised the vacancies, the President of the relatively moderate Pakistani Friends League issued a public statement on behalf of the League urging 'workers in general and Pakistanis in particular, not to take any of the vacant jobs until this matter is fully resolved'.[6] Although some native whites did apply for the vacancies it seems that not a single coloured worker applied.

The second dispute proved much more intractable and complicated and eventually the Secretary of State for Employment set up a Committee of Inquiry to look into it.[7] It too involved Asian workers – on this occasion those employed by the Mansfield Hosiery Mills Ltd, in two factories at Loughborough. They comprised 40 per cent of the work-force in the case of one factory and 51 per cent in the other. The dispute centred around four kinds of workers. The most skilled and best paid were those who operated full-fashioned knitting machines. The next best paid were those who worked non-fashioned machines. They were followed by the less skilled 'runners-on' (who prepare strips of fabric knitted on non-fashioned machines for transfer onto fully-fashioned machines). All three of these grades were paid on a piece-rate basis. The final group of workers, 'bar-loaders' (who transfer the material prepared by the 'runners-on' to the fully-fashioned machines) were paid on a time rate basis and earned very much less than the others. The Asian and white workers were not distributed amongst the four grades in a uniform way. On the contrary, at one factory, all of the fully-fashioned knitters were white workers. In marked contrast all of the bar-loaders and over 90 per cent of the runners-on were Asians. Although the dispute began, at least ostensibly, with the refusal of the company to pay the bar-loaders an increase of £5 per week, it quickly became apparent that the real dispute was over the limited opportunities available for the Asians to become knitters.

The company had made attempts to alter this pattern in the ten year period leading up to the dispute but had on each occasion met with opposition from the white workers. In 1962–3 the appointment of Asians as runners-on provoked a strike of those white workers already involved in the operation – although their reluctant acceptance was eventually obtained. In 1968–9 the management discussed the possibility of training Asian workers as knitters but capitulated when they met strong resistance from both the knitters and the Union. In 1969, three Asians were actually transferred to full-fashioned knitting but when the existing knitters withdrew their labour the management again capitulated and subsequently negotiated (with the Union and the Shop Committee) their transference to non-fashioned machines. When in 1972 the management re-opened talks on the subject it became clear that if it gave effect to its proposal to train Asian knitters then another strike would ensue. Once again the management gave way to the white workers. At about the same time, however, acting on a complaint by an Asian employee, the Race Relations Board investigated the situation and formed the opinion that both the Company and the Union had contravened the Race Relations Act. It failed to take the matter further only because of the appointment of the Committee of Inquiry.

The particular dispute which resulted in the setting up of the Committee of Inquiry began when a Union claim for a pay increase of £5 per week for the bar-loaders was turned down in October 1972. The company offer was rejected and against the advice of the Union the bar-loaders went on strike. A return to work was secured when the mediation of a Community Relations Worker from Birmingham (who emphasised that the lack of opportunities for Asians to become knitters was an important element in the dispute) resulted in an undertaking by the Company to train two Asian knitters. The selection of the knitters provoked a strike on the part of established knitters which was settled only when the Union and Company agreed on at least a temporary return to the *status quo*. After a further pay offer was rejected the bar-loaders withdrew their labour a second time. This time they were joined by other Asian workers. The Company held that the strikers were in breach of their contract and took on replacement labour. After a series of negotiations the dismissal notices were withdrawn and the strikers returned to work. On doing so they discovered that forty-one of the new employees were being trained as knitters and came out on strike again. This time the Union gave the strike official recognition.

The Committee of Inquiry found that the Company had done 'insufficient to satisfy the legitimate aspirations of the Asian workers and the requirements of natural justice' and had not shown enough courage in the face of 'what can only be described as a racialist attitude on the part of some of their white employees'. It was also critical of the role of the Union in the affair and argued that 'there is clearly much the Union can do to increase the confidence of the Asian membership that it will in fact champion their legitimate aspirations'.[8]

Despite the compromise position recommended by the Committee, and the assurances it received from the parties concerned, the dispute was still not fully resolved at the time of writing. Clearly, not even when the existing machinery for improving race relations is supplemented by an official inquiry can there be any guarantee that such deeply rooted problems will be brought to a conclusion satisfactory to all.

The reasons for the relative impotence of the Community Relations machinery has already been discussed at length in Chapter 7. Less attention has been given to the weaknesses in the machinery set up under the 1968 Race Relations Act. It is especially noteworthy that, even though more than ten years old, the discrimination at the Mansfield Hosiery Mills came to the attention of the East Midlands Conciliation Committee (the local unit of the Race Relations Board), in a form in which action could be taken, as long as four years after it had actually been made illegal. This underlines the point made elsewhere in the book, that the Board is often rendered powerless by its virtual dependence on the registration of specific complaints. Only if it is able and willing to initiate enquiries can it hope to be more effective than at present. Such a proposal is one of the main recommendations of Lester and Bindman who have conducted the most searching examination of both the 1968 Act and the way in which it operates.

> The Race Relations Board's power to investigate suspected instances of unlawful discrimination in the absence of any specific complaint (Section 17) should be widened, so that the Board is able to investigate any situation which it

regards as important, without the need for the Board to suspect that a particular person may have been discriminated against. This would free the Board from its excessive dependence upon individual complaints.[9]

There are many reasons why such a change is necessary. Some immigrants may still be ignorant of the legislation or the way in which complaints are made. Furthermore, as was noted during the discussion of Jowell and Clarke's study of discrimination in Chapter 5, it is very often the case that a victim of discrimination may have no possible way of knowing that it has taken place. Those who know how to make a complaint may, of course, choose not to do so for any of several reasons. They may, for example, have little confidence that a satisfactory outcome will result. Certainly many of those interviewed expressed the general view that legislation was not a very effective way of dealing with a problem like racial discrimination. Over one third of those interviewed (36 per cent) said that they had little or no confidence in legislation and four respondents even said that it could make things worse.

> It's people's feelings that make trouble and you can't change them by passing a law.

> It would be forcing someone to do something against their will – and that might just make things worse.

> People will just find ways round it.

> If you make them give you a job then what would you feel like at work? They would not want you and it would make everybody feel bad.

> If you should say to a man, I'm sorry there's no vacancy – what can you do about it? He doesn't tell you its because of your colour – he tells you there's no vacancy. Passing a law won't make no difference.

There are many specific reasons why those who are familiar with the 1968 Act and its machinery may lack confidence in it. At present the procedures tend to work slowly and the voluntary industrial machinery for the investigation of employment complaints is particularly cumbersome. The Board is not empowered to compel the attendance of witnesses or the disclosure of documents, neither can it insist on the keeping of the kind of records necessary for it to check on possible discrimination. In other words, it must at present win the co-operation of the person against whom an allegation is made in order to obtain the necessary information with which to evaluate the complaint against him. It has no power to apply for an interim order restraining any further violation of the law until a complaint has been fully investigated. Even in cases where conciliation proves impossible and the Board takes a discriminator to Court, there is no provision to make the defendant put right the specific wrong committed (e.g. reinstate the employee). Neither is there any provision for the Court to award damages for any distress that may have been caused by the discrimination. One very obvious further feature of the present legislation which makes for suspicion on the part of immigrants is that a victim of discrimination must wait upon the Race Relations Board for any redress and is not entitled to pursue a complaint in the courts on his own behalf.

Although the 1968 Race Relations Act is much more comprehensive in scope than the 1965 Act which preceded it, it is still far from fully comprehensive. For example, it is possible for racial discrimination to be practised in the guise of religious discrimination (which is not yet an offence), and it can exist in its own right in 'private' clubs (e.g. working-men's clubs) and advertisements for jobs overseas. Given such exceptions and the procedural weakness which have been outlined, as well as the several and sometimes sweeping criticisms which have been made by employees or former employees of the Board, it ought not to be suprising that some of the immigrants familiar with the Act lack confidence in it.

The Race Relations Board and Community Relations Councils are not the only official bodies in which some coloured immigrants lack confidence. In recent years, and in many parts of the country, complaints have also been made about the police. This is an especially serious problem since it is the police who are expected to act as guardians of law and order in industrial disputes, in cases of rows between neighbours and similar situations where no actual criminal behaviour is involved. In other words, the police are able to play a crucial role in either mitigating or exacerbating outbreaks of inter-racial hostility. If they are seen as agents for the native white population, rather than as neutral law-enforcers, then this could very easily influence the outcome of any given situation. The chief officers of the police force in Nottingham seem alive to such a possibility. For many years one of their number has had special responsibility for liaison work, and talks and discussions on matters relating to race relations

Table 31 Police treatment of coloured immigrants

Claim	West Indians %	Indians %	Pakistanis %	All %
Same treatment	42	52	50	45
Less favourable treatment	31	19	36	29
Don't know	26	30	9	25
Would not answer	1	—	5	2
No. respondents	72	27	22	121

and immigration have been provided during training courses at their college in nearby Epperstone. What has been derived from these sessions it is impossible to say. That there is a need for something like them is undeniable. Towards the end of one meeting, led by a mild and quietly spoken community relations worker, a large section of the experienced policemen present (i.e. with twenty or more years in the force) stood up and began to chant, 'Enoch, Enoch, we want Enoch'!

In the course of the interviews all immigrant respondents were asked: 'Do you think that the police treat immigrants and English people in the same way or do they treat them differently?' As Table 31 shows, 45 per cent believed that they were treated in the same way. A few of these went out of their way to praise the police.

> Such policemen can only be found in Heaven! We don't get such police in India or Pakistan. This society and government works only because of the police. If you ask a PC for a place he would not go to his duty without guiding you. We are here because of the police. They treat blacks and whites alike. The police do not take sides. They apply the law strictly.

> Nowhere else in the world are the police like these. These police are really intelligent men. They listen – they really listen to what things are. Oh, our police is far rougher than these. These men use their intelligence you see.

A further quarter said that they were not able to offer any answer to the question. The remaining 29 per cent said that coloured people were treated differently. All of these meant by this that coloured people were treated *less favourably*.

The charge made most often (by 57 per cent) was that the police ignore complaints made by coloured people.

> Well my lad was beaten-up by an Englishman and some Englishman saw it and came and told me. He was hurt bad so I went to the police – but they wouldn't do anything. But if *I* had hit *his* lad things would have been different!

> Once I went to Goose Fair along with other friends. We were standing near a merry-go-round. The operator, who was drunk, came up to me and slapped me – for no reason at all. I was going to ring the police but an officer appeared on the scene. We reported the matter to him but he did not take any action. This made us think they take our complaints very lightly.

> The boy next door broke our window and we called the police on the advice of a friend. The policeman came and was sympathetic. He said he would be able to get damages or a conviction. But when he found our neighbours were white – previously he had been under the impression they were West Indian – his whole manner changed and he wiped his hands of the whole affair. It is this sort of incident which really undermines your confidence.

Some 29 per cent of those who alleged differential treatment claimed the police 'picked-on' coloured people.

Well I have seen these things for myself. If any Indian is involved the police get annoyed very quickly. Oh yes – they're very prejudiced – they're very rough!

If there's a dispute between me and a white even if I'm in the right they favour the white man – Oh yes.

They supposed to treat everybody equally but they don't. They don't listen to what we say. If we phone up and they come they always have a bias against us. For instance, they sided with the Englishman who parked outside our house – yet we're not even allowed to park our own car there. It is sheer colour prejudice.

Finally, some 23 per cent claimed that the police sometimes 'beat-up' coloured people.

Actually I think the Nottingham police are bastards. I've met decent policemen –but not in Nottingham. They're really hostile here. There's a lot of people been beaten-up by them.

I don't know anything of the police personally – but lots of stories have come out and some must be true. They beat-up lots of people of course – but they give it to us much worse.

A friend went to make a complaint at a police station and a plain clothes man told him to get out and assaulted him.

There can be no doubt that confidence in the police has slumped further since the interviews were conducted. The fact that there is still not a coloured policeman in the city has not helped the situation. But more important to the deterioration in relations are the circumstances surrounding the trial in which three Nottingham policemen were charged with conspiring to pervert the course of justice. The charges were brought on the advice of the Director of Public Prosecutions after allegations that the policemen had planted drugs on coloured men in the Nottingham area.[d] The trial, which lasted from 5 Oc-

[d]   The charges were: (1) that between 2 February 1967 and 13 August 1969 they conspired to obstruct and pervert the course of justice by acting contrary to their public duties as police officers in relation to the administration of the law. They were accused of making unlawful gifts of cannabis to diverse persons by threatening diverse persons with arrest and prosecution in order to induce them to give information and assistance to the police, of permitting unlawful drinking and of permitting soliciting for the purpose of prosecution; and of promising to show favour to persons charged with offences in order to induce them to give information and assistance to the police; (2) conspiring to pervert and obstruct the course of justice between the same dates by causing false evidence to be fabricated and false charges to be preferred against diverse persons by planting cannabis on these persons; (3) that, between 13 September 1968 and 24 January 1969, they conspired together with Vincent Lloyd Robinson to pervert and obstruct the course of justice by causing false charges to be preferred against Keith McLean and Audrey Letts, and by causing Robinson to give false witness against Letts and McLean.

tober 1970 to 20 November 1970, received extensive publicity, and the proceedings were often made the subject of the main front page story in the local newspapers.

Several features of the trial, quite apart from the charges themselves, caused disquiet. For example, it seems that for the first time in many years there were no black men on the jury list.[10] Then, a number of tape recordings on which the prosecution's case rested heavily, and which had been accepted as evidence at the committal proceedings, were judged to be inadmissible as evidence by the trial judge. Since the recordings had been authenticated as a genuine record of actual conversations by an expert on tape recordings, and had been arranged and made under the close supervision of a nationally known journalist, this seemed to many to be an unfair as well as crippling judgement.[11] Unhappiness has also been expressed about the performance of the prosecuting counsel – not least his failure to call a number of key witnesses; about the fact that subsequent charges were not brought against a West Indian witness who admitted under oath to having committed perjury at an earlier trial which resulted in the conviction and imprisonment of a fellow West Indian; and about the failure of the Home Office to take any steps to formally re-open the case involving the latter man – who has always insisted on his innocence.

However just or unjust the criticisms made about the way in which the trial was conducted, there is no doubt that many coloured people remain convinced that the policemen were guilty as charged and that justice was not done or seen to be done. To put these findings and comments in perspective it must be added that police-immigrant relations in Nottingham have not reached the same low ebb as in some London boroughs. Nevertheless, fears and suspicions are very common and the absence of coloured policemen and circumstances of the kind described above serve only to reinforce them. The sporting activities and other ventures arranged by the police to try to bridge the gap do not go very far in dispelling such feelings.

Most of the coloured respondents were very apprehensive about the future of race relations in Nottingham and doubtful about the possibility of eliminating racial discrimination. When they were asked: 'What do you think should be done about the racial discrimination that seems to take place in Britain?' suggestions were made which ranged from 'skinning the colour people' and 'taking the word of Jesus into our hearts' to more practical suggestions for reforms in the Race Relations Act. But the large majority either said that they had no idea what could be done or despaired that anything at all could be done.

Nothing can be done – you cannot stop it.

There's no remedy – it's in the people – until death it won't leave them.

Nothing can be done. The heart of the English – their 'superiority' – will not change. Only the Creator can change it.

The difference of 'black' and 'white' will not come to an end even after centuries. The white man will never give up his belief that he is better than black and brown – even if they are more educated, intellectually superior and have a better way of life. I work hard to live better so that the Englishman cannot say that we are scruffy. We pray for the prosperity of their country. We try to treat the white man as a real brother. But if we show him affection he answers with hatred.

The apprehension of the immigrants showed itself in other ways. Towards the end of each interview, respondents were asked what, if anything, they knew about the 1958 racial disturbances. Although only about half had been in Britain at the time, 77 per cent were able to offer comments on them. These were also asked: 'Do you think that sort of thing could happen again?' As many as 68 per cent said 'yes' and only 21 per cent said that they did not think that it could happen again.

One day, next year, year after – it *will* happen again.

I think it is going to happen – yes.

At any time!

When asked: 'What do you think could make it happen again?' the respondents offered a great variety of possible precipitants.

Well there's a lot of things, quite a lot of our people are afraid for their safety – oh it will happen again. There are signs of it coming back. There's a pub in Alfreton Road – a fella went in there and 'she' said – 'we don't serve niggers here' – this fella felt pretty bad and knocked down a glass of beer. The landlord grabbed him and shook him and took him to court. Those sorts of thing could start it off again.

It's going to be worse – even worse than America I think. When these children grow up and cannot get good jobs – that's when it will start. *They* won't stand for it.

Any little incident might get out of hand. Michael X might stir it up going around preaching about the white people. Just the same with Jordan.

It's hard to predict – but when a man hates it can always happen.

As Table 32 shows, the widespread apprehension of the coloured immigrants is shared by most of their white neighbours. The native white respondents were also asked if they thought there could be a repetition of the 1958 disturbances and as many as 74 per cent said that they thought that it was possible. Only 21 per cent ruled out the possibility of a recurrence. Like the immigrants, the native whites suggested a wide range of circumstances over which violence might erupt.

It's to do with these council houses – like you're asking me. They're getting them before us – some of us can't even get on the waiting list. It's brewing all the time – look at the flow of Asians coming now. Some day the bubble's got to burst. It's been done once in Nottingham. It could happen again just as easily.

It will happen again – wait and see what happens to the Yankee dollar. It will affect this country. The employment situation will be affected – that'll spark off the trouble. Too many will be unemployed and too many of them will be white!

Some blokes hate the whites and why they come here in the first place feeling like this I don't know. Some whites hate the blacks. A bloke where we last lived, an Indian, played his radio at 7 o'clock every morning – including Sunday. It's little silly things like that'll start it off.

It started over women in the pub before – it could happen that way again. A darkie trying to get off with a white woman started it before and it'll probably start it again.

The Indians and Pakistanis have taken over the pubs round here. If we go in now they stare at us. The English don't like it – there's usually a fight here every Saturday night anyway.

The problem will start when they can't get houses – work is short as it is. When they get no job or house, that's when the trouble will start. They'll stir up trouble amongst themselves and it'll spread to us.

Table 32 Anticipation of further racial violence

	Native whites %	West Indians %	Indians and Pakistanis %
Recurrence likely	74	70	63
Recurrence unlikely	21	20	26
Other	5	11	11
No. respondents	124	66	27

In anticipating further violence the respondents were not engaging in a purely speculative exercise. To some extent they were extrapolating from the small-scale incidents which they know take place fairly frequently in Nottingham. It is true that there has been no large-scale violence since 1958. However, there have continued to be violent clashes between individuals, or small groups of coloured immigrants and native whites, in which the racial element has been to the fore.

For example, in July 1967 a West Indian was fined and bound over for a year after being found guilty of assaulting and occasioning actual bodily harm to a white woman. The prosecution claimed that the assault was part of an attempt to intimidate the woman who was likely to be giving evidence in a pending case involving another coloured man charged with living off immoral earnings. The accused claimed that the woman had struck him first, had thrown a bunch of keys in his face and called him 'nigger'.[12] In October of the same year a West Indian was fined for assaulting the landlady of a public house and causing her bodily harm. It was alleged that an argument broke out between him and a Scotsman and flared into violence. The scuffle was settled by the landlady and a barman but, soon afterwards, it began again and the accused was claimed to have picked up a stool, knocked aside the barman who tried to take it from him, and struck the landlady over the head with it. The West Indian denied that he had even been involved in the struggle and asserted that he and his brother had actually left the public house soon after the fight began.[13]

In January 1968, it was reported in the local press that the police were trying to trace four Jamaicans who had been in dispute with a white man and, it was alleged, had subsequently stabbed him.[14] In February, a white man from the Meadows district was charged and found guilty of threatening behaviour with intent to provoke a breach of the peace under the Race Relations Act. It seems that he threatened an Indian immigrant by using extremely abusive language and taking off his jacket with the apparent intention of attacking him.[15]

In October 1970, an incident involving a white woman and a West Indian man was described by the prosecuting councel as 'a classic case of black against white'. The West Indian was charged with causing actual bodily harm to the woman. She claimed that a friend accidentally brushed against the accused whilst they were out one Saturday afternoon exercising a dog. She asserted that, although they both apologised to him, he called her a 'white bastard' and followed her across the street where he hit her across the face. The accused's version of the incident was very different. He agreed that the woman's *friend* had apologised to him but that, on the contrary, she had said that there was no need to do so to a 'black bastard who should never be in the country'. He then walked on, only to be pursued by the woman who began to scream and swear and threatened to set the dog onto him. It was when she swung her shoulder bag at him and he raised his arm to fend her off that he accidentally struck her. The West Indian was cleared of the charge. However, both he and the woman were bound over to keep the peace for twelve months.[16] In another incident in 1970 a West Indian was gaoled for six years after being found guilty of wounding a Nottingham policeman. He was stopped by two detectives, for what was described as a 'routine-check', in an area in which there had recently been several burglaries. He was alleged to have said to them, 'you are not stopping me, kid' and then made three slashes with a penknife causing a serious wound to the forearm of one of the detectives. The accused pleaded not guilty and denied having ever seen the penknife produced in evidence in court. It was emphasised, during the proceedings, that he had no previous convictions and a good work record and he claimed that after his arrest he was kicked and beaten by the officers and attacked again by a circle of policemen at Nottingham Guildhall.[17]

There have been many other incidents of the kind described over the past few years. Whilst those mentioned do not constitute any sort of representative sample they are certainly fairly typical and do illustrate the kind of pattern which many of them take. The participants in such incidents are probably not representative members of either the immigrant or the native white populations. In some instances they are clearly unrepresentative. However, violent clashes do occur — and fairly frequently — and even for onlookers and those who read newspaper accounts of them, quite apart from those more directly involved, they probably serve to reinforce both prejudice and feelings of apprehension.

In the introduction to the book reference was made to Nottingham's reputation for tolerance and harmony and to what many have claimed to be a much more positive approach to race relations than that found in other cities. I emphasised that such conclusions had not been based upon any systematic study of the situation and that, on the contrary, the city's officially supported public image had been built up by paying virtually no attention to the views and experiences of the ordinary men and women between whom race relations take place. If nothing else this investigation seems to have demonstrated that Nottingham does not enjoy harmonious race relations. Similarly, it does not seem that its inhabitants are unusually tolerant towards coloured people. This is not to say that race relations in Nottingham may not be less 'abrasive' than those found elsewhere — but care must be taken not to draw inappropriate conclusions from what may be nothing other than surface manifestations. And, even if it could be shown that, on the basis of what would have to be very carefully formulated criteria, another town did appear less harmonious, this would not allow anything other than a conclusion about 'relative' harmony to be made.[e] Obviously the more harmonious of the two towns might still have very serious racial problems as measured by a more 'absolute' yardstick.

The contention that Nottingham's approach to race relations has been more positive than that found elsewhere is no more easy to sustain than its reputation for tolerance and harmony. It is true that it has had one voluntary body devoted to the problem since as early as 1955. It is also true that it can claim the country's first coloured JP. Yet the City Council has on several issues

[e]   Much more so than the measure used by A. Marsh, 'Race, Community and Anxiety', *New Society*, vol. 23, no. 542 (22 July 1973).

trailed far behind many similarly placed local authorities and it cannot be said to have adopted a particularly positive approach to them. One of the first acts of the Commonwealth Citizens Consultative Committee when it was established in 1955 was to ask the City Council to appoint a special welfare officer to help ease the transitional problems of the newcomers. Its request was refused on this and a number of subsequent occasions. Only after the 1958 disturbances had thrust the city into the nation's headlines was such an appointment made. Similarly, from an early date, the Consultative Committee requested financial and other help from the Council. It was not forthcoming. Indeed the small grant of £500 which was eventually made came only when the Corporation seemed likely to be embarrassed by the collapse of the Consultative Committee. The financial aid given by the Council over the years to the Committee is small when judged by the support given to similar bodies elsewhere and it has been reminded of this on several occasions. For example, in a letter to the Town Clerk in November 1969 the Secretary of the Consultative Committee wrote:

> ... As you are aware, the White Paper, *Immigration from the Commonwealth 1965* provided that grants from the Community Relations Commission (which was then the National Committee for Commonwealth Immigrants) should only be available if matched by a grant from the appropriate local authority. For some years past the Consultative Committee has received £750 net from the Corporation. This does not compare favourably with the grants which other Community Relations Councils receive from their respective authorities. Examples of such grants are as follows:

Borough	Local Authority Contribution to Community Relations Council	Total population
Camden	£7,500	240,970
Derby	£1,600	128,430
Ealing	£4,100 + rent, rates, lighting and heating of offices	303,660
Hackney	£5,100	253,810
Hammersmith	£4,000	215,240
Luton	£2,500	146,000
Sheffiield	£6,500 + 2 welfare officers and 2 secretaries	
Slough	£3,000	
Westminster	£3,500	

You will observe that the number of Boroughs with populations far smaller than that of Nottingham contribute much more towards their Community Relations Councils. If only for the sake of her reputation, I am sure that the Queen of the Midlands would not wish to be outdone by smaller Authorities . . .

The Committee's grant was not increased. Indeed, three years later in the year 1972–3 it was still only £1,000.

It is also revealing that over the years, and compared with other LEAs, Nottingham has made relatively little extra provision for its coloured immigrant schoolchildren. It was pointed out in Chapter 5, that it is one of only a few authorities which have tried to get by without providing reception classes or an equivalent form of in-school provision for them. It is equally significant that the concession to Sikh bus conductors and drivers, which enabled them to wear turbans, came grudgingly and some time after similar concessions had been made elsewhere – including Wolverhampton which is often contrasted with Nottingham as having a less positive approach to race relations. Despite this record, as Katznelson showed in his enquiry, most of Nottingham's councillors seem to think that they have coped well or reasonably well with the problems arising from coloured immigration.[18]

It is not possible to derive recommendations for the improvement of race relations directly from the data contained in this book. However, it is possible to note some of the implications for policy formation which are suggested by it.

Given the continuation of existing trends it seems more likely that race relations will deteriorate than improve. The Nottingham Community Relations Council and the East Midlands Conciliation Committee of the Race Relations Board, the two existing bodies supported by the central government to try to improve race relations and combat racial discrimination, do not appear to be making any marked impact on the situation. This is because they are not well conceived rather than because they are relatively new or short of manpower and resources. The Community Relations Council has no clear or coherent strategy and its new parent-body, the Community Relations Commission, has not helped it to evolve one. Indeed it is possible to argue that the Commission itself lacks a clear and coherent strategy.[19] Whether it is in principle possible for it to develop an effective set of policies is doubtful. Two of the main themes running through this book have been the extent to which patterns of race relations are historically rooted and how much they may be affected by apparently unrelated decisions which are made without any serious consideration of the effect which they may have on race relations. For such reasons it is difficult to see how bodies resembling the present Community Relations Commission and its local Councils can bring about anything other than the most marginal of changes in race relations. Certainly it is difficult to envisage what steps could be taken by a local Community Relations Council to prevent the development of situations, in areas such as housing and employment, likely to cause a deterioration in race relations. It is also difficult to see how the existing machinery and mode of operation of the Race Relations Board and its local Conciliation Committees can bring about an end to racial discrimination. Moreover, if these latter bodies were to be more conspicuously successful then it is possible that, by creating resentment on the part of native whites, they might actually undermine the kind of work undertaken by Community Relations Councils. Without a new departure in policy there can be little hope of a genuine improvement in race relations.

The only alternative policy which seems to be under active consideration at present is the large-scale voluntary repatriation of coloured immigrants. This is strongly advocated by Enoch Powell, the Monday Club, the National Front and large sections of the native white population. There is nothing novel about the concept of repatriation. Indeed it is likely to emerge whenever those who do not understand the dynamics of the situation are in search of a simple solution to it. As Dilip Hiro has pointed out: 'The repatriation of blacks in England was first ordered by the Privy Council of Queen Elizabeth I in 1596 and concerned "divers blackamoores" who had "crept into the realm since the troubles between her Highness and the King of Spain".'[20] The same solution was proposed for the problem of the 'St Giles Blackbirds' in the eighteenth century – the mainly freed but unemployed slaves who had become concentrated in the common lodging-houses for the destitute in the St Giles area of London. They were offered free passage with £12 per head subsistence allowance to leave Britain and, in 1787, 351 blacks (and 60 white prostitutes, were shipped off to Sierra Leone.[21] Again, after the 1919 racial disturbances in Cardiff and other towns, there was a campaign for the repatriation of coloured people and a few of them did take advantage of free passages home.[22] But, however ancient the idea of repatriation, there is little reason to suppose that the schemes which are advocated at present will achieve what is intended for them.

Many immigrants still express an intention to return home and others are actually returning. But, unless the situation in Britain becomes desperate, it is unlikely that very many will choose to take advantage of a free passage home – even if they are also offered small financial inducements. Few immigrants wish to return home virtually empty-handed. To do so under the conditions envisaged by the advocates of repatriation would be an open admission of defeat. It would mean that the long period of time spent in Britain, with its attendant hardship and humiliation in many cases, would have been wasted. And, since conditions have changed so little in their countries of origin, a return might make them worse off than when they left. Provided that they are not virtually hounded out of the country most of them will probably stay on should a repatriation policy be introduced – but in an even more insecure and suspicious frame of mind than at present. This would be intensified by the harassment which would inevitably accompany such a policy. For those who see repatriation as a panacea there would be great disappointment and exasperation were it found not to work. It is hard to avoid the conclusion that some of the more exasperated of them might then try to *make* the policy succeed. All that is likely to follow either the continual demand for, or the actual introduction of, a large-scale scheme of repatriation is a further deterioration in race relations.[f]

Race relations are just as likely to deteriorate further if measures are not taken to ensure the ending of discrimination against those coloured people who remain in Britain. It is in this area, in particular, that a new departure in policy seems necessary. At the very least a complete recasting of the anti-discrimination machinery may be required. The extent of the change which will be needed may be illustrated by drawing an analogy between the prevention of disease and the prevention of discrimination. Although they are not exactly analogous, the comparison may be useful. At the present time the Conciliation Committees of the Race Relations Board are like poorly equipped, widely separated first-aid stations which are unknown to, too far away from, or which do not enjoy the confidence of many of those they are intended to help. Obviously if this were the only form of medical help available to the British people then disease would be much more prevalent than at present. Yet it is about the only sort of help available to those susceptible to discrimination. There is no equivalent of the general practitioner and casualty department services which ensure that prompt help is available to those who need it. Much more important, there is no equivalent of the public health system. However unglamorous it may be, there can be no doubt that it is this prophylactic form of medicine which has produced the most significant inroads into the incidence of disease in Britain over the past 150 years. Without such a system, the

[f]   This is apart from the havoc which would accompany a '*successful*' repatriation scheme. In June 1969, the Rt. Hon. Enoch Powell outlined a scheme for the repatriation of 600,000 to 700,000 immigrants over a period of 'ten years or more'. Unless such a scheme included a legally enforceable provision to *prevent* immigrants from leaving the country unless and until the administrators of the scheme thought fit, it would be remarkable if the outflow did not create very great difficulties in Britain. The hospital and public transport systems and many other industries and individual firms would experience the most acute problems and could even collapse if tens of thousands (quite apart from hundreds of thousands) of immigrants were to leave. Yet neither this nor the likely consequences of retaliatory measures from other countries has been publicly discussed by Powell. His claim that his views and proposals derive from the fact that he, unlike other politicians, is acting responsibly about the problem must be judged against his failure to give close attention to such eventualities.

provision of curative medicine would be hopelessly inadequate. If racial discrimination is to be effectively ended it seems imperative that an equivalent form of control be introduced. Thus, in addition to an improved complaints and conciliation procedure, there seems to be a need for a regular and systematic monitoring of such things as recruitment and promotions, and housing enquiries and allocations. This must be combined with more adequate means to enforce compliance with the law. At the moment there is no equivalent of the public health inspectorate in the machinery devised to prevent discrimination. Yet there can be no doubt that the efficiency of the public health system rests very much upon the size and vigilance of its inspectorate. No one today would consider that it should rely solely or even mainly on the goodwill of those it supervises. However, this is precisely what those who work to try to prevent racial discrimination are expected to do. It may be argued that the kind of approach which has been outlined is impracticable. Others will argue that such means of ensuring fair and equal opportunities are no less objectionable, and perhaps even more objectionable, than discrimination itself. Nevertheless, it is difficult to see how discrimination can be prevented without recourse to this kind of machinery.

It may also be objected that, given the existing prevalence of antipathy towards coloured people, the more successful such measures to curb discrimination the more hostility is likely to be aroused in the native white population. In other words, the successful pursuance of racial equality is likely to exacerbate race relations. This is certainly a very real possibility. But, as it seems that the nature of British feelings towards coloured people are such that they are not easily changed, they must, at least for the present, be taken as a 'given' in any analysis. The likely consequence of yielding to expressions of hostility seems to have been made abundantly clear by the events at the Mansfield Hosiery Mills. Retreats of the kind practised by the management of that firm buy only a temporary peace and, in the long run, some kind of confrontation is probably inevitable. The short period of relief which may be earned by giving way is only likely to increase the intensity of a later confrontation. This does not mean that there is no point in being sensitive to such possibilities and that it is not worth trying to minimise their effects. Nor does it mean that there should not be continued efforts to improve race relations by educational means. It does mean that it would be courting a further deterioration in race relations if curbs on discrimination were to wait on the uncertain effects of such measures.

The degree of any native white hostility which does arise will in part be a function of the kind of circumstances which exist at the time that curbs on discrimination begin to bite. If the conditions are of a sort which increase feelings of insecurity and threat then hostility may be marked. If they are more favourable then an improvement in the position of coloured people may go virtually unchallenged. This seems to be one of the clearest implications of the analysis presented in this book. It means that there is unlikely to be a great improvement in race relations until there is a change in the distribution of resources and opportunities within the wider society. So long as large numbers of native whites feel conspicuously deprived there is likely to be opposition to any advances made by coloured people. A marked, long-term improvement in race relations seems impossible without conditions of full employment, an adequate supply of decent housing and a sufficient redistribution of resources to at least ensure that the effects of inflation are felt more uniformly than at present. Any attempt to improve race relations which relies on an attack on a more narrow front is unlikely to succeed.

The removal of such sources of insecurity would not eliminate all the factors which make for conflict between racial groups. For example, the difficulties which result from differences in culture and from a simple dislike of being in close proximity to members of another racial group would remain. I must also emphasise that the changes which I have suggested may be required to obtain an improvement in race relations do not constitute, and are not offered as, a 'solution'. No blue-print can be prepared for such a complex and deeply-rooted problem. But some avenues are more likely to lead to desirable results than others – and those that are being followed and most vociferously advocated at present do not look promising.

Appendix 1
The survey

The research on which this book is based began, not as a study of race relations, but as a study of the political views and activities of coloured immigrants in Nottingham. I mention this because by the time the focus had shifted from that of a narrowly-conceived exercise in political sociology, to a broader study of race relations, several irrevocable decisions had been taken on the research design. The most important is that it had already been decided that the most profitable use of the resources available would derive from concentrating attention on a single Parliamentary constituency. Of the three feasible alternatives Nottingham Central had been selected for it contained a larger number of coloured immigrants than either Nottingham South or Nottingham West.

This early decision meant that two areas of high immigrant concentration (Lenton and the Meadows), which would otherwise have been included in the research area, were excluded. Nevertheless, the research area did still contain, according to the 1966 Sample Census, 58·25 per cent of all those coloured Commonwealth immigrants who lived in the city. So, especially as the excluded areas were not markedly different from those included, it does not seem improper to refer to the sample as one of coloured immigrants *in Nottingham*.

To obtain a representative sample of any minority group is no easy matter.[1] Indeed the difficulty of obtaining adequate sampling frames often makes it impossible. In this instance, the only ready-made frame which could be considered for use was the electoral register. It was quite inappropriate, however, for I was just as interested in those immigrants who had not registered as those who had. The absence of a suitable frame seemed to leave only three possibilities. One, the use of quota sampling; two, some form of participant observation; or, three, the construction of a special sampling frame. Of these three alternatives quota sampling could not be used because it demanded a degree of advance information on the structure of the population to be studied which did not exist. Participant observation was also out of the question, not least because it would have required a more or less full-time commitment which my circumstances did not allow. Thus, even though the resources at my disposal would not enable a complete frame to be constructed, of the three possible alternatives the third seemed to be the most sensible choice.

A sample of 150 streets was drawn from the electoral register and each dwelling in them was visited.[a] Every male of voting age who could be contacted was asked if he

[a] This particular number was chosen simply because it did not seem possible to cover more than 150 streets with the resources available.

had been registered to vote in the 1966 General Election. If so, he was also asked if he had voted. Respondents were *not* asked to disclose the name of the candidate for whom they had voted. After the answers to these questions had been noted, along with the name and address of the respondent, the interviewer recorded his impression of the respondent's racial origin.

2,436 males of voting age were contacted in this way. Although it is not known how many were not contacted, it is possible to give a reasonable estimate. The Electoral Register in operation at the time of the 1966 Election showed the 150 streets to contain approximately 3,870 male voters.[b] However, the results of a study carried out by the Government Social Survey suggest that between 3·5 per cent and 4 per cent of those eligible to be registered would not have been registered.[2] If in this case, a figure of 3·75 per cent is assumed, and if it is further assumed that exactly half of those who were not registered were women, then the figure of 3,870 represents just over 98 per cent of the potential male electorate of the 150 streets concerned. In short, the potential male electorate must have been in the region of 3,940. But between the qualifying date for the register (late 1965) and the period when the frame was constructed (late 1966) three other factors may have altered this figure. They are: (1) movement from the 150 streets; (2) movement into them; and (3) deaths amongst the potential male electorate of the streets. By comparing the number of males on the 1966–7 register with those on the 1967–8 register, in the streets concerned, it was possible to estimate the size and direction of such changes. It was found that the latter register contained 201 fewer male names than the earlier one. Thus it is reasonable to work on the assumption that the number of males of voting age who could have been contacted was about 3,740. In other words those actually contacted constitute, so far as is possible to judge, at least 65 per cent of those who could have been contacted.

Had more money been available (the total research grant was only £750) it would have been very easy to improve upon this figure by making further calls to those dwellings where it was known that respondents had been missed. Nevertheless, as such a sizeable minority does seem to have been missed, it is important to note the result of the one check it is possible to make on the representativeness of those contacted.

The official turnout rate recorded for Nottingham Central in the 1966 General Election was 67·74 per cent. That calculated for those interviewed in the 150 streets who were registered to vote was 69·03 per cent. Some slight discrepancy in this direction is to be expected, of course, and does not suggest a bias in the sample. This is because electoral registers are always out of date to some extent when an election takes place and, as a result, the official turnout recorded is always less than the 'real' turnout. Consequently, though this does not constitute proof of the representativeness of the sampling frame, the very close similarity between the figures certainly does not suggest the existence of any particular bias.

Of the respondents contacted, 291 were coloured immigrants. As it did not seem likely that it would be possible to conduct more than about 300 interviews in total, it was

[b]   It is not possible to give an exact figure because the fore-names of electors are not always recorded and because it is not always clear from a fore-name whether or not an elector is male.

decided to interview a 50 per cent random sample of them, i.e. 145. A sample of the same size was drawn from the remaining white respondents.

The interviews with the white respondents were conducted by students from Nottingham University and a response rate of 85·5 per cent was achieved. Though no special problems were involved in this part of the research, up to eight visits were necessary, in some cases, to obtain such a satisfactory response rate.

The interviews with the immigrants did present special problems. The most obvious difficulty was that of communication. No less important, however, and much more difficult to overcome, was the suspicion of the immigrants. I would certainly agree with Marsh's observation that: 'Any sociologist who simply goes along to interview Punjabis armed with a notebook and interview schedule expecting to get replies to direct questions is in for a rude shock.'[3] Indeed I would add that the same applies to West Indian immigrants. However, (and here I differ with Marsh) this understandable suspicion does not rule out the use of relatively formal interviews. By taking the following precautions a response rate of 84 per cent was obtained and, in all but a handful of cases, those involved felt convinced at the end of the interviews that the respondents had been frank with us.

1. A great deal of time, both prior to and during the interviewing programme, was spent amongst the immigrants in ways not connected with the research. This involved formal occasions, for instance Independence Day celebrations and visits to the Sikh Temple; more informal occasions such as meals with families on feast days; and quite informal occasions in pubs and similar contexts. Though the pay-off from such contact cannot be quantified I believe it was considerable. Perhaps the most important aspect of it was that it helped to remove something of the gulf which usually exists between the researcher and his respondents, and certainly this contact did prove helpful on two occasions when interviews were made possible by suggesting that uncertain respondents seek advice from respected mutual acquaintances.

2. Wherever possible I was accompanied by a friend of a similar ethnic origin to the respondent at the initial contact. These 'sponsors' played a vital role and without them both the number and quality of the interviews would have been severely impaired. Indeed when it proved necessary to conduct some interviews with West Indians, towards the end of the interviewing programme, without the help of a sponsor, the response rate was markedly low. This is undoubtedly because the sponsors were much more capable of reassuring respondents about the objectives of the research and overcoming the suspicion to which reference has been made. It is also worth noting that those sponsors who most often accompanied me did not belong to Nottingham. This avoided the possibility of their being identified as members of particular factions within Nottingham's immigrant communities.

3. The reason for our visit was stated at the beginning of each contact. However, the interview did not proceed until it was felt that a satisfactory rapport had been established. This sometimes meant that considerable time was spent in various kinds of 'preliminaries'. In such cases, when it was felt appropriate, the purpose of our visit was re-introduced and usually it was then possible to proceed without difficulty. Those who remained uncertain were encouraged to take time to consider, rather than make up their

mind on the spot, and a return visit arranged. In almost all cases considerable hospitality was received and, in the large majority, respondents clearly welcomed the opportunity to air their views and tell their stories.

4. If the sponsor judged that my presence would limit the frankness of the interview I would leave and he or she would continue alone. But, even in such cases, our impression was that meeting the person directly responsible for the research served only to reassure respondents. Had I not been present at any stage it would have only served to create more suspicion.

5. Though the interview schedule was quite structured, it was usually possible to create a relatively informal and relaxed atmosphere during the interviews. This was made easier by the inclusion of a large number of open-ended questions in the schedule; tape-recording most of the interviews (which had the virtue of allowing the respondent to digress as and when he pleased, as well as freeing the interviewer from the burden of note-taking); and conducting the interview in the respondent's mother tongue.

As in the case of the white sample up to eight visits were made in an effort to contact some respondents. Flexibility was also demanded. After eight unsuccessful visits to one Indian respondent it was learned (from one of his Indian workmates) that he knew of our visits and would very much like to be interviewed. Unfortunately his hours of work had caused us to miss him on each occasion. Eventually an interview was held – beginning at 6.45 a.m.

Appendix 2
Nottingham's future housing programme

In April 1972 Nottingham Corporation issued its new Clearance and Improvement
Programme. Extracts from the statement which accompanied the programme and
details of the programme are included below. Perhaps the most significant feature of the
proposals is the new emphasis on house improvement – as against the wholesale demolition of areas of poor housing. Even so, of the estimated 35,013 houses involved in the
programme over the period 1971–81, 20,500 will come down as compared to the
14,513 which will be improved, i.e. 59 per cent of the total will be pulled down. Although
the proportion of houses demolished rather than improved will fall over the ten year
period, even in the last year of the programme there will still be more houses being
demolished than improved. This is likely to mean a further significant reduction in the
number of dwelling units in the central city area available to the city's households
(assuming that they remain at a constant number). So, although this new departure in
the programme may slow down the trends outlined in Chapter 4, it will certainly not halt
or reverse them and there seems to be no need for any of the conclusions in that chapter
to be revised.

The Corporation's Clearance and Improvement Programme

Following a city-wide survey into the condition of housing in Nottingham, the
appropriate Committee of the City Council have recently approved a further
programme of clearance areas and a new programme for the declaration of
general improvement areas has also been approved . . .

   . . . It should be clearly noted that both programmes may be altered in the light
of changing circumstances. Indeed consideration is being given at present to the
possibility of achieving some acceleration in the clearance programme.

   As far as the clearance programme is concerned, this constitutes an extension
of the earlier clearance programme and covers the period from 1974–5 onwards.
At that time clearance in the St Ann's Well Area will be well advanced . . . The
improvement programme is a new departure on the part of the Corporation and
is intended to try to avoid the disadvantages of wholesale clearance. In this way
it will be possible to preserve existing communities at the same time as improving
their standard of housing. This approach can only be adopted where the
majority of houses in the area are sufficiently sound to justify retention for at
least 30 years after improvement.

   The main aim will be to secure the improvement of the houses, especially by the installation of amenities such as kitchens, bathrooms, internal WCs and hot and cold running water, which the houses may lack at present. Under existing legislation improvement grants will be available.

Once the area is declared a general improvement area, the Corporation will themselves improve the environment by providing such amenities as garaging or play spaces; they may carry out tree planting, etc. and in some cases may introduce traffic management schemes. When each prospective improvement area is surveyed in detail, some individual houses may be found to be unfit for human habitation; if so, they will be made the subject of official representations under Parts II or III of the Housing Act 1957 with a view to their clearance.

P. M. Vine, MA, LLB.

Town Clerk and Chief Executive Officer

Table 33 Nottingham's clearance and improvement programme, 1971–81

	No. houses to be cleared	No. houses to be improved
1971–2	1,905	69
1972–3	2,155	883
1973–4	2,070	1,645
1974–5	2,140	1,652
1975–6	2,180	1,661
1976–7	2,150	1,763
1977–8	2,150	1,910
1978–9	2,080	1,649
1979–80	2,030	1,645
1980–1	1,640	1,636
No. houses	20,500	14,513

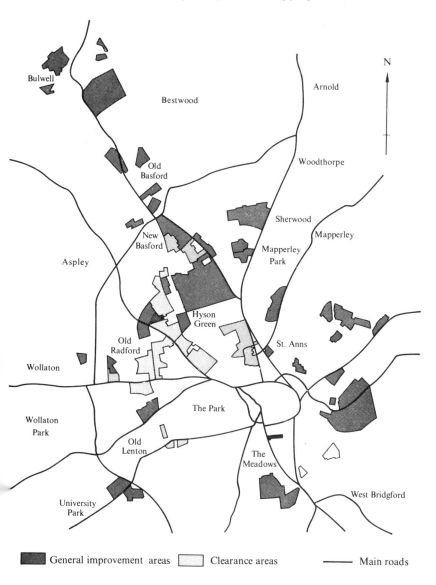

Map 3 Programme of clearance and general improvement areas

Notes to chapters

Chapter 1: Introduction

1. Nottingham Commonwealth Citizens Consultative Committee, 'Reports of Surveys on West Indians at Work in Nottingham and the Employment Experiences of Asians in Nottingham' (1969).
2. Elizabeth Burney, *Housing on Trial* (London, Oxford University Press, for Institute of Race Relations, 1967), Chapters 7 and 8.
3. Ira Katznelson, 'The Politics of Racial Buffering in Nottingham, 1954–68', *Race*, vol. 11, no. 4 (April 1970).
4. E. J. B. Rose and associates, *Colour and Citizenship* (London, Oxford University Press, for Institute of Race Relations, 1969), Chapter 28.
5. *Daily Sketch*, 1 September 1958.
6. Robert A. Burt, 'Colour Prejudice in Britain' (Unpublished thesis, University of Princeton, 1960), p. 49.
7. Burney (1967), p. 204; W. W. Daniel, *Racial Discrimination in England* (London, Pelican, 1968), Introduction by M. Abrams p. 10 and Mary Grigg, *The White Question* (London, Secker and Warburg, 1967), p. 138.
8. James Wickenden, *Colour in Britain* (London, Oxford University Press, for Institute of Race Relations, 1958).
9. R. B. Davison, *Commonwealth Immigrants* (London, Oxford University Press, for Institute of Race Relations, 1958), p. 53.
10. Grigg (1967), p. 138.
11. Quoted by Katznelson, 'The Politics of Racial Buffering in Nottingham', *Race*, 11 (1970), pp. 431–2.
12. Burt (1960), p. 49.
13. Quoted by Katznelson, 'The Politics of Racial Buffering in Nottingham', pp. 431–2.
14. *Evening Post*, 8 August 1964.
15. Grigg (1967), p. 139.
16. *Evening Post*, 1968.
17. *Evening Post*, 'Special Supplement on School Leavers', May 1968.
18. Commonwealth Citizens Consultative Committee, 'Minutes', 28 November 1967.
19. *Evening Post*, 16 January 1970.
20. *Evening Post*, 27 April 1967.
21. *Evening Post*, 29 April 1968.
22. Rose (1969), p. 553.
23. *Evening Post*, 19 November 1968.
24. John Heilpern and Dilip Hiro, 'The Town We Were Told Was Tolerant', *Observer*, 1 December 1968.
25. Katznelson, 'The Politics of Racial Buffering in Nottingham', p. 445.
26. A. Marsh, 'Race, Community and Anxiety', *New Society*, vol. 23, no. 542 (22 February 1973).
27. Katznelson, 'The Politics of Racial Buffering in Nottingham', p. 441.

Chapter 2: The immigrants

1. M. Banton, *Race Relations* (London, Tavistock, 1967), Chapter 15.
2. For a useful introduction to the views of the Rt. Hon. J. Enoch Powell on repatriation see B. Smithies and P. Fiddick, *Enoch Powell and Immigration* (London, Sphere Books, 1969).
3. Orlando Patterson, *The Sociology of Slavery* (London, Macgibbon and Kee, 1967), p. 9.
4. Katrin Norris, *Jamaica, The Search for Identity* (London, Oxford University Press, for Institute of Race Relations, 1962), p. 2.
5. Norris (1962), p. 5.
6. Ibid. pp. 5, 11 and 40.
7. Ibid. p. 11.
8. Ibid. p. 7.
9. Ibid. p. 79.
10. Ibid. p. 73.
11. Ibid. p. 12.
12. Ibid. pp. 39 and 77.
13. M. G. Smith, *The Plural Society in the British West Indies* (Berkeley, University of California Press, 1965), pp. 166–7.
14. Norris (1962), p. 7.
15. Ceri Peach, *West Indian Migration to Britain* (London, Oxford University Press, for Institute of Race Relations, 1968), pp. 2–3.
16. G. W. Roberts, 'Review of *West Indian Migration to Britain*', *Race*, vol. 12, no. 2 (October 1970).
17. Peach (1968), p. 92.
18. Ibid. p. 93.
19. Roberts, 'Review of *West Indian Migration to Britain*', *Race*, 12 (1970), p. 247.
20. P. Marsh, *The Anatomy of a Strike* (London, Institute of Race Relations Special Research Series, 1967), p. 5.
21. Rose (1969), p. 52.
22. Marsh (1967), p. 3.
23. Ibid. p. 5.
24. Ibid. p. 7.
25. Kusum Nair, *Blossoms in the Dust* (London, Duckworth, 1961), p. 112.
26. Ibid. footnote to p. 112.
27. Rose (1969), p. 54.
28. Marsh (1967), pp. 7–8.
29. Rose (1969), p. 59.
30. Ibid. p. 70.
31. Ibid.
32. Stuart B. Philpott, 'Remittances, Social Networks and Choice among Montserratian Migrants in Britain', *Man*, vol. 3, no. 3 (September 1968).
33. Sheila Patterson, *Dark Strangers* (London, Pelican, 1965), p. 71.
34. W. H. Israel, *Colour and Community* (Slough Council of Social Service, 1964), p. 73.
35. D. Brooks, 'Who Will Go Back?', *Race Today*, vol. 1, no. 5 (September 1969).
36. Rose (1969), footnote on p. 473.
37. Israel (1964), p. 73.
38. Rose (1969), p. 473.
39. J. Rex and R. Moore, *Race, Community and Conflict* (London, Oxford University Press, for Institute of Race Relations, 1967), p. 111.
40. R. B. Davison, *Black British* (London, Oxford University Press, for Institute of Race Relations, 1966), p. 106.
41. Lord Walston, 'Repatriation: Why is it Wrong', *Race Today*, vol. 1, no. 1 (May 1969), p. 7.

42. See, for example, Brooks, 'Who Will Go Back?', *Race Today*, 1 (1969), p. 132 and R. Jowell and G. Hoinville, 'Do Polls Influence Voters?', *New Society*, no. 358, p. 206.
43. Brooks, 'Who Will Go Back?', p. 132.
44. Ibid. p. 134.
45. Address to the Annual Conference of Rotary Clubs of London at Eastbourne, 16 November 1968. Quoted by Smithies and Fiddick (1969), pp. 75–6.
46. Philpott, 'Remittances, Social Networks and Choice', *Man*, 3 (1968), pp. 465–6.
47. Ibid. p. 468.
48. Ibid. p. 474.
49. Paul C. P. Siu, 'The Sojourner', *American Journal of Sociology*, vol. 58 (July 1952).
50. Nottingham Commonwealth Citizens Consultative Committee, 'West Indians at Work', (1969), p. 3.
51. Nottingham Commonwealth Citizens Consultative Committee, 'Employment Experiences of Indians and Pakistanis', (1969), pp. 4–5.
52. Betty Davison, 'No Place Back Home: A Study of Jamaicans Returning to Kingston, Jamaica', *Race*, vol. 9, no. 4 (April 1968).
53. R. Desai, *Indian Immigrants in Britain* (London, Oxford University Press, for Institute of Race Relations, 1963).
54. Rose (1969), p. 434.

Chapter 3: Prejudice and the indigenous population

1. E. J. B. Rose and associates, *Colour and Citizenship* (London, Oxford University Press, for Institute of Race Relations, 1969), Chapter 28.
2. Rose (1969), p. 551.
3. M. Abrams, 'Attitudes of Whites towards Blacks', *Listener*, (6 November 1969), p. 623.
4. Rose (1969), p. 737.
5. Brian Lapping, 'Review of *Colour and Citizenship*', *New Society* (10 July 1969).
6. Rose (1969), p. 603.
7. Ibid. p. 552.
8. Ibid.
9. Daniel Lawrence, 'How Prejudiced Are We?', *Race Today*, vol. 1, no. 6 (October 1969) and 'The Incidence of Race Prejudice in Britain', paper presented to the Race Relations Group of the British Sociological Association (January 1970).
10. Oliver C. Cox, *Caste, Class and Race* (New York, Doubleday, 1948), p. 393.
11. Nathan Ackerman and Marie Jahoda, *Antisemitism and Emotional Disorder* (New York, Harper and Row, 1950), pp. 3–4.
12. G. E. Simpson and J. M. Yinger, *Racial and Cultural Minorities* (New York, Harper and Row, 1965), p. 12.
13. Rose (1969), pp. 567 and 571.
14. For a discussion of the content of school history books see Frank Glendenning, 'Racial Stereotypes in History Textbooks', *Race Today*, vol. 3, no. 2 (February 1971), pp. 52–4.
15. Rose (1969), p. 552.
16. Nicholas Deakin, *Colour, Citizenship and British Society* (London, Panther, 1970).
17. Ibid. p. 10.
18. Ibid. pp. 318–19.
19. Carey McWilliams, *Brothers Under the Skin*, rev. edn. (New York, Little Brown, 1951), pp. 315–17. Quoted by Simpson and Yinger (1965), p. 14.
20. Central Statistical Office, *Social Trends*, no. 1 (HMSO, 1970), p. 82.
21. K. Coates and R. Silburn, *Poverty: The Forgotten Englishmen* (London, Penguin Special, 1970).

Chapter 4: Race relations and housing

1.   C. J. Thomas, 'Geographical Aspects of the Growth of the Residential Area of Greater Nottingham' (Unpublished Ph.D thesis, University of Nottingham, 1968), p. 38.
2.   J. D. Chambers, *Modern Nottingham in the Making* (Nottingham Journal Ltd, 1945), p. 1.
3.   S. D. Chapman (ed.), *The History of Working-Class Housing* (London, David and Charles, 1971), p. 135.
4.   Ibid. p. 153.
5.   Ibid. p. 150.
6.   Quoted by Chapman, Ibid. p. 152.
7.   Quoted by Chapman, Ibid. p. 157.
8.   Quoted by Chapman, Ibid. p. 158.
9.   T. H. Marshall, *Social Policy* (London, Hutchinson, 1965), p. 70.
10. Department of the Environment, *Fair Deal for Housing*, Cmnd. 4728 (HMSO, 1971), p. 1.
11. Susan Stone, 'Private Landlords in Nottingham. Problems, Prospects and Policies', (Unpublished M.A. thesis, University of Nottingham, 1968), p. 111.
12. *Fair Deal for Housing* (1971), p. 1.
13. For a brief discussion of this classification see Select Committee on Race Relations and Immigration, Visit to Nottingham in the Session 1970–1, 'Minutes of Evidence' (HMSO, 1971), p. 346.
14. J. Rex and R. Moore, *Race, Community and Conflict. A Study of Sparkbrook* (London, Oxford University Press, for Institute of Race Relations, 1967); J. Rex, 'The Sociology of a Zone of Transition', in R. E. Pahl (ed.), *Readings in Urban Sociology* (London, Pergamon, 1968); and J: Rex, 'The Concept of Housing Class and the Sociology of Race Relations', *Race*, vol. 12, no. 3 (January 1971).
15. Rex and Moore (1967), p. 36.
16. Rex, 'The Sociology of a Zone of Transition', in Pahl (1968), pp. 214–15.
17. Rex and Moore (1967), pp. 273–4.
18. Rex, 'The Sociology of a Zone of Transition', p. 214.
19. Rex and Moore (1967), p. 275.
20. Ibid. p. 9.
21. Rex, 'The Sociology of a Zone of Transition', p. 214.
22. Ibid. p. 216.
23. Ibid. p. 215.
24. Ibid. p. 223.
25. Ibid. p. 227.
26. Valerie Karn, 'A Note on *Race, Community and Conflict. A Study of Sparkbrook*', *Race*, vol. 9, no. 1 (July 1967); J. Rex and R. Moore, 'A Reply to Valerie Karn', *Race*, vol. 9, no. 1 (July 1967); J. G. Davies and J. Taylor, 'Race, Community and No Conflict', *New Society*, (9 July 1970); and A. H. Richmond, 'Housing and Racial Attitudes in Bristol', *Race*, vol. 12, no. 1 (July 1970).
27. Richmond, 'Housing and Racial Attitudes in Bristol', *Race*, 12 (1970).
28. Rex and Moore (1967), pp. 73–4.
29. Ibid. p. 93.
30. Ibid. p. 109.
31. Ibid. p. 127.
32. J. R. Lambert and Camilla Filkin, 'Race Relations and Research: Some Issues of Approach and Application', *Race*, vol. 12, no. 3 (January 1971), p. 332.
33. Rex, 'The Concept of Housing Class and the Sociology of Race Relations', *Race*, 12 (1971), p. 298.
34. Ibid.
35. K. Coates and R. Silburn, *St Anns: Poverty, Deprivation and Morale in a Nottingham Community* (University of Nottingham Adult Education Department, 1967), p. 81.

36. *Evening Post*, 5 February 1972.
37. R. Gosling, *St Anns* (Nottingham Civic Society, 1967), p. 2.
38. Rex, 'The Sociology of a Zone of Transition', p. 212.
39. Ibid. p. 216.
40. Rex, 'The Concept of Housing Class and the Sociology of Race Relations', p. 296.
41. Rex and Moore (1967), p. 30.
42. Karn, 'A Note on *Race, Community and Conflict*', *Race*, 9 (1967).
43. W. G. Runciman, *Relative Deprivation and Social Justice. A Study of Attitudes to Social Inequality in Twentieth-Century England* (London, Routledge and Kegan Paul, 1966), particularly pp. 192–208.
44. See, for example, the evidence given by the Nottingham and District Estate Agents Association and Mr. G. W. Webster of the Nottingham Building Society to the Select Committee on Race Relations and Immigration during its visit to Nottingham, 'Minutes of Evidence, 1970–1' (HMSO, 1971), pp. 304–12.
45. W. W. Daniel, *Racial Discrimination in England* (London, Pelican, 1968).
46. For a discussion of the techniques employed by the PEP research team see R. Ward, 'A Note on the Testing of Discrimination', *Race*, vol. 11, no. 2 (October 1969); and the contributions by W. W. Daniel and Robin Ward, *Race*, vol. 11, no. 3 (January 1970), pp. 352–70.
47. PEP, *Report on Racial Discrimination* (London, PEP, 1967) p. 11.
48. For a series of articles on the workings of the Race Relations Act see *Race Today*, vol. 3, nos. 10 and 11 (October and November 1971).
49. PEP, *Report on Racial Discrimination* (1967), p. 10.
50. Select Committee on Race Relations and Immigration, 'Minutes of Evidence', p. 305.
51. Ibid. p. 309.
52. Ibid. p. 277.
53. Morris Janowitz (ed.), *W. I. Thomas on Social Organisations and Social Personality, Selected Papers* (Chicago, University of Chicago Press, 1966), p. 301.
54. Select Committee, 'Minutes of Evidence', p. 336.
55. Ibid. p. 348.
56. Ibid. pp. 319–20.
57. Elizabeth Burney, *Housing on Trial* (London, Oxford University Press, for Institute of Race Relations, 1967), p. 200.
58. Select Committee, 'Minutes of Evidence', p. 344.
59. Nottingham Corporation Housing Department, 'Annual Report 1966–7'.
60. R. Silburn, 'Housing Problems and Performance in Nottingham' (unpublished paper, 1970), p. 5.
61. Burney (1967), p. 199.
62. Nottingham Corporation City Planning Department, *St Anns. Renewal in Progress* (1970), p. 4.
63. Nottingham Corporation City Planning Department, *The Meadows District Plan* (1971), p. 8.
64. Nottingham Fair Housing Group, 'Annual Report' (1969–70).
65. C. Bagley, 'Those Not Rehoused', *New Society*, (21 May 1970).
66. Select Committee, 'Minutes of Evidence', pp. 297 and 353.
67. Nottingham Fair Housing Group, 'Annual Report' (1971–2), p. 6.
68. Nottingham Fair Housing Group, *Somewhere to Live* (1971), p. 13.

Chapter 5: Race relations and employment

1. Ceri Peach, *West Indian Migration to Britain. A Social Geography* (London, Oxford University Press, for Institute of Race Relations, 1968), p. 67.
2. Ibid. p. 70.
3. Ibid. p. 75.

4.   Ibid. p. 79.
5.   Ibid. p. 82.
6.   Peter L. Wright, *The Coloured Worker in British Industry* (London, Oxford University Press, for Institute of Race Relations, 1968), pp. 42–50.
7.   Ibid. pp. 46–7:
8.   Ibid. p. 49.
9.   East Midlands Planning Council, *The East Midlands Study* (HMSO, 1967), p. 2.
10.   Ibid. p. 7.
11.   I am grateful to the East Midlands Planning Council who provided me with the figures on which Table 18 is based.
12.   East Midlands Planning Council, *The East Midlands Study*, p. 21.
13.   Ibid. p. 23.
14.   J. D. Chambers, *Modern Nottingham in the Making* (Nottingham Journal Ltd, 1945), p. 4.
15.   S. D. Chapman, 'Inventors and Technologists', in K. C. Edwards (ed.), *Nottingham and its Region* (British Association for the Advancement of Science, 1966), p. 515.
16.   F. A. Wells, 'Industrial Structure', in Edwards (1966), p. 406.
17.   Ibid. p. 407.
18.   Ibid. p. 410.
19.   F. A. Wells, 'Present Day Economic Structure', in Edwards (1966).
20.   These figures are taken from the 1966 Sample Census Economic Activity Leaflet for Nottinghamshire.
21.   F. A. Wells, 'Industrial Structure', in Edwards (1966), p. 412.
22.   Ruth Glass, *The Newcomers* (London, Allen and Unwin, 1960).
23.   The official journal of the then Ministry of Labour Staff Association.
24.   W. F. Maunder, 'The New Jamaican Migration', Social and Economic Studies, vol. 4 (1955); G. E. Cumper, 'Working-Class Migrants to the U.K., October 1955', *Social and Economic Studies*, vol. 6 (1957); G. W. Roberts and D. O. Mills, 'Study of External Migration Affecting Jamaica, 1953–5', *Social and Economic Studies*, vol. 7 (1958); and R. B. Davison, *West Indian Migrants* (London, Oxford University Press, for Institute of Race Relations, 1962). The main findings of these studies are summarised and discussed by Wright (1968), pp. 30–40.
25.   Wright (1968), p. 35.
26.   Ibid. pp. 36–7.
27.   D. Beetham, *Immigrant School Leavers and the Youth Employment Services in Birmingham* (London, Institute of Race Relations Special Research Series, 1968) and Dipak Nandy, 'Unrealistic Aspirations', *Race Today*, vol. 1, no. 1 (May 1969), pp. 9–11.
28.   I am grateful to the Nottingham Office of the Department of Employment and Productivity for making this information available to me.
29.   For a discussion of the DEP's policy of keeping statistics on the unemployment of coloured immigrants see Michael Marshall, 'Counting the Black Unemployed', *Race Today*, vol. 3, no. 2 (February 1971).
30.   I am grateful to Mr Everett and Mr Haworth of the London Office of the Department of Employment for drawing my attention to the unpublished Census data on which Table 20 is based.
31.   Nottingham Commonwealth Citizens Consultative Committee, 'Reports of Surveys on West Indians at Work in Nottingham and of the Employment Experiences of Asians in Nottingham in 1966' (1969), Tables 12 and 11 respectively.
32.   K. Little, *Negroes in Britain* (London, Kegan Paul Trench, Trubner and Co. Ltd, 1947), p. 61.
33.   S. Collins, *Coloured Minorities in Britain* (London, Lutterworth, 1957), pp. 213–14.
34.   Ibid. pp. 214–15.
35.   Carole Blair, 'Two Bills, One Fight', *Race Today*, vol. 3, no. 3 (March 1971).
36.   Nottingham Commonwealth Citizens Consultative Committee, 'Minutes of Employment Sub-Committee', 28 November 1967.

37. Race Relations Board, 'Annual Report 1971–2' (HMSO, 1972), pp. 38–9.
38. Roger Jowell and Patricia Prescott-Clarke, 'Discrimination and White Collar Workers in Britain', *Race*, vol. 11, no. 4 (April 1970).
39. Ibid. p. 412.
40. Ibid. p. 413.
41. For a study of immigrant achievement in the Schools of Inner London see Alan Little *et al*, 'The Education of Immigrant Pupils in Inner London Primary Schools', *Race*, vol. 9, no. 4 (April 1968).
42. George Jackson, 'The Education of Immigrant Children in Nottingham', *Institute of Race Relations Newsletter* (February 1966), pp. 10–11.
43. For a survey of the various administrative arrangements see N. Hawkes, *Immigrant Children in British Schools* (London, Pall Mall Press, 1966).
44. Department of Education and Science, *The Education of Immigrants: Education Survey 13* (HMSO, 1971), p. 33.
45. Hawkes (1966), pp. 46–7.
46. Letter to the Acting Secretary of the Commonwealth Citizens Consultative Committee dated 1 January 1970.
47. Jackson, 'The Education of Immigrant Children in Nottingham' (1966), p. 11.
48. Commonwealth Citizens Consultative Committee, 'Minutes of Integration Sub-Committee', 10 January 1967.
49. 'Minutes of Integration Sub-Committee', 6 March 1967.
50. 'Minutes of Integration Sub-Committee', 17 July 1967.
51. 'Minutes of Integration Sub-Committee', 4 December 1968.
52. Commonwealth Citizens Consultative Committee, 'Minutes', 7 July 1969.
53. Letter from Nottingham's Director of Education to the Commonwealth Citizens Consultative Committee (by then renamed the Community Relations Council) 22 April 1970.
54. For more details see the Community Relations Council Report on the Summer School.
55. Letter to the Community Relations Council, 8 March 1971.
56. Richard Bourne, 'One Summer of Acrimony', *Guardian*, 10 September 1971.
57. See the Report on the 1971 Summer School.
58. Lancelot Christopher, 'West Indian Education in Crisis', *Race Today*, vol. 4, no. 6 (June 1972).
59. Letter to Commonwealth Citizens Consultative Committee, 1 January 1970.
60. These figures have been calculated from the statistics contained in three documents issued by Nottingham Corporation's Education Committee
    1. Immigrant Children Return (to the DES, January 1972).
    2. Report of the Director on the Number of Coloured Pupils: March 1972.
    3. Twelfth Report of the Organiser for Work with the Coloured Immigrant Community (1971–2).
61. What is known is reported annually by the Organiser for Work with the Coloured Immigrant Community in his Report to the Education Committee. At the time of writing a study of white and coloured school-leavers was being undertaken by Mr. P. Vincent, a research student in the Sociology Department, University of Nottingham.
62. Nottingham Corporation Education Committee, 'Twelfth Report of the Organiser for Work with the Coloured Immigrant Community' (1971–2), p. 8.
63. Notts./Derbys. Sub-Regional Planning Unit, *Nottinghamshire and Derbyshire Sub-Regional Study* (1969), pp. 4–5.

Chapter 6: Race relations and politics

1. Paul Foot, *Immigration and Race in British Politics* (London, Penguin Special, 1965), p. 136.
2. N. Deakin (ed.), *Colour and the British Electorate*, 1964 (London, Pall Mall Press, 1965), p. 10.

3.   M. Hartley-Brewer, 'Smethwick', in Deakin (1965), p. 85.
4.   Ibid. p. 102.
5.   D. Butler and D. Stokes, *Political Change in Britain. Forces Shaping Electoral Choice* (London, Pelican, 1971), p. 411.
6.   N. Deakin, 'The Minorities and the General Election, 1970', *Race Today*, vol. 2, no. 7 (July 1970), p. 205.
7.   N. Deakin *et al.*, 'Colour and the 1966 General Election', *Race*, vol. 8, no. 1 (July 1966), p. 17.
8.   Ira Katznelson, 'The Politics of Race under the Impact of Migration: The United States (1900–30) and the United Kingdom (1948–68)' (Ph.D. thesis, University of Cambridge, 1969), p. 17.
9.   *Evening Post*, 23 March 1966.
10. Butler and Stokes (1971), pp. 90–1.
11. For a critical examination of some of the studies which have drawn this conclusion see H. Daudt, *Floating Voters and the Floating Vote* (Leyden, Stensert Kroese, 1961).
12. R. Alford, *Party and Society* (London, Rand McNally, 1964).
13. Butler and Stokes (1971), p. 558.
14. Ibid. p. 155.
15. Ibid. p. 582.
16. Ibid. pp. 599–600.

Chapter 7: Race relations organisations

1.   Ira Katznelson, 'The Politics of Race under the Impact of Migration: The United States (1900–30) and the United Kingdom (1948–68)' (Ph.D. thesis, University of Cambridge, 1969); Ira Katznelson, 'The Politics of Racial Buffering in Nottingham, 1954–68', *Race*, vol. 11, no. 4 (April 1970); A. F. Laird and D. Wood, 'Reply to Ira Katznelson on "The Politics of Racial Buffering in Nottingham 1954–68" ', *Race*, vol. 12, no. 2 (October 1970); and Ira Katznelson, 'Reply to Letter by Miss Wood and Mr. Laird,' *Race*, vol. 12, no. 2 (October 1970).
2.   Katznelson, 'The Politics of Racial Buffering in Nottingham', *Race*, 11 (1970), p. 433.
3.   Ibid.
4.   Ibid. p. 435.
5.   Ibid. p. 436.
6.   Ibid. pp. 440–2.
7.   Katznelson, 'The Politics of Race Under the Impact of Migration' (1969), pp. 24–34.
8.   Katznelson, 'The Politics of Racial Buffering in Nottingham', p. 433.
9.   Ibid. p. 434.
10. Laird and Wood, 'Reply to Katznelson', *Race*, 12 (1970), p. 237.
11. Katznelson, 'Reply to Wood and Laird', *Race*, 12 (1970), p. 239.
12. Consultative Committee for the Welfare of Coloured People, 'Minutes', 16 February 1955.
13. Consultative Committee, 'Minutes', 14 September 1955, 13 October 1955, 6 December 1955 and 10 January 1956.
14. Consultative Committee, 'Minutes', 14 March 1957, 11 April 1957, 9 May 1957, 12 June 1957, 17 July 1957, 3 September 1957 and 8 October 1957.
15. Katznelson, 'The Politics of Racial Buffering in Nottingham', pp. 435–8.
16. Ibid. p. 436.
17. The quotations are from publicity hand-outs prepared by the Campaign.
18. Consultative Committee, 'Minutes', 6 March 1961 and 10 April 1961.
19. Consultative Committee, 'Minutes', 5 June 1961.
20. On 8 August 1961 when a further meeting was arranged for 7 September 1961. Consultative Committee, 'Minutes', 4 September 1961.

21. Consultative Committee, 'Minutes', 4 February 1962.
22. Katznelson, 'The Politics of Racial Buffering in Nottingham', pp. 435–6.
23. Ibid. p. 441.
24. Consultative Committee, 'Minutes', 6 November 1958.
25. Consultative Committee, 'Minutes', 3 March 1960.
26. Consultative Committee, 'Minutes', 21 March 1956.
27. Consultative Committee, 'Minutes', 7 May 1959.
28. Katznelson, 'The Politics of Racial Buffering in Nottingham', p. 438.
29. See, for example, Consultative Committee, 'Minutes', 2 March 1964, 7 September 1964 and 1 June 1966.
30. Katznelson, 'The Politics of Racial Buffering in Nottingham', p. 439.
31. Consultative Committee, 'Minutes', 7 December 1964.
32. Katznelson, 'The Politics of Racial Buffering in Nottingham', p. 439.
33. Consultative Committee, 'Minutes', 9 January 1967.
34. Consultative Committee, 'Minutes', 7 August 1960.
35. Consultative Committee, Finance Sub-Committee, 'Minutes', 11 November 1964.
36. Consultative Committee, 'Minutes', 17 January 1966.
37. Katznelson, 'The Politics of Racial Buffering in Nottingham', p. 439.
38. Consultative Committee, 'Minutes', 18 April 1966.
39. Consultative Committee, 'Minutes', 17 October 1966.
40. Afro-Asian West Indian Union, 'Information Bulletin', vol. 1, no. 1, p. 5.
41. Katznelson, 'The Politics of Racial Buffering in Nottingham', p. 437.
42. Laird and Wood, 'Reply to Katznelson', p. 237.
43. Katznelson, 'Reply to Laird and Wood', p. 239.
44. Nottingham Council of Social Service, 'Twenty-first Annual Report', p. 19.
45. Nottingham Council of Social Service, 'Twenty-fourth Annual Report', p. 35.
46. Nottingham and District Community Relations Council, 'Annual Report 1969–70', pp. 3–4.
47. Laird and Wood, 'Reply to Katznelson', p. 237.
48. Consultative Committee, 'Minutes', 14 September 1955.
49. Consultative Committee, 'Minutes', 13 October 1955.
50. Consultative Committee, 'Minutes', 6 December 1955.
51. Consultative Committee, 'Minutes', 10 January 1956.
52. Consultative Committee, 'Minutes', 6 March 1961.
53. Consultative Committee, 'Minutes', 10 April 1961.
54. Consultative Committee, 'Minutes', 5 June 1961.
55. Consultative Committee, 'Minutes', 4 September 1961.
56. Consultative Committee, 'Minutes', 4 February 1962.
57. Consultative Committee, 'Minutes', 7 October 1963.
58. Consultative Committee, Employment Sub-Committee, 'Minutes', 8 December 1965.
59. For example, see the report in the *Evening Post*, 6 January 1971.
60. Consultative Committee, Finance Sub-Committee, 'Minutes', 3 June 1966.
61. Consultative Committee, 'Minutes', 11 July 1966.
62. Consultative Committee, 'Minutes', 17 October 1966.
63. Consultative Committee, Integration Sub-Committee, 'Minutes', 6 March 1967.
64. Consultative Committee, Integration Sub-Committee, 'Minutes', 22 May 1967.
65. Consultative Committee, Integration Sub-Committee, 'Minutes', 17 July 1967.
66. Consultative Committee, Integration Sub-Committee, 'Minutes', 17 January 1968.
67. Consultative Committee, 'Minutes', 5 May 1970.
68. Consultative Committee, 'Annual Report, 1971–2'.
69. Michael J. Hill and Ruth M. Issacharoff, *Community Action and Race Relations. A Study of Community Relations in Britain* (London, Oxford University Press, for Institute of Race Relations, 1971), p. 284.
70. Ibid.

71. Nottingham Council of Social Service, 'Twenty-first Annual Report', p. 16.
72. Nottingham Council of Social Service, 'Twenty-fourth Annual Report', p. 33.
73. Nottingham and District Community Relations Council, 'Annual Report 1969–70', p. 2.
74. Ibid. p. 4.
75. Nottingham and District Community Relations Council, 'Annual Report 1971–2', p. 3.
76. Hill and Issacharoff (1971), p. 287.
77. Ibid. pp. 193–4.
78. Ibid. p. 179.
79. Ibid. pp. 188–9.
80. Ibid. p. 288.
81. Katznelson, 'The Politics of Racial Buffering in Nottingham', p. 441.
82. O. G. Powe, *Don't Blame the Blacks* (Afro-Asian West Indian Union).
83. This quotation is from one of the Campaign's hand-outs, 'Apartheid in its Infancy'.
84. *Evening Post*, 6 February 1967.
85. *Evening Post*, 18 April 1968.
86. *Evening Post*, 9 May 1968.
87. Indian Welfare Association, 'Annual Report 1968'.
88. Address by Mohammad Aslam J. P., Pakistan Day, 7 April 1968.
89. See, for example, the following editions of the *Evening Post*, 10 April 1969, 11 April 1969, 28 April 1969, 24 June 1969 and 25 June 1969.
90. *Evening Post*, 12 December 1969.
91. *Evening Post*, 2 March 1971.
92. *Guardian Journal*, 1 November 1967.
93. *Evening Post*, 28 February 1970.
94. Mary Grigg, *The White Question* (London, Secker and Warburg, 1967), p. 138.
95. Quoted by Katznelson, 'The Politics of Racial Buffering in Nottingham', pp. 431–2.

Chapter 8: Conclusions

1. J. Giggs, 'The Distribution of Schizophrenics in Nottingham', *Transactions of the Institute of British Geographers*, no. 58 (July 1973).
2. C. Bagley, 'Schizophrenia amongst Immigrant Groups', *Race Today*, vol. 1, no. 6 (October 1969), p. 172.
3. *Nottingham Weekly Post*, 25 January 1973.
4. *Evening Post*, 31 May 1972.
5. *Guardian Journal*, 1 June 1972.
6. *Evening Post*, 1 June 1972.
7. Department of Employment, 'Report of a Committee of Inquiry into a dispute between employees of the Mansfield Hosiery Mills Ltd, Loughborough and their employer' (HMSO, December 1972).
8. Ibid. pp. 14–16.
9. Anthony Lester and Geoffrey Bindman, *Race and Law* (London, Penguin, 1972), p. 378.
10. This point was made during a discussion of the case in *Private Eye*, Issue 234 (4 December 1970).
11. Mr. Simon Regan, a freelance journalist.
12. *Evening Post*, 7 January 1967.
13. *Evening Post*, October 1967.
14. *Evening Post*, 31 January 1968.
15. *Evening Post*, 27 February 1968.
16. *Evening Post*, 6 October 1970.
17. *Evening Post*, 29 September 1970.
18. Katznelson, 'The Politics of Racial Buffering in Nottingham', p. 442.

19. Michael J. Hill and Ruth M. Issacharoff, *Community Action and Race Relations. A Study of Community Relations Committees in Britain* (London, Oxford University Press, for Institute of Race Relations, 1971).
20. Dilip Hiro, *Black British White British* (London, Eyre and Spottiswoode, 1971), pp. 3 and 5.
21. E. Scobie, *Black Britannia. A History of Blacks in Britain* (Chicago, Johnson, 1972), pp. 62–75.
22. Anthony Richmond, *The Colour Problem* (London, Pelican, 1955), p. 238.

Appendix 1

1. For a discussion of this problem see E. Krausz, 'Sampling Ethnic Minorities', *Race*, vol. 10, no. 3 (January 1969).
2. P. G. Gray and Frances A. Gee, *Electoral Registration for Parliamentary Elections. An Enquiry made for the Home Office by the Government Social Survey* (HMSO, S.S. 391, May 1967).
3. P. Marsh, *Anatomy of a Strike* (London, Institute of Race Relations Special Research Series, 1968), p. vi.

Bibliography

Abrams, M. 'Attitudes of Whites towards Blacks', *Listener* (6 November 1969).

Ackerman, Nathan and Jahoda, Marie, *Antisemitism and Emotional Disorder* (New York, Harper and Row, 1950).

Alford, R. *Party and Society* (London, Rand McNally, 1964).

Allen, S. *New Minorities, Old Conflicts, Asian and Indian Migrants in Britain* (New York, Random House, 1971).

Bagley, C. 'Schizophrenia amongst Immigrant Groups', *Race Today* , vol. 1, no. 6 (October 1969).

Bagley, C. 'Those Not Rehoused', *New Society* (21 May 1970).

Banton, M. *Race Relations* (London, Tavistock, 1967).

Bayliss, F. J. and Coates, J. B. 'West Indians at Work in Nottingham', *Race*, vol. 7, no. 2 (October 1965).

Beer, Samuel H. *Modern British Politics* (London, Faber and Faber, 1965).

Beetham, D. *Immigrant School Leavers and the Youth Employment Service in Birmingham* (London, Institute of Race Relations Special Research Series, 1968).

Blair, Carole, 'Two Bills, One Fight, *Race Today*, vol. 3, no. 3 (March 1971).

Blake, Judith, *Family Structure in Jamaica* (New York, Free Press of Glencoe, 1961).

Bourne, R. 'One Summer of Acrimony', *Guardian*, 10 September 1971.

Brooks, D. 'Who Will Go Back?' *Race Today*, vol. 1, no. 5 (September 1969).

Burney, Elizabeth, *Housing on Trial* (London, Oxford University Press, for Institute of Race Relations, 1967).

Burt, Robert A. 'Colour Prejudice in Britain' (Unpublished thesis, University of Princeton, 1960).

Butler, D. and Stokes, D. *Political Change in Britain. Forces Shaping Electrical Choice* (London, Pelican, 1971).

Calley, M. J. C. *God's People* (London, Oxford University Press, for Institute of Race Relations, 1965).

Chambers, J. D. *Modern Nottingham in the Making* (Nottingham, Nottingham Journal Ltd, 1945).

Chapman, S. D. (ed.), *The History of Working-Class Housing* (London, David and Charles, 1971).

Christopher, Lancelot, 'West Indian Education in Crisis', *Race Today*, vol. 4, no. 6 (June 1972).

Clarke, Edith, *My Mother Who Fathered Me.* 2nd edn. (London, Allen and Unwin, 1966).

Coates, K. and Silburn, R. *St Anns: Poverty, Deprivation and Morale in a Nottingham Community* (Nottingham, University of Nottingham Adult Education Department, 1967).

Coates, K. and Silburn, R. *Poverty: The Forgotten Englishmen* (London, Penguin Special, 1970).

Collins, S. *Coloured Minorities in Britain* (London, Lutterworth, 1957).

Commonwealth Citizens Consultative Committee (now the Nottingham and District Community Relations Council), 'Minutes' and Annual Reports, 1955–72.

Commonwealth Citizens Consultative Committee, 'Reports of Surveys on West Indians at Work in Nottingham and the Employment Experiences of Asians in Nottingham', (1969).

Commonwealth Citizens Consultative Committee, 'Report on the 1971 Summer School', (1971).

Cox, O. C. *Caste, Class and Race* (New York, Doubleday, 1948).

Craig, F. W. S. *British Parliamentary Election Results, 1950–1970* (London, Political Reference Publications, 1971).

Cumper, G. E. 'Working Class Migrants to the UK, October 1955', *Social and Economic Studies*, vol. 6 (1957).

Daniel, W. W. *Racial Discrimination in England* (London, Pelican, 1968).

Daniel, W. W. 'Reply to R. Ward', *Race*, vol. 11, no. 3 (January 1970).

Daudt, H. *Floating Voters and the Floating Vote* (Leyden, Stensert Kroese, 1961).

Davies, J. and Taylor, J. 'Race, Community and No Conflict', *New Society*, (9 July 1970).

Davison, Betty, 'No Place Back Home: A Study of Jamaicans Returning to Kingston, Jamaica', *Race*, vol. 9, no. 4 (April 1968).

Davison, R. B. *Commonwealth Immigrants* (London, Oxford University Press, for Institute of Race Relations, 1958).

Davison, R. B. *West Indian Migrants* (London, Oxford University Press, for Institute of Race Relations, 1962).

Davison, R. B. *Black British* (London, Oxford University Press, for Institute of Race Relations, 1966).

Deakin, N. (ed.), *Colour and the British Electorate 1964* (London, Pall Mall Press, 1965).

Deakin, N. *et al.*, 'Colour and the 1966 General Election', *Race*, vol. 8, no. 1 (July 1966).

Deakin, N. *Colour, Citizenship and British Society* (London, Panther, 1970).

Deakin, N. 'The Minorities and the General Election, 1970', *Race Today*, vol. 2, no. 7 (July 1970).

Desai, R. *Indian Immigrants in Britain* (London, Oxford University Press, for Institute of Race Relations, 1963).

Edwards, K. C. (ed.), *Nottingham and Its Region.* (British Association for the Advancement of Science, 1966).

Foot, Paul, *Immigration and Race in British Politics* (London, Penguin Special, 1965).

Giggs, J. 'The Distribution of Schizophrenics in Nottingham', *Transactions of the Institute of British Geographers*, no. 58 (July 1973).

Glass, R. *The Newcomers* (London, Allen and Unwin, 1960).

Glendenning, F. 'Racial Stereotypes in History Textbooks', *Race Today*, vol. 3, no. 2 (February 1971).

Gosling, R. *St Anns* (Nottingham Civic Society, 1967).

Grigg, Mary, *The White Question* (London, Secker and Warburg, 1967).

Hawkes, N. *Immigrant Children in British Schools* (London, Pall Mall Press, 1966).

Heilpern, John and Hiro, Dilip, 'The Town We Were Told Was Tolerant', *Observer*, 1 December 1968.

Hepple, Bob, *Race, Jobs and the Law* (London, The Penguin Press, 1968).

Hill, M. J. and Issacharoff, Ruth M. *Community Action and Race Relations. A Study of Community Relations Committees in Britain* (London, Oxford University Press for Institute of Race Relations, 1971)

Hinds, D. *Journey to an Illusion* (London, Heinemann, 1966).

Hiro, D. *Black British White British* (London, Eyre and Spottiswoode, 1971).

Israel, W. H. *Colour and Community* (Slough Council of Social Service, 1964).

Jackson, G. 'The Education of Immigrant Children', *Institute of Race Relations Newsletter*, (February 1965).

John, DeWitt, *Indian Workers' Associations in Britain*, (London, Oxford University Press, for Institute of Race Relations, 1969).

Jowell, R. and Hoinville, G. 'Do Polls Influence Voters', *New Society*, no. 358.

Jowell, R. and Prescott-Clarke, Patricia, 'Discrimination and White Collar Workers in Britain', *Race*, vol. 11, no. 4 (April 1970).

Karn, Valerie, 'A Note on *Race, Community and Conflict. A study of Sparkbrook*', *Race*, vol. 9, no. 1 (July 1967).

Katznelson, Ira, 'The Politics of Race under the Impact of Migration: The United States (1900–1930) and The United Kingdom (1948–1968)', (Ph. D. thesis, University of Cambridge, 1969).

Katznelson, Ira, 'The Politics of Racial Buffering in Nottingham, 1954–68', *Race*, vol. 11, no. 4 (April 1970).

Katznelson, Ira, 'Reply to Miss Wood and Mr Laird', *Race*, vol. 12, no. 2 (October 1970).

Krausz, E. 'Sampling Ethnic Minorities', *Race*, vol. 10, no. 3 (January 1969).

Kusum, Nair, *Blossoms in the Dust* (London, Duckworth, 1961).

Laird, A. F. and Wood, D. 'Reply to Katznelson, "The Politics of Racial Buffering in Nottingham, 1954–68" ', *Race*, vol. 12, no. 2 (October 1970).

Lambert, J. and Filkin, Camilla, 'Race Relations and Research: Some Issues of Approach and Application', *Race*, vol. 12, no. 3 (January 1971).

Lawrence, D. 'How Prejudiced Are We?', *Race Today*, vol. 1, no. 6 (October 1969).

Lawrence, D. 'The Incidence of Race Prejudice in Britain' (paper presented to the Race Relations Group of the British Sociological Association, January 1970).

Lester, A. and Bindman, G. *Race and Law* (London, Penguin, 1972).

Little, A. 'The Education of Immigrant Pupils in Inner London Primary Schools', *Race*, vol. 9, no. 4 (April 1968).

Little, K. *Negroes in Britain* (London, Kegan Paul Trench, Trubner and Co. Ltd., 1947).

McKenzie, R. T. and Silver, A. *Angels in Marble* (London, Heinemann, 1968).

McWilliams, Carey, *Brothers under the Skin*, rev. edn. (New York, Little Brown, 1951).

Mailer, Norman, *Miami and the Siege of Chicago* (London, Penguin, 1969).

Marsh, A. 'Race, Community and Anxiety', *New Society*, vol. 23, no. 542 (22 February 1973).

Marsh, P. *The Anatomy of a Strike* (London, Institute of Race Relations Special Research Series, 1967).

Marshall, M. 'Counting the Black Unemployed', *Race Today*, vol. 3, no. 2 (February 1971).

Marshall, T. H. *Social Policy* (London, Hutchinson, 1965).

Maunder, W. F. 'The New Jamaican Migration', *Social and Economic Studies*, vol. 4 (1955).

Nandy, Dipak, 'Unrealistic Aspirations', *Race Today*, vol. 1, no. 1 (May 1969).

Nordlinger, E. *Working-Class Tories* (London, Macgibbon and Kee, 1967).

Norris, Katrin, *Jamaica. The Search for Identity* (London, Oxford University Press, for Institute of Race Relations, 1962).

Nottingham Fair Housing Group, 'Annual Reports 1969-72'.

Nottingham Fair Housing Group, *Somewhere to Live* (1971).

Pahl, R. E. *Readings in Urban Sociology* (London, Pergamon, 1968).

Patterson, Orlando, *The Sociology of Slavery* (London, Macgibbon and Kee, 1967).

Patterson, Orlando, 'West Indians Returning Home', *Race*, vol. 10, no. 1 (July 1968).

Patterson, Sheila, *Dark Strangers* (London, Pelican, 1965).

Peach, Ceri, *West Indian Migration to Britain. A Social Geography* (London, Oxford University Press, for Institute of Race Relations, 1968).

Philpott, Stuart B. 'Remittances, Social Networks and Choice among Montserratian Migrants in Britain', *Man*, vol. 3, no. 3 (September 1968).

Political and Economic Planning, *Report on Racial Discrimination*, (London, PEP, 1967).

Powe, O. G. *Don't Blame the Blacks* (Afro-Asian West Indian Union).

Radin, Beryl, 'Coloured Workers and the British Trades Unions', *Race*, vol. 8, no. 2 (October 1968).

Rex, J. 'The Sociology of a Zone of Transition' in Pahl, R. E. (ed.) *Readings in Urban Sociology*, (London, Pergamon, 1968).

Rex, J. 'The Concept of Housing Class and the Sociology of Race Relations', *Race*, vol. 12, no. 3 (January 1971).

Rex, J. and Moore, R. *Race, Community and Conflict. A Study of Sparkbrook* (London, Oxford University Press, for Institute of Race Relations, 1967).

Rex, J. and Moore, R. 'A Rejoinder to Valerie Karn', *Race*, vol. 9, no. 1 (July 1970).

Richmond, A. H. *The Colour Problem* rev. edn. (London, Pelican, 1961).

Richmond, A. H. 'Housing and Racial Attitudes in Bristol', *Race*, vol. 12, no. 1 (July 1970).

Roberts, G. W. and Mills, D. O. 'A Study of External Migration Affecting Jamaica: 1953–5', *Social and Economic Studies*, vol. 7 (1958).

Rose, E. J. B. and associates, *Colour and Citizenship* (London, Oxford University Press, for Institute of Race Relations, 1969).

Runciman, W. G. *Relative Deprivation and Social Justice. A Study of Attitudes to Social Inequality in Twentieth-Century England* (London, Routledge and Kegan Paul, 1966).

Scobie, E. *Black Britannia. A History of Blacks in Britain* (Chicago, Johnson, 1972).

Silburn, R. 'Housing Problems and Performance in Nottingham'. (unpublished paper, 1970).

Simpson, G. E. and Yinger, J. M. *Racial and Cultural Minorites* (New York, Harper and Row, 1965).

Singh, Kushwant, *A History of the Sikhs 1839–1964* vol. 2 (Princeton. Princeton University Press, 1966).

Siu, Paul C. P. 'The Sojourner', *American Journal of Sociology*, vol. 58 (July 1952).

Smith, M. G. *The Plural Society in the British West Indies* (Berkeley, University of California Press, 1965).

Smithies, B. and Fiddick, P. *Enoch Powell and Immigration* (London, Sphere Books, 1969).

Stevenson, D. 'Second Generation West Indians: A Study in Alienation', *Race Today*, vol. 2, no. 8 (August 1970).

Stone, Susan, 'Private Landlords in Nottingham: Problems, Prospects and Policies' (Unpublished M. A. thesis, University of Nottingham, 1968).

Thomas, C. J. 'Geographical Aspects of the Growth of the Residential Area of Greater Nottingham' (Unpublished Ph.D. thesis, University of Nottingham, 1968).

Walston, Lord, 'Repatriation: Why it is wrong', *Race Today*, vol. 1, no. 1 (May 1969).

Ward, R. 'A Note on the Testing of Discrimination', *Race*, vol. 11, no, 1 (May 1969).

Wickenden, J. *Colour in Britain* (London, Oxford University Press, for Institute of Race Relations, 1958).

Wright, Peter L. *The Coloured Worker in British Industry* (London, Oxford University Press, for Institute of Race Relations, 1968).

Official publications

East Midlands Study, East Midlands Planning Council (HMSO, 1967).

Economic Activity Leaflet, Nottinghamshire, 1966 Sample Census (HMSO).

The Education of Immigrants: Education Survey 13, Department of Education and Science (HMSO, 1971).

Fair Deal for Housing, Cmnd. no. 4728 (HMSO, 1971).

The Housing Programme 1965–70, Cmnd. no. 2838 (HMSO, 1965).

The Meadows District Plan, Nottingham Corporation City Planning Department (1971).

Nottinghamshire and Derbyshire Sub-Regional Study, Notts./Derbys. Sub-Regional Planning Unit (1969).

Our Older Homes: A Call for Action, Report of the Sub-Committee on Standards of Housing Fitness (HMSO, 1965).

Race Relations Board Annual Report 1972 (HMSO).

Report of a Committee of Inquiry into a dispute between employees of the Mansfield Hosiery Mills Ltd, Loughborough and their employer, Department of Employment (HMSO, 1972).

Reports of the Organiser for Work with the Coloured Immigrant Community 1959–72, Nottingham Corporation Education Department.

St. Anns. Renewal in Progress, Nottingham Corporation City Planning Department (1970).

Select Committee on Race Relations and Immigration, Minutes of Evidence vol. 2 (HMSO, 1971).

Social Trends no, 1, Central Statistical Office (HMSO, 1970).

Index

Glass, Ruth, 105, 234n
Glendenning, F., 231n
Gordon-Walker, Rt Hon. Patrick, 130
Gosling, R., 82, 233n
Gray, P. G., 239n
Griffiths, P., 130–1, 136–7
Grigg, Mary, 1, 3–4, 194, 229n, 238n

Halpern, M., 164
Hartley-Brewer, M., 236n
Hawkes, N., 123, 235n
Hayworth, Mr, 234n
Heath, Rt Hon. Edward, 131, 136–7
Heilpern, J., 5, 229n
Hill, M. J., 185–6, 188–9, 237–9n
Hiro, D., 5, 216, 229n, 239n
Hoinville, G., 231n
housing
  and race relations, 76–100
  classes, 76–89
  decline in private rented sector, 73
  desire for suburban, 77, 79–84, 86–7
  extent of substandard, 74
  dissatisfaction with, 77–84
  future policies, 225–7
  growth of council sector, 73, 94
  growth of owner-occupation, 73
  origins of problem, 69–73
  quality in areas of immigrant concentration, 75–6

immigration control
  as election issue, 130–1
  immigrants views on, 34, 159–60
  native whites views on, 62, 159–60
  opposed by Commonwealth Citizens Consultative Committee, 169–70, 180–2
  opposed by immigrant organisations, 192
  possible effect on native white attitudes, 55–6
  unexpected consequences of, 34, 38–9, 114–15
Indian Association, 174–5, 179
Indians in Nottingham (*see also* settlement intentions)
  age structure, 63–4
  anti-discrimination legislation, 205
  apprehensions for future, 209–11
  Commonwealth Citizens Consultative Committee, opinion of, 173–9
  content of messages home, 43–4
  discrimination against in employment, 116–22
  discrimination against in housing, 89–96

educational and occupational background, 24–5, 105–7
employment aspirations, 107
employment, degree of satisfaction with, 115–16, 202–4
employment pattern, 109–12
English, opinion of, 41–3, 155–6
estimated number, 9–10
financial commitments at home, 32
housing, degree of satisfaction with, 80–4, 99–100
housing, pattern of tenure, 86–9
identification with Britain and British, 21, 35–6, 44–5, 155–6
immigrant organisations, membership of, 153–4
length of stay, 63–4
migration, reasons for, 22–7
place of origin, 13–14, 21
police, opinion of, 206–9
political parties, opinion of, 143–50
political tactics, 150–4, 156–8
settlement intentions, 28
surprise and disillusionment with Britain, 39–41
trade union membership, 114
unemployment, 107–9
voting behaviour, 134–41
West Indians, opinion of, 155–6
Indian Welfare Association, 119, 134, 174–7, 179, 191–2
Indian Workers Association, 119, 134, 151, 161, 163, 168, 171, 174–8, 191–2
International Social Club, 187
Irons, E., 126
Israel, W. H., 27, 230n
Issacharoff, Ruth, 185–6, 188–9, 237–9n

Jackson, G., 122–6, 174, 235n
Jahoda, Marie, 53, 231n
Jamaica
  economic problems, 14–16
  educational system, 15–16
  migratory tradition, 16, 19–20
  slave heritage, 13–14
Jamaicans in Nottingham (*see* West Indians in Nottingham)
Janowitz, M., 233n
Jenkins, Rt Hon. Roy, 136–7
Joshi, Mr, 191
Jowell, R., 120–1, 126, 205, 231n, 235n

Kandola, S. S., 119, 191
Karn, Valerie, 87–8, 232–3n